MW00577088

LIGHT FROM LIGHT

Scientists and Theologians in Dialogue

Edited by

Gerald O'Collins, S.J., & Mary Ann Meyers

WILLIAM B. EERDMANS PUBLISHING COMPANY
GRAND RAPIDS, MICHIGAN / CAMBRIDGE, U.K.

Published 2012 by

Wm. B. Eerdmans Publishing Co.

2140 Oak Industrial Drive N.E., Grand Rapids, Michigan 49505 /

P.O. Box 163, Cambridge CB3 9PU U.K.

Printed in the United States of America

18 17 16 15 14 13 12   7 6 5 4 3 2 1

Library of Congress Cataloging-in-Publication Data

Light from light: scientists and theologians in dialogue /
    edited by Gerald O'Collins & Mary Ann Meyers.
        p.   cm.
    Proceedings of symposiums held Apr. 27-29, 2009 in Istanbul, Turkey
    and Apr. 15-17, 2010 in Oxford, England.
    Includes index.
    ISBN 978-0-8028-6667-7 (pbk.: alk. paper)
    1. Light — Religious aspects — Christianity — Congresses.
    2. Religion and science — Congresses.   I. O'Collins, Gerald.
    II. Meyers, Mary Ann.

BL265.L5L54   2012
201'.65 — dc23

2011031086

www.eerdmans.com

Contents

Introduction   1

     Mary Ann Meyers and Gerald O'Collins, S.J.

Part One

Some Light from Physics   17

     John Polkinghorne

Light in the Beginning: Georges Lemaître's
Cosmological Inspirations   28

     Michael Heller

On the Development of Physical Characteristics
Through Interactions   43

     Andrew M. Steane

Light on Quantum Physics from Experiments
with Quanta of Light   56

     Markus Aspelmeyer and Anton Zeilinger

Studies of the Velocity of Light and Causality   68

     Robert W. Boyd

Light in the Beginning   80

     Marco Bersanelli

Contents

Part Two

"Light from Light": The Divine Light Reflected in and by
the Son and the Holy Spirit   103
Gerald O'Collins, S.J.

The Use of Perceived Properties of Light as a
Theological Analogy   122
Kathryn E. Tanner

Light and Darkness in the Mystical Theology
of the Greek Fathers   131
Kallistos Ware, Metropolitan of Diokleia

"The Darkness and the Light Are Both Alike to Thee":
Light as Symbol and Its Transformations   160
David Brown

"Let There Be Light!": A Byzantine Theology of Light   183
John Behr

Light in the Thought of St. Augustine   195
Robert Dodaro, O.S.A.

Uncreated Light: From Irenaeus and Torrance
to Aquinas and Barth   208
George Hunsinger

Contributors   236

Index   244

Introduction

The glories of ancient Constantinople, the capital of the Eastern Roman Empire, continue to shine through modern Istanbul. The only city located on two continents, it straddles the Bosphorus, the narrow strait separating Europe and Asia. On the Asian side, the city incorporates the site of Chalcedon, the town where in 451 CE an ecumenical council of bishops re-affirmed the Nicene Creed of 325 CE that in its fuller form had been established by the First Council of Constantinople in 381 CE. The John Templeton Foundation drew a phrase from that Creed, when inviting fourteen scientists and theologians to a symposium on "Light from Light" in Istanbul (April 27-29, 2009) to explore the physics and metaphysics of light. The conversation drew together these scholars to share insights and research on a theme linked to core issues in both theology and science.

In all the great religions of the world, light has served as a metaphor for ultimate reality. The Abrahamic faiths, in particular, associate God with uncreated, primal light and the creation itself with the (first) divine command: "Let there be light *(fiat lux)*." But the link between divinity and light also exists in archaic Greek literature, where gods glowed with brightness. In Plato's cave, goodness enters the material realm "as sunlight enters darkness." Among later Greeks, Plotinus writes of the One coming into the world as light that will not be confined.

For Christians, it is light that frames the messianic hope developed through the prophets of Israel. Above all, it is light (John 8:12) that provides an answer to the question of who Jesus is — the self-description that theologians through the ages have sought to explicate by examining Jesus' claim and what it means for us. The rich and elusive Chalcedonian Definition gestured towards Christ's paradoxical (though *not* self-contradictory)

1

identity as the luminous, divine Word made flesh. St. Athanasius, in writing about the far-reaching deliberations at the earlier Council of Nicaea (325 CE), pressed an analogy for the unique relationship of the incarnate Son to the Father in the relationship between the sun and the radiance of its light. The theme of God as light was a leitmotif in the writings of St. Gregory Nazianzen (d. 389). More than two centuries later, St. Maximus the Confessor (d. 662) found in the light streaming forth from the transfigured Christ a parable for God's relationship to creation.

From the perspective of physics, to ask the question "What is light?" is to address an issue fundamental to our understanding of material reality. Discoveries resulting from modern scientific research into the properties of light would seem to deepen our sense of its spiritual significance. But even the sixth-century science of John Philoponus, taking issue with Aristotle, understood light as something dynamic. From Robert Grosseteste (d. 1253), the author of a highly original cosmogony who wrote of light as the "first form" of all things, to Christiaan Huygens (d. 1695), father of the wave theory of light, to James Clerk Maxwell (d. 1879), who proposed that light was a form of electromagnetic radiation, and on to Albert Einstein (d. 1955), who saw that electromagnetic radiation can behave as both wave and particle, our increasing knowledge of the physics of light has been tied to an increasing knowledge of how the physical world works in general. Observations made during the past century have linked light to the origin and evolution of the universe. The Big Bang is described as a burst of radiant energy that expanded dramatically outward from an infinitesimal point 13.7 billion years ago. Our earliest knowledge of the state of the universe is provided by the background radiation that fills the cosmos.

We know that no signal can travel faster than light, and Einstein's assumptions about the constancy of the speed of light enabled him to grasp the reality of a dynamic invariance inherent in the order of the world that is the basis of his theory of special relativity, which radically altered our understanding of space and time. The observation that gravity bends the path of light helped confirm the theory of general relativity, Einstein's great discovery on which modern cosmology rests. Now with the Glashow-Weinberg-Salam model describing how the electromagnetic force and the weak nuclear force might be united in a single "electroweak" force, physics is moving closer to a grand unified theory (GUT) that would include the strong nuclear force as well. Even more audacious than the dream of a GUT is the speculation that it may one day be possible to merge gravity with the other three gauge symmetries and create a "theory of everything" that links together all physical phenomena. Could what is yet to be known about light provide further insight into the basic ontology of nature?

Key theological questions considered in the Istanbul symposium included: What could it have meant when, in John's Gospel, Jesus described himself as the "Light of the world" (John 8:12; 9:5)? Or what did St. Paul mean when he wrote to the church in Corinth: "For God, who commanded the light to shine out of darkness, has shone in our hearts, to give the light of the knowledge of the glory of God in the face of Jesus Christ" (2 Cor. 4:6)? What might the author of Revelation have been suggesting by portraying the heavenly Jerusalem as the city with "no need of sun or moon to shine on it, for the glory of God is its light, and its lamp is the Lamb" (Rev. 21:23)? What can contemporary scholarship tell us about the origins of the Nicaean formulation "Light from Light"? And its interpretation afterwards, especially in the great mystical works of the Greek Fathers? Does the formulation help us grasp the inner ontological coherence of the gospel as mediated through apostolic Scripture? How might the phrase be interpreted in systematic theology, both Eastern and Western, today?

Then, in terms of scientific understanding, one can ask: How are new experiments deepening our knowledge of light? What significance attaches to the quantum entanglement of photons? What might theologians offer to scientists seeking a richer and fuller comprehension of created light? And what might scientists provide theologians who probe the mystery of uncreated Light? The discussion of such questions at the Istanbul symposium was aimed at contributing to the ongoing dialogue between science and religion.

The Symposium

The Istanbul symposium and its follow-up in Oxford (April 15-17, 2010), which put the last touches on this volume, was part of the Templeton Foundation's Humble Approach Initiative. The goal of the initiative is to bring about the discovery of new spiritual information by furthering high-quality scientific research. The "humble approach" is inherently interdisciplinary, sensitive to nuance, and biased in favor of building linkages and connections. It assumes an openness to new ideas and a willingness to experiment. Placing high value upon patience and perseverance, it retains a sense of wondering expectation because it recognizes, in Loren Eiseley's haunting phrase, "a constant emergent novelty in nature that does not lie totally behind us, or we would not be where we are." A fundamental principle of the Foundation, in the words of its founder, is that "humility is a gateway to greater understanding and open[s] the doors to progress" in all endeavors. Sir John Templeton believed that in their quest to comprehend foundational realities, scientists, philosophers, and theologians have much to learn about and from one another. The humble approach is intended as a corrective to parochialism. It encourages discovery and seeks to accelerate its pace.

At Istanbul and then in Oxford, the Humble Initiative Approach brought into conversation two cultures that both differ from each other and resemble each other. Seven themes serve to express these differences and similarities.

Two Cultures in Conversation

First, scientists come to such discussions after working in laboratories and seminar rooms, as well as at desks in their own offices. Those places provide the *contexts* or specific settings in which Markus Aspelmeyer, Robert Boyd, Anton Zeilinger, and other scientists investigate light, its velocity, and a range of other properties. Theologians enter such conversations with questions and convictions about the biblical and Christian symbol of light that have emerged through pursuing truth in classrooms and libraries. Academic study forms one setting for developing theological views of "Light from Light." But theologians also operate in two further contexts: those of prayer and service. Community worship and individual prayer (e.g., the devout reading the Scriptures) should gift theologians with insights about the light of God and their participation in it. When prompted by this participation to serve others — especially, those in terrible distress — they can appreciate more deeply how the divine light shines in the darkness of this world. In short, theologians learn about and grow in communion with the light of God in three contexts: study, prayer, and sharing that light through the practice of Christian love.

Second, scientists and theologians share some similar presuppositions when they reflect together on light. In particular, both groups presuppose that, like other realities, light is *intelligible* in itself. While recognizing that light may be subtle, elusive, surprising, and even paradoxical, they hold that, at least in some sense and to some degree, it can be understood and interpreted — but only in some sense and to some degree. Scientists and theologians accept that the reality of light can resist their spontaneous expectations. As Aspelmeyer and Zeilinger remark in their chapter below, "some observable quantum phenomena are dramatically inconsistent with our 'intuitive' understanding of 'how the world should work.'" Yet both scientists and theologians agree that they should let it constrain and shape the way they think about it. Trusting in the fundamental intelligibility of light, they seek to conform their thought to it, as John Polkinghorne insisted at the Istanbul symposium.

Third, even if so much reality remains veiled and our knowledge of it continues to be "patchy," scientists and theologians make *truth claims* about light, albeit limited and qualified claims. While far from pretending to describe and explain everything completely, both groups intend to affirm something when they state the properties of light as particles and waves (the scientists) and find meanings involved in confessing Christ as "Light from Light" (the theologians).

Fourth, as regards the *methods* by which they come to make their claims about light, scientists and theologians appeal to *experience*. Scientists come to their claims through what Polkinghorne calls "bottom-up thinking," involving experiments or carefully prepared and highly controlled experiences. At the same time, they need to be open to surprising and unexpected results emerging from their experiments. They do not merely find what they have planned and hoped to establish. Theologians seem to differ by basing their claims on a "top-down" method, the personal self-revelation (or self-communication) of the transcendent God as (1) recorded and interpreted in the inspired Scriptures and (2) experienced, embodied, and expressed in the worship, teaching, and practice of Christians down through the centuries. Yet, as Polkinghorne points out, theology also entails a "bottom-up approach," since it too is grounded in "actual experience."[1] The witness of Scripture and tradition to the divine self-disclosure, which constrains theologians, is derived from *experiences* of God in the periods of the Old and New Testaments and in the history of Christianity.

After Robert Dodaro's chapter on light according to St. Augustine illustrated the role of the Bible (in particular, the psalms) in shaping Augustine's thought and language, Kallistos Ware reminded the symposium of how the biblical witness itself derives from human experience of God. Like

---

1. J. Polkinghorne, *Theology in the Context of Science* (New Haven: Yale University Press, 2009), p. xvi.

John Behr and Gerald O'Collins, Bishop Ware appealed to St. Symeon the New Theologian (d. 1022), an outstanding mystic whose spiritual experiences were shaped by the divine light. He embraced monastic life at the famous monastery of Studios and later transferred to the monastery of St. Mamas. The ruins of both monasteries are only a few miles from where the Templeton Foundation symposium met in Istanbul. The story of Symeon personified for us the significance of experience for any theological and mystical grasp of light, just as the work on light by Aspelmeyer, Boyd, Zeilinger, and others expresses a similar (but not identical) role of experience (in the form of scientific experiments) for progress in optics.

Fifth, when proposing their conclusions about light, scientists and theologians say things that seem to be analogous and "resonate" mutually: for instance, each group points to *correlations* rather than isolated entities and offers information contained in those correlations. At the Istanbul symposium, theologians explored the correlation implied by "Light from Light." In his chapter below, Andrew Steane indicates what developments in physics, including relativity and quantum theory, involve: "physical statements are primarily about relationships." This allows Polkinghorne to write about "the remarkable degree of interconnectedness in the physical world."[2]

Sixth, the discoveries that scientists have made about light (e.g., by Boyd and his collaborators) enable them not only to conduct further experiments but also to construct new devices for technology. By developing intellectual understanding, they can *do further things with light.* Their beliefs and conclusions about light enable theologians, on their side, to do further things personally and for others. Insights about light drawn from the sacred Scriptures and the Christian tradition can help them to pray better, to participate more generously in the divine light, and to guide others to experience "the light of life" in their prayer and daily existence.

Seventh, any assessment of a conversation between scientists and theologians about light raises questions about the mutual impact between the two groups. What impact, for instance, has the new, scientific knowledge of light had on the religious power of the central New Testament *metaphor,* "God is Light" (1 John 1:5)? How could physical light, as understood and interpreted by modern science, illuminate Christian faith and life? Would scientists expect this to happen?

Here metaphor, analogy, and symbol, while all truly ascribing proper-

---

2. Polkinghorne, *Theology in the Context of Science,* p. xxi.

ties to reality, need to be distinguished. Metaphor involves an extended use of language, which, while being false in the literal sense, makes a true statement about reality: e.g., "The Lord is my Shepherd." While God is not literally a shepherd, there is something about God's caring behavior towards "me" that justifies this metaphorical statement.

Analogy uses a common term to designate realities that are both like and unlike with regard to the same point (e.g., "love" as predicated of God and human beings). Analogy is distinguished from (a) the case of equivocal terms, i.e., terms that are the same but designate totally dissimilar realities (e.g., "pen" as an enclosure for cattle and as a writing instrument); and (b) the case of univocal or synonymous terms, i.e., different terms that refer to an identical reality (e.g., "king" and "sovereign" for the male hereditary ruler of an independent nation). When comparing two realities, analogies "carry over" some core meaning but qualify it. In our book a precise grasp of analogy is central to the contribution by George Hunsinger. The chapter by Kathryn Tanner draws attention to the similarities and dissimilarities (or necessary qualifications to be made) involved in comparing the creative work of God to the force of light.

A symbol is something perceptible that represents something else, either naturally (e.g., light symbolizing understanding) or conventionally (e.g., the lotus symbolizing fullness in Hinduism). By making other things present, symbols enter our imagination, affect our feelings, influence our behavior, and invite our *participation*. Rational explanations will always fall short of the potential range of meanings conveyed by given symbols. By representing ultimate, transcendent realities, religious symbols prove inexhaustibly deep in their significance.

As a metaphor, "God is Light" functions powerfully within Judaism and Christianity, as well as beyond. There is something about experiences of God, especially mystical experiences, that encourages and justifies the pervasive use of the metaphor of light when witnessing to such experiences. On the one hand, it may seem to be a *nonpersonal* metaphor, unlike such personal metaphors as "the Lord is my shepherd." But, on the other hand, its use in religious discourse points to the intelligibility, beauty, warmth, and life-giving quality of God. Theologians and scientists can share a sense of wonder and awe when faced with light and its properties. This sense of wonder at the awesome mystery of light can be reinforced not only by mystical experiences (see the chapters below by Behr and Ware) but also by the astonishing discoveries and theories about the physical nature of light coming from scientists.

At the Istanbul symposium and its follow-up in Oxford, the scientists reached out effectively to the theologians. For their part, the theologians were intrigued by the scientific insights and data. The result was a shared sense that light can continue to function not only as an effective metaphor for God but also as a deep symbol that invites participation in the divine light and life.

A Summary of the Contents

Part One

John Polkinghorne asks: Is the use of the image of light in theology a metaphor or something more? How has modern scientific discovery enhanced or diminished the use of this image? In physics, light has an absolutely unusual velocity and photons have only a subtly qualified participation in temporality. Quantum theory has its own formal logic that underlies the counterintuitive possibility of wave/particle duality. Quantum entanglement makes clear the irreducibly relational character of physical reality. The universe is bathed in the Cosmic Background Radiation, a universal signal of cosmic circumstances half a million years after the Big Bang. How can theologians make use of these remarkable scientific insights in their employment of the image of light?

Michael Heller discusses the "Primeval Atom" hypothesis developed by Georges Lemaître (1894-1966), one of the founders of modern cosmology. This hypothesis differs from the present Big Bang theory, but there remains a clear genetic connection between the hypothesis and the widely accepted Big Bang theory. Dr. Heller follows the track of thought that led from Lemaître's early ideas on the role light played in the origin of the universe and a popular commentary on the first verses of Genesis (1921) to his now classic 1927 paper, which broke new ground by comparing predictions of a relativistic world model with real astronomical observations. His "Primeval Atom" hypothesis used principles of quantum physics in reconstructing the early history of the universe, as well as aiming to avoid the discrepancy between the age of the universe derived from theory and as deduced from observational data. Lemaître argued that the products of the "Primeval Atom" disintegration had the properties of corpuscular radiation. In this sense, he could be regarded as the first cosmologist to predict the existence of the radiation era in the early universe, even if there are striking differences between the mechanism producing radiation proposed by Lemaître and as elaborated in the present standard model of the universe. Dr. Heller completes his chapter by summarizing the evolution of Lemaître's views on the mutual relations between science and religion.

Andrew Steane describes for the nonexpert some aspects of quantum field theory and quantum entanglement. Fundamental physics is primarily concerned with relationships between entities rather than characteristics of individual entities. The mathematical language that expresses this fact also shows that, when considered in isolation, physical systems can lose their individual properties. Well-defined properties such as spatial orientation can be acquired through a process involving interaction among three systems, where the third acts as an environment or context for the other two. Two characteristics of physical reality are emphasized by this: first, a permanently isolated or self-contained system is tantamount to a nonexistent system. Second, basic physical existence is richer and subtler than was widely supposed a century ago. If existence comes from God, then the act of "allowing the world to be itself" would, in the case of our world, more naturally suggest a continuing active relationship rather than a deistic passivity.

Markus Aspelmeyer and Anton Zeilinger describe how the predictions of quantum theory run against our spontaneous intuition. Quantum experiments confirm these very counterintuitive features. There are several ways out of this dilemma, but each of them has peculiar consequences for our worldview. Eventually, we may have to accept the possibility of an "open" world, in which physical realism is a concept without ontological meaning independent of epistemology.

Robert Boyd describes some recent experimental studies showing that the velocity of light can be significantly modified through the use of nonlinear optical effects. Under certain circumstances, light pulses are observed to propagate with velocities that exceed the velocity of light in vacuum c. Boyd then reviews theoretical arguments which show that the principle of causality limits the maximum velocity, with which signals can be transmitted, to the velocity of light in a vacuum. This apparent paradox is resolved by showing that the velocity at which the peak of the pulse moves through a material (known as the group velocity) is not the same as the velocity at which information is transmitted through a material. Finally, Boyd speculates about what it could mean to live in a universe in which the principle of causality can be violated. The broad conclusion to be drawn from this work is that studies of the properties of light can provide insight for more general questions of a philosophical nature.

Marco Bersanelli points to the background of the sky, which glows with a faint, diffuse light that brings us an image of the universe in its infancy. Cosmic expansion has transferred the primordial light from the visible to the microwave range of the electromagnetic spectrum, at wavelengths of the order of a few millimeters. The new generation of experiments provides us with an opportunity to investigate at unprecedented depth the physics of the early universe. The central role of light in the structure of the universe, as modern cosmology has shown, enjoys remarkable analogies with the cosmic vision of medieval authors such as Robert Grosseteste and Dante Alighieri.

This chapter concludes the contributions scientists made to the symposium on "Light from Light."

Part Two

Gerald O'Collins shows how in the Hebrew Scriptures light symbolized the divine otherness and holiness and was understood to be the most perfect manifestation of God's reality and operations. The New Testament — especially, the Gospel of John — presented Christ as the Light of the world. The theme of Christ as "Light from Light" developed from Justin Martyr in the second century and was incorporated in the Nicene Creed (325). The theme of the Holy Spirit as "Light" and "Light-giver" developed from the fourth century to be deployed by St. Symeon the New Theologian (d. 1022) and others in the Middle Ages. As Kathryn Tanner proposes, the analogy of light has its limits, as well as values, in elucidating (1) the unity of persons within the Trinity, (2) God's action in creating the world, and (3) the divine presence to and within all created things. Despite its intercultural values, light is strictly speaking an impersonal analogy for God and hence takes second place to such personal analogies as love and what love entails.

Kathryn Tanner sets out the ways in which the perceived properties of light provided analogies for three main topics in patristic and medieval theology: (a) the relationships between the persons of the Trinity, (b) God's creation of the world, and (c) God's presence within the world. As regards (a), thirteen considerations show how light imagery conveys the unity between the Trinitarian persons. Yet this imagery might suggest that the second and third persons are merely properties or powers of the first person. As regards (b), an artisan analogy has often served better to express God's creation of the world. Here analogies with light have proved strongest when the self-diffusiveness of God is stressed (e.g., by Bonaventure). (c) The analogy of light has been successful in portraying God's immanent presence, even to sinful human beings.

Kallistos Ware begins by recalling that in the Christian tradition the presence of God is associated with darkness on Mt. Sinai and with dazzling light on Mt. Tabor. After distinguishing four "levels" of light and four somewhat similar "levels" of darkness, Bishop Ware reviews how light and darkness are interpreted in Hellenic philosophy and Scripture. He then examines the "solar" and "nocturnal" mystics from Irenaeus to Gregory of Nyssa, before turning to two outstanding "mystics of light," St. Symeon the New Theologian and St. Gregory Palamas (d. 1359). Summing up seven things Palamas indicated about divine light, Bishop Ware concludes that for the Greek Fathers the divine light is an objective reality revealed through grace to the saints. Yet what the saints experience far transcends the physical light presence in the material world, and for this reason it may equally be termed "darkness." This theme of "darkness" will be taken up in the following two chapters.

David Brown explores some of the more unexpected uses of light imagery in relation to God. The first part examines two biblical images and the uses to which they are put in later biblical exegesis. First, there is the theme of God as darkness, most obviously on Mt. Sinai and in the Temple but also elsewhere. Used to emphasize divine mysteriousness, it could possibly be older than light imagery. Although eventually equated with dazzling light in the dominant strand of the mystical tradition, other approaches also continued. The second image considered is that of God as cloud and shade. The warrior/judgmental content of the original biblical use is contrasted with a later, gentler application in the blind poet and preacher George Matheson.

In the second part of Brown's chapter, two paradoxes in the history of art and architecture are explored. The rationale given for Gothic architecture focuses on light; yet it came eventually to be associated with "a dim religious light," and clear daylight was even explicitly rejected as part of its purpose. In the second example the influence of Birgitta of Sweden's vision of the nativity is explored, in which the strongest light comes from Christ at his most vulnerable.

In the third part, the treatment of modern scientific theories of light and artificial light by artists and poets is explored: in the atheism of Italian Futurist art, in the Christianity of Salvator Dalì and John Updike (drawing nonetheless opposed conclusions about the potential implications), and finally in the agnostic light sculptures of Dan Flavin. The openness of the last is also seen as potentially the most fruitful. To close, some more general conclusions are drawn about the way to read imagery such as this within Christian theology.

John Behr explains the Eastern Christian tradition that the light shining from Christ in his transfiguration is nothing less than the eschatological light of the kingdom to come. This light of Tabor, according to St. Gregory Palamas, illuminates the hesychasts and others who are, therefore, already living the eschatological life. This focus on the transfiguration understands Tabor to be the paradigmatic moment of revelation, a moment, as Origen recognizes, that illuminates retrospectively the Law and the Prophets. Finally, Christ shows us what it is to be divine by the manner in which he undergoes death.

Robert Dodaro illustrates how St. Augustine, drawing on biblical and philosophical sources, proposed an original and influential interpretation of light *(lux, lumen)* in relation to God, creation, and human beings. In his chapter, Dodaro examines three aspects of Augustine's doctrine: God as Father, Son, and Holy Spirit in relation to light; the relationship of light to spiritual and material reality; and the relationship of light to human intelligence. He concludes by suggesting three possible correlations between Augustine's theory of divine illumination and the contemporary physics of light.

George Hunsinger begins by exploring how Irenaeus saw the idea of light in relation to God. His statement that "God is light and yet God is unlike any light that we know" is unpacked and then taken as paradigmatic for analogical discourse in theology. Such discourse holds real predications in tension with God's radical otherness. A contrast case is seen in the Fourth Lateran Council. This council famously stated that God's similarity to the world must be seen in relation to his "infinitely greater" dissimilarity. Whatever the spirit of this statement may have been, it seems, taken strictly, less than adequate, because no common scale can properly be thought to embrace both God and the world. An example of ambiguity is then noted in T. F. Torrance. Although Torrance generally thinks in accord with Irenaeus when relating created light to Uncreated Light, he sometimes seems to move in another direction, especially when discussing "contingency." By turning to Aquinas and Barth, the second half of the chapter attempts to explore these themes more deeply. Recent Aquinas scholarship makes it possible to see Barth and Aquinas as existing not in conflict but in convergence. A broad typology of how revelation and reason may be related is sketched in conclusion. It suggests how the views of Aquinas and Barth, which would both accept the Irenaean statement in particular ways, can be placed in chastened correlation.

*   *   *

It has been a joy for us to coordinate and facilitate this meeting of outstanding scientists and theologians. In a world that desperately needs more sharing and cooperation at every level, we hope, in the spirit of the Templeton Foundation's Humble Approach Initiative, that our symposium and the volume it produced will build more bridges and establish further connections.

MARY ANN MEYERS *and* GERALD O'COLLINS, S.J.

PART ONE

Some Light from Physics

John Polkinghorne

In the grand narrative of Genesis 1, the first creative word spoken by God is "Let there be light." The picture given us by modern cosmologists of the very early universe as it emerges from the singularity of the Big Bang is that of an almost uniform expanding ball of energy. In the stories that they have to tell, both theology and physics assign a significant role to light, understood by the latter as being the energy of electromagnetic radiation. In the scientific account, light can also serve as an example of the nature of the world described by quantum physics. In the Bible, and in theological discourse generally, light is often employed as an image to represent the goodness and purity of the divine nature. "This is the message we have heard from him and proclaim to you, that God is light and in him is no darkness at all" (1 John 1:5). This theme is extensively present in the Johannine writings, where Jesus says "I am the light of the world" (John 8:18). The Orthodox tradition makes use of the concept of uncreated light, manifested for example at the transfiguration of Jesus on Mt. Tabor. The extensive analyses given in the later chapters of this book of the ways in which the image of light has repeatedly been employed in scriptural and theological writings, make it clear that there is a need for a careful consideration of what might be the character and force of this light-centered discourse.

An important issue is to explore whether what is involved in the theological appeal to light is more than simply the use of a powerful literary trope. The employment of metaphor is doubtless a significant strategy to convey meaning in a manner more illuminating and allusive than is possible by way of plain statements of matters of fact. Yet, in metaphor there is a degree of arbitrariness in the choice of the image that is selected. Robert Burns tells us that his love is like "a red, red rose," but he might have replaced that image of freshness by different words, such as "the pearly dew of dawn." There is nothing intrinsic and indispensable in the words that Burns actually chose to employ. Something much deeper would be implied by the concept of symbol. In this case, what is involved is the idea of an intrinsic relationship of participation by the symbol in the reality symbolized. Paul Ricoeur wrote, "The symbol gives: I do not posit the meaning, the symbol gives it."[1] A Union Jack sewn on an anorak is simply a sign that the wearer is British; the regimental color carried at the anniversary of a famous battle possesses the symbolic power to invoke the glory and ambiguity of war and to invite a present participation. "Only a symbol? He who asks the question shows he has not understood the difference between signs and symbols, nor the power of symbolic language."[2]

Yet deeper even than symbol is the concept of analogy, as it is understood in Christian theological thought. An intrinsic, if necessarily qualified, relationship is implied between the nature of the Creator and the nature of creation. The world is held to be a reflection, however pale, of the One who holds it in being. It is certainly important to sustain the fundamental distinction between the infinite Creator, who possesses aseity (i.e., Being itself), and finite creatures, whose existence is contingent on the will of their Creator. Yet, one may reasonably expect that creation will, to a degree, bear the impress of the character of the One who ordains and sustains it. David Brown quotes the remark of Dionysius: "So, then, forms, even those drawn from the lowliest matter, can be used not unfittingly, with regard to heavenly beings." Thomas Aquinas appealed to just such an *analogia entis* in framing his theology. The analogy of being may surely be expected to have some role to play in the attempts of finite humanity to find some appropriate manner in which to attempt to speak of the infinite reality of deity.

The discussions of this volume revolve around two questions relating to the theological use of the image of light. The first is whether this usage is indeed a true example of analogical reasoning, and therefore whether the image of light is in some way indispensable to theological discourse and it is not simply being used as a metaphorical convenience. A positive answer to this first question raises a second question, central to an interdisciplinary project of this kind, concerning the extent to which the analogical em-

---

1. P. Ricoeur, *The Conflict of Interpretations* (Evanston, IL: Northwestern University Press, 1974), p. 288.

2. P. Tillich, *Dynamics of Faith* (London: Allen & Unwin, 1957), p. 45.

ployment of light has been affected by modern discoveries about its actual physical nature, revealing unexpected properties unknown before the nineteenth century. Have these discoveries enhanced or diminished the value of the light analogy to theology? There can be no doubt that a need for some degree of necessary revision has arisen from these developments in physics.

An example would be the classical appeal, made by several of the Fathers, to the supposed distinctions between the source of light, the rays of light, and the surrounding radiance. This was cited as affording some analogy to the relationships between the Divine Persons of the Holy Trinity. However, for modern scientific thinking these "distinctions" simply correspond to three different manners in which we may perceive the single reality of electromagnetic radiation. Ironically, use of this analogy today would lead to a modalist way of thinking about the nature of God (Father, Son, and Spirit are simply three aspects of a single divine reality — a view that the church rejected as heretical)!

In the nineteenth century, the deep insights of James Clerk Maxwell had made it plain that the nature of light was that of excitations of electromagnetic energy. When these excitations lie in a certain limited band of frequency, they are perceptible by us as visible light. Outside this band, the excitations correspond to what the physicists call either infrared or ultraviolet radiation. From the point of view of physics, visibility is simply an idiosyncratic fact of human physiology, and in this chapter we shall use "light" to refer to all forms of electromagnetic radiation. We shall also use light as a paradigmatic example of quantum physics in general, a strategy that is quite appropriate since quantum theory was, in fact, discovered through attempts to understand some unexpected and counterintuitive properties of light.

The remainder of the chapter is devoted to a concise survey of what contemporary physics can tell us about the nature of light, together with some discussion of what analogical resource these properties might be held to offer to the discourse of theology.

1. Relativity

Einstein's theory of special relativity abolished the Newtonian concepts of absolute space and absolute time, but replaced them with two different universal concepts. The first of these was the absolute character of the velocity of light. Contrary to everyday expectation, the velocity of light is found to be the same for all observers, irrespective of their states of motion. It represents an absolute limit on the rate at which information can be transferred from one observer to another. In relativity theory, causal influences originating from a particular point event in the spacetime continuum are confined within the forward light-cone of that point, the region bounded by light rays originating from there.[3] The relativistic universe is not simply a world of instantaneous effects. It is also found that the judgments that different observers make of the simultaneity of distant events will depend upon those observers' states of motion. This latter property has led some to believe that the true reality must be the so-called "block universe," i.e., the entire spacetime continuum treated as a whole, and that our human perception of the passage of time is no more than a phenomenon of human psychological perspective. However, careful analysis shows that this is not an inevitable conclusion from relativistic physics. No observer is aware of a distant event until it is in his past light-cone, that is to say, unambiguously past. The different judgments that observers make of simultaneity simply reflect the different ways in which they organize their accounts of the past. This can do nothing to establish the reality of an already-existing future. The question of the nature of temporality is constrained by physics but not settled by it alone, for it requires also an act of metaphysical decision.[4]

The block universe would correspond to the way in which classical theology, following Boethius, believed that God saw the whole of history laid out before the divine gaze *totum simul,* all at once, but that is just one metaphysical way of interpreting a relativistic universe. Another possibility is that of a universe of unfolding becoming, in which the experience of the passage of time is not a trick of human perspective but a fundamental aspect of reality. In such a universe there would be a moving cosmic "present," with relativity simply requiring that it could not be uniquely identified by local physical experiments. In fact, cosmologists appeal to just such

3. In fact, the phenomenon of quantum entanglement, discussed later, means that this statement needs a subtle qualification. However, the instantaneous influence associated with entanglement cannot be used to convey information. For a careful and sophisticated discussion of this issue, see B. d'Espagnat, *On Physics and Philosophy* (Princeton: Princeton University Press, 2006).

4. For a much fuller discussion of these issues, see J. C. Polkinghorne, *Exploring Reality* (London: SPCK and New Haven: Yale University Press, 2005), ch. 6; *Theology in the Context of Science* (London and New Haven: SPCK, 2008; Yale University Press, 2009), ch. 3.

a cosmic time when they say that the universe is 13.7 billion years old. Since God surely knows things truly, i.e., according to their actual natures, one might expect that the Creator of such a temporal world would know it in its temporal succession, a conclusion implying a kind of divine dipolar engagement with both time and eternity. These contentious theological issues cannot be pursued further here, but one can note that problems of simultaneity cannot arise for an omnipresent Observer, since for such an Observer there would be no distant events.

While space and time are not themselves absolutes, there is a "distance" in four-dimensional spacetime, called "proper time" or "interval," which is invariant, the same for all observers. This fact allows the consistent reconciliation of the accounts that different observers give of physical process, and it is the second absolute of relativity theory, for which not everything is relative. Along a light ray, proper time is zero. In consequence, photons, the particles of light, have a kind of timeless existence, something that is correlated with the fact that they also have zero mass. However, great care would have to be taken if one were to attempt to make analogical use of this scientific fact. The phenomenon is subtle. Photons certainly participate in time (they interact with matter at specific instants) and it is only in their internal nature that there is a kind of timelessness, since, so to speak, they have no clock ticking away to make them age in themselves.

2. Quantum Theory

We can use the properties of light to illustrate the surprising character of the quantum world.[5] The most famous of its counterintuitive properties is wave/particle duality. In the nineteenth century, diffraction experiments had shown conclusively that light displays wavelike properties. However, at the start of the twentieth century the discoveries of Max Planck concerning the character of blackbody radiation, and Albert Einstein's explanation of the photoelectric effect, showed equally conclusively that light also manifests particle-like properties. For more than twenty-five years physicists faced the threat of an apparent paradox. After all, particles are small, bullet-like objects and waves are spread out and flappy. How could something sometimes behave like one and sometimes like the other? In

5. See, for example, J. C. Polkinghorne, *Quantum Theory: A Very Short Introduction* (Oxford: Oxford University Press, 2002).

1927, Paul Dirac dissolved the paradox by his discovery of quantum field theory. Because fields are spread out and vary through space and time, they manifest wavelike properties. The effect of applying quantum theory is to induce a discreteness into their structure, so that their energy comes in countable packets (quanta), resulting in a particle-like behavior. For light, these particles are called photons. Looking more deeply into this duality, it becomes clear that wavelike states (technically, states with a definite phase) are composed of an *indefinite* number of particles. This is possible in quantum physics because of the superposition principle, the fundamental property that distinguishes quantum mechanics from classical Newtonian mechanics. In the quantum world there are states composed of the addition (superposition) of states that common sense would say could never be mixed together, for example, a counterintuitive mixture of being "here" and being "there." In the clear world of Newtonian physics there would always have to be a specific number of photons present (just look and see how many), but in quantum physics states with different numbers of particles present can be superposed to form a state with an indefinite particle number. It is precisely this indefiniteness that turns out to permit wave/particle duality.

Another way of thinking about the consequences of quantum superposition is to recognize that it implies that a new kind of logic applies to the quantum world, different from the classical logic of Aristotle.[6] The latter depends upon the law of the excluded middle, that there is no state intermediate between A and not-A. In the quantum world there are very many such intermediate states, formed by different superpositions of A ("here") and not-A ("there").

The Orthodox concept of uncreated light forming part of the divine energies would certainly seem to encourage the thought of an analogical connection between the physical and the spiritual. Moreover, one can surely acknowledge that there might seem to be some sort of parallel between the seeming paradox of wave/particle duality and the seeming paradox of the duality of humanity and divinity in Jesus Christ. However, the latter is so profound a mystery that I doubt that one should appeal to anything as strong as an analogical connection in this case. Instead, wave/particle duality can be used to make an important point about the nature of rationality, the human attempt to conform our thinking to the nature of whatever it is that we are endeavoring to think about.

6. Polkinghorne, *Quantum Theory,* pp. 37-38.

Science teaches us that the world is surprising, often displaying a character that would have been beyond our power to anticipate. No one in 1899 could have considered wave/particle duality to be a conceivable possibility. Consequently, the natural question for a scientist to ask about any particular claim, whether within science or beyond it, is not, "Is it reasonable?" as if we felt we knew beforehand the shape that rationality had to take. Rather, the instinctive question for the scientist to ask is one that is at once more open and more demanding: "What makes you think that might be the case?" No prior restriction is being placed on what is an acceptable answer about the actual nature of reality, but if an unexpected proposal is made, it will have to be backed up by well-winnowed motivating evidence. I believe that it is both possible and desirable to approach theological assertions in the same manner. The New Testament writers were all struggling to express in some adequate fashion their experience of the new life that they had been given by the risen Christ. In doing so, these monotheistic Jews were driven time and again to use divine-sounding language about Jesus (such as attributing to him the title "Lord," which really belongs to the one true God of Israel), yet knowing that within living memory he had lived the life of a human being. Wrestling with this seeming paradox eventually led the church to the doctrine of the two natures, proclaimed at Chalcedon in 451.

The elusively veiled nature of quantum entities has led to much philosophical discussion of what degree of reality might be attributed to them. Perhaps the idea of photons is no more than a convenient manner of speaking about luminous phenomena. However, almost all physicists are stoutly realist in their quantum beliefs, which they defend by appeal to the intelligibility that these beliefs confer. For example, quarks (the fundamental constituents of nuclear matter) are intrinsically invisible, confined within the larger entities that they constitute. No one has ever detected a single isolated quark, and we believe that no one ever will. Nevertheless, we believe in quark reality because that belief makes sense of great swaths of directly accessible physical phenomena. Belief in the reality of photons grants just such a satisfying breadth of understanding. Theology owes science no apology for its belief in the unseen reality of God, which makes sense of great swaths of spiritual experience. The emphasis on intelligibility as the criterion of reality has been powerfully expressed in the theological writings of Bernard Lonergan.[7]

7. B. Lonergan, *Insight* (London: Darton, Longman & Todd, 1958).

3. Relationality

Einstein had been one of the grandfathers of quantum theory, but as it grew into maturity he came to repudiate his grandchild. He detested the cloudy fitfulness that it seemed to imply in nature and he was always looking for some way to demonstrate its inadequacy. His dissatisfaction seems to have arisen from the mistaken belief that the assertion of a straightforward objectivity would be the only way to defend the reality of the physical world.

In 1935 Einstein felt he had succeeded in identifying a flaw in quantum theory. Working with two young collaborators, he showed that quantum mechanics implied a counterintuitive nonlocality, an altogether unexpected degree of togetherness-in-separation. In certain well-defined circumstances, two quantum entities, such as two photons that have interacted with each other, remain mutually entangled however far they may then separate spatially. Acting on the one "here" will induce an instantaneous change in the other, even if it were "beyond the Moon," as we conventionally say. Effectively they remain a single system despite their spatial separation. Einstein thought that this was too "spooky" to be acceptable. However, much later, in the 1980s very delicate and clever experiments showed that quantum entanglement is indeed an actual property of nature. (The chapters by Anton Zeilinger and Markus Aspelmeyer and by Andrew Steane have much more to say about this.) Physics has shown us that the world is much stranger than we had originally thought. Mere atomistic reductionism is not enough, even in physics. The subatomic world is not one that can be fully understood atomistically.

Another form of relationality present in the physical world is manifested by the principles controlling the behavior of groups of particles of the same kind. In quantum theory there are identical particles (all photons are intrinsically the same), just as there are in classical physics. However, in the latter case these particles are nevertheless distinguishable, since one can follow the individual trajectories and identify which is which throughout their interaction. The cloudiness of the quantum world means that for quantum entities this is not the case. It has no clear trajectories, and quantum particles are therefore indistinguishable. We can start with two photons A and B and end with two photons, but we cannot say that one of these is definitely A and the other definitely B. Physicists call the way in which collections of the same particles behave their "statistics." It turns out that a consequence of the indistinguishability of quantum entities is that in their case there are two possible forms that statistics might take, each different from the statistics of classical physics. One of these ways is bose statistics, in which particles have a strong tendency to associate together in the same state, and the other is fermi statistics, in which no two particles can ever be in exactly the same state. Photons are bosons, "togetherness particles" one might say in an anthropomorphic manner of speaking. This property of light is the basis of devices such as the laser. Laser light is powerful because it is what the physicists call coherent. It is easier to explain this in terms of a wave picture. If one just adds waves together in a fairly random way there will be interference effects, cancellations due to the crest of one wave coinciding with the trough of another. However, if the waves are added coherently (that is, all in step), then all the crests will combine to add up, and all the troughs combine to add down, to give the maximum possible effect.

Thus physics has learned that Reality is Relational. This will come as no surprise to Trinitarian theologians, who have long believed in Being as Communion.[8] Christian thinkers can perceive the intrinsic interconnectedness of the created universe as being a kind of pale reflection of the relationship of the perichoretic exchange of love between the three Divine Persons in the Godhead. Of course, entanglement does not imply the mystery of the Trinity, and even less does it explain it. I think that to claim analogy here might be too strong an assertion to make, but there is certainly a satisfying degree of consonance discernible between the relationality of the physical world and the Trinitarian character of its Creator.

4. Cosmic Properties

Two properties of light in relation to the cosmos itself are worth noting.

The universe that we observe sprang forth from the fiery singularity of the Big Bang 13.7 billion years ago. Initially it was extremely simple, just an almost uniform expanding ball of energy, made up of photons and other fundamental particles. As the cosmos expanded it cooled, and after less than half a million years its temperature dropped below the level at which the photons would be sufficiently energetic to disrupt the formation of atoms. These photons then became effectively noninteractive and they sim-

8. J. Zizioulas, *Being as Communion* (Crestwood, NY: St. Vladimir's Seminary Press, 1985).

ply continued to cool in the course of further expansion. Today this body of radiation is very cold, just over three degrees above absolute zero, forming the celebrated Cosmic Background Radiation that fills the whole universe. It is a kind of preserved signature of the early state of the cosmos, a dying echo of events following closely on the Big Bang. This Background Radiation tells us much of importance about the early universe, playing the role of a kind of witness to primeval times.

The second property of interest relates to the fact that in quantum physics the vacuum, defined as the lowest energy state, is not mere emptiness but a buzzing hive of energetic activity. This is due to the fact that Heisenberg's uncertainty principle does not permit any quantum entity to be at complete rest, for then it would have both a definite position and a definite state of (zero) motion, which is not allowed. In consequence, the quantum world is full of a kind of perpetual quivering, which the physicists call "zero point motion." This phenomenon implies the universal presence of an energy associated with space itself. This energy has most likely been observed as the so-called "dark energy" that is partly driving the expansion of the universe. A straightforward estimation of the magnitude of this energy yields an immense value, some 120 powers of 10 greater than that observed! Some sort of tremendous cancellation has reduced its value in our universe, and we would not be here if that had not been the case, for otherwise the cosmos would have blown apart so rapidly that no stars or galaxies would have been able to form. This fact is the most striking example of the so-called cosmic "fine-tuning" of the given physical fabric of the universe that was necessary for it to have been able to evolve carbon-based life.[9]

These two properties tell us significant facts about the cosmos, but I doubt whether they lend themselves to any form of theological development in terms of analogical reasoning.

The physics of light gives us a picture of a world whose character is quite different from that of everyday experience. In it, a different kind of logic permits the consistent complementarity of seemingly antithetic properties, such as in wave/particle duality. When Christian theology is driven by its experience to speak of the deeper duality of divinity and humanity in Christ, something not altogether different is happening. If the physical world has proved stranger than we could have anticipated, may

---

9. See, for example, R. D. Holder, *God, the Multiverse and Everything* (London: Ashgate, 2004).

this not also be true of divine reality? Through the phenomena of quantum entanglement and bose statistics, light is seen to manifest the presence of a deep-seated relationality present in the physical world. Those who believe that the Creator of that world is the triune God will not find this altogether surprising. The insights that physics can bring to theological thinking are modest for sure, but at the very least they provide metaphorical resources of a kind that the biblical writers could never have imagined. The question of the degree to which they also present an opportunity for analogical reasoning is a more difficult and delicate matter to decide, which requires careful consideration by the theologians.

Light in the Beginning: Georges Lemaître's Cosmological Inspirations

Michael Heller

1. The First Three Words of God

Among the papers and notes left by Georges Lemaître and now preserved in his archive at Louvain-la-Neuve (Belgium), there is a short manuscript titled *Les Trois Premières Paroles de Dieu* ("The First Three Words of God").[1] It contains a popular commentary on the first few verses of Genesis 1 and bears the date of June 21, 1921. At that time Lemaître, who became one of the founders of modern cosmology, was attending the seminary of Malines and about to finish his first year of studies with a view to becoming a Catholic priest. I found this manuscript when, together with Professor Odon Godart, Lemaître's former assistant, I was organizing what later became Lemaître's archive at the Institute of Astronomy and Geophysics in Louvain-la-Neuve. When I first came across the manuscript, I thought it was of a sermon or essay written in connection with his theological studies. The true significance of these notes has been discovered by Dominique Lambert, a biographer of Lemaître.[2] Using them as a starting point, Lambert was able to reveal the extraordinary track of thoughts that led the future "father of Big Bang" to one of his most important ideas.[3]

In 2001 a Flemish journalist, Daniël Vanacker, published some letters

---

1. The manuscript is published in *Mgr Georges Lemaître savant et croyant suivi de la physique d'Einstein*, ed. J.-F. Stoffel, *Reminiscences* 3 (Louvain-la-Neuve: UCL, 1996), pp. 107-11.

2. See his fundamental book: *Un atome d'univers. La vie et l'œuvre de Georges Lemaître* (Bruxelles: Lessius-Racine, 2000).

3. See D. Lambert, *L'itinéraire spirituel de Georges Lemaître* (Bruxelles: Lessius, 2007), chs. 2 and 3.

exchanged between Lemaître and his friend Joris Van Severen in the period 1917-21.[4] The latter kept a diary, also published by Vanacker,[5] in which he often alluded to discussions and events concerning his friend. It turns out that the young Lemaître presented to Van Severen his ideas concerning the beginning of the universe in almost exactly the same words as he used in *Les Trois Premières Paroles de Dieu*. His ideas made a big impression on Van Severen. Lambert convincingly argues that these ideas were not the transient imaginings of a young enthusiast but rather lasting inspirations that, after having matured and been transformed, led the trained cosmologist to his most fruitful scientific works.

In what follows I tell the story of this maturation and transformation. I start with Lemaître's wartime experience and his early ideas concerning the role that light played in the origin of the universe (Section 2). I will then take a closer look at the manuscript *Les Trois Premières Paroles de Dieu* and Lemaître's formative years in the seminary of Malines (Section 3). In 1927, he published his fundamental cosmological paper in which he broke new ground by comparing, for the first time in history, predictions of a "relativity" world model with real astronomical observations. Strangely enough, in this purely scientific paper there are quite clear traces of his early speculations about light (Section 4). Lemaître's famous Primeval Atom hypothesis was motivated by purely scientific reasons: the wish to take into account principles of quantum physics in reconstructing the early history of the universe, as well as a desire to avoid the discrepancy between the age of the universe as derived from theory and as deduced from observational data. The motif of light is overwhelmingly present in Lemaître's hypothesis, but this time the role of radiation (light) follows from the inner structure of the model rather than from any external sources (Section 5). Lemaître argued that products of the "Primeval Atom" disintegration had the properties of corpuscular radiation, and he tried to identify it with cosmic rays. In this sense, he could be regarded as the first cosmologist to predict the existence of the radiation era in the early universe. There are, however, striking differences between the mechanism producing this radiation as proposed by Lemaître and as elaborated in the present standard model of the universe (Section 6). Finally, I briefly sum-

4. D. Vanacker, "Het absolute geloof van Georges Lemaître," in *Joris Van Severen. Zijn person, zijn gedachten, zijn invloed, zijn werk* (Ypres: Studien Coördinatiecentrum Joris Van Severen, Jaarboek 5, 2001), pp. 5-40.

5. J. Van Severen, *Die Vervloekte Oorlog. Dagboek 1914-1918*, ed. D. Vanacker (Ypres: Studiencentrum Joris Van Severen, Kapellen, Pleckmans, 2005).

marize the evolution of Lemaître's views on the mutual relations between science and religion (Section 7).

Much of this essay is based on the two books by Dominique Lambert mentioned above, especially his *L'itinéraire spirituel de Georges Lemaître*. Neither of these books has been translated into English, and both of them contain a good deal of hitherto unknown material that is important for the history of modern cosmology. I thank Dominique for keeping me informed about developments in his research into the life and work of Georges Lemaître.

2. The War Experience

Georges Henri Joseph Édouard Lemaître was born in 1894 into a religious family. His father Joseph, a lawyer in Charleroi, died when his son was still a child. Lemaître retained a close relationship with his mother, Marguerite Lannoy, until her death in 1956. He was educated at Jesuit schools, and very early expressed his wish to become a Catholic priest. But his father persuaded him to enroll first at a university and complete technical studies. In 1914 he obtained the diploma *d'ingénieur des mines* at the Catholic University of Louvain, and at the start of the First World War, he volunteered for the army (together with his brother Jacques). He served first in the infantry and then in the artillery, almost always on the front line. During his free time he continued his scientific reading (no longer in the field of technology but rather in the field of theoretical science), studying in particular Poincaré's *Électricité et optique*. The copy of this book, with ample annotations in Lemaître's hand, is now preserved in his archive in Louvain-la-Neuve.

It was during the war (probably in 1916) that he established a friendship and correspondence with Joris Van Severen. At that time Van Severen was an officer in the Belgian army. He was a young man of passionate temperament with the soul of an artist, and his spiritual life was marked with some instability. His political views were strongly pro-Flemish, and his activities in the separatist movement of Flanders caused many problems with the Belgian Sûreté. At the beginning of the Second World War, he was arrested on suspicion of treason and moved to a French prison at Abbeville. During a German air attack on May 20, 1940, he and a group of fellow prisoners were executed by French soldiers who believed they were spies.

Both Lemaître and Van Severen were devout Christians, and perhaps their faith provided a starting point for their friendship, because psychologically they were very different. In the first reference to Lemaître in his diary, Van Severen characterized him as very orderly and clear but "lacking the fiber of an artist." It was Joris who suggested that Georges read the French author Léon Bloy.

At that time Bloy was a fashionable Catholic writer and philosopher in France. His strong objections to the "pharisaic Church" with its legal concept of religion earned him the reputation of an "anticlerical Catholic." He objected to the positivist views of other scientists and, by adopting a kind of symbolic exegesis, tried to show the value of the Bible in its meeting with modern science. This certainly attracted young Lemaître, but it was Bloy's radical attitude towards spiritual life that made a lasting impression on him. Under the influence of Bloy's writings, Lemaître decided to give up, for some time, his scientific reading "in the trenches," as a kind of gift made to God of what was for him the most precious thing.

According to Lambert,[6] it was at this time that Lemaître, giving up Poincaré's *Électricité et optique,* started thinking about light as an "essence of the universe." In his diary, Joris Van Severen recalls that on April 17, 1917, he met Lemaître (who was probably then on a short leave from a training course in Audresselles) in Wulpen and presented his idea concerning the role that light played in the origin of the universe. Van Severen recounts that his friend had for a long time been looking for a "fundamental essence of matter." Initially he had believed that it was of the electrical nature (an echo of the *Électricité et optique*?), but recently he found that it was light. In this way, Lemaître found a link with the first verses of Genesis. Van Severen was greatly impressed by Lemaître's vision. "Today," he wrote in his diary, "I have seen with my own eyes an éclat of genius."

A month later (in a letter of May 28, 1917) Lemaître wrote to his friend that it was Léon Bloy who inspired him to regard the *Fiat lux* as the *raison de l'univers.* Lemaître prepared an essay explaining his ideas and sent it to Léon Bloy, but he never received an answer. In early June 1917, during a short visit to Paris (on his way back from a trip to Le Havre on military business), he paid a visit to Bloy but was not well received. Bloy, who seemed to be dissatisfied with Lemaître's ideas, advised him to study the Church Fathers. Lemaître continued, nevertheless, to be greatly influenced by Bloy's thinking, even if he never mentioned him by name in any of his own writings.

6. Lambert, *L'itinéraire spirituel de Georges Lemaître,* p. 27.

After the war, Lemaître resumed his university studies, but this time he turned to mathematics and physics. In 1920, he obtained a doctorate in this field with *la plus grande distinction,* and decided to enter the seminary in Malines and become a priest.

3. Light from Darkness

A comparison of *Les Trois Premières Paroles de Dieu,* written by Lemaître during his theological studies, with information contained in the correspondence between Lemaître and Van Severen, and especially with that contained in the latter's diary, reveals that the essay *Les Trois Premières Paroles* is no more than an elaborated formulation of almost exactly the same ideas Lemaître already had at the end of the war. Is this essay based on the text Lemaître sent to Bloy? We can only speculate, because the text in question has not been preserved.

The essay of Lemaître shows some traces of his theological studies. He employs principles of biblical exegesis that at that time were obligatory in Catholic seminaries. He quotes the following declaration from the 1893 Encyclical Letter *Providentissimus Deus* of Pope Leo XIII: "The Holy Ghost who spoke by them [i.e., sacred writers] did not intend to teach men these things [that is to say, the essential nature of the things of the visible universe], things in no way profitable unto salvation."[7] It seems that Lemaître wants to justify his own interpretation of the biblical creation story against such a clear exegetical principle when he writes that "the Holy Ghost Creator, who led Moses [believed to be the author or editor of Genesis], knew perfectly well the Universe, His deed." Therefore, what cannot be excluded is that the Scripture contains some sort of scientific information in a "hidden form" that could be revealed at a certain stage when human knowledge is mature enough.

I am not going to analyze the whole of Lemaître's essay; my objective is to pick up a single idea contained in it that later became an inspiration for

---

7. *Providentissimus Deus,* no. 18. Leo XIII comments here on "the rule so wisely laid down by St. Augustine," according to which one should not "depart from the literal and obvious sense [of the Bible], except only when reason makes it untenable or necessity requires." After the passage quoted in the text the pope continues: "Hence they [sacred writers] did not seek to penetrate the secrets of nature, but rather described and dealt with things in more or less figurative language, or in terms which were commonly used at the time, and which in many instances are in daily use at this day, even by the most eminent men of science."

his future cosmological work. The idea that struck Lemaître, when still "in the trenches," was that every body at a temperature above absolute zero necessarily emits radiation. "It is impossible for any body to subsist without emitting light. In fact, every body at a certain temperature emits radiation of all wavelengths [the black body theory]. From the physical point of view, darkness is absolute nothingness. . . . Before the *Fiat lux* there was absolutely no light; consequently, there was absolutely nothing."[8] In this sense, the separation of light from darkness is fully equivalent to the creation out of nothingness.

In the text of Genesis, the second act of God, after separating light from darkness, was the separation of the waters above the firmament from the waters under the firmament. Following the principles of his symbolic exegesis, Lemaître interprets the waters as "an ensemble of light, crossing itself in all directions" and forming "something like a fluid with no distinct contours" — and the appearance of the dry land as a "partial condensation" of light.[9]

As we can see, Lemaître read into the text of Genesis his own, earlier idea that light is, as expressed by him, "la substance 'originaire,' le fondement de toute la matière du monde."[10]

4. Lemaître's Classical Paper

In 1923, Lemaître completed his theological studies in Malines and was ordained a Catholic priest. During his seminary years he studied extensively Einstein's theory of relativity. At the end of these years he won a scholarship for study abroad, and first went to Cambridge to study relativity under Eddington. He then traveled to Canada and the United States, obtaining in 1927 a Ph.D. in physics from the Massachusetts Institute of Technology,[11] published his first scientific works, and became a full-fledged scientist.

It might be expected that, engulfed by the world of science and immersed in his scientific works, he would forget his earlier, purely qualitative idea. Indeed, in his published papers from this period one can find no

8. "Les Trois Premières Paroles de Dieu," in *Mgr Georges Lemaître savant et croyant*, pp. 110-11.

9. "Les Trois Premières Paroles de Dieu," pp. 110-11.

10. Lambert, *L'itinéraire spirituel de Georges Lemaître*, p. 47.

11. The title of his thesis was: *The Gravitational Field in a Fluid Sphere of Uniform Invariant Density according to the Theory of Relativity*.

trace of it. But, suddenly, in his first really important cosmological paper a hint surfaces that the old idea is still at work.

The importance of the paper in question stems from the fact that in it Lemaître was the first scientist ever to compare predictions derived from a "relativistic" world model with actual astronomical data. In this paper, two so far independent lines of research met: the theoretical line, which consisted of solving Einstein's equations representing various possible universes, and the observational line, which consisted of measuring red shifts and distances to galaxies (at that time called nebulas). Lemaître selected one particular world model and demonstrated that its predictions do not contradict currently available data. Relativistic cosmology as an observational discipline had been founded.

Lemaître's paper, written in French, appeared in 1927 in the Belgian scientific journal *Annales de la Société Scientifiques de Bruxelles,*[12] and for some time remained unknown to the broader scientific community. It was only when Eddington, in 1931, arranged for the English translation of Lemaître's paper and its publication in the *Monthly Notices of the Royal Astronomical Society* that the paper became a classic text of modern cosmology.

Lemaître begins by sketching the issue. There are two known cosmological solutions to Einstein's gravitational field equations: Einstein's solution and de Sitter's solution. Both solutions represent a homogeneous universe, i.e., "such that all positions in space are completely equivalent." Einstein's solution is static and contains matter. De Sitter's solution is nonstatic, but the density of matter in it is zero. Each of these two world models has its advantages. "One [de Sitter's model] is in agreement with the observed radial velocities of nebulae, the other [Einstein's model] with the existence of matter, giving a satisfactory relation between the radius and the mass of the universe." This determines the goal of Lemaître's work: "It seems desirable to find an intermediate solution which could combine the advantages of both," i.e., to find a world model that would contain matter and would account for the radial velocities of galaxies. This is exactly what Lemaître does in his paper.

He was not aware (and only very few scientists in the West were) that for some time such "intermediate" solutions (not only one but many) had been found by a Russian mathematician and meteorologist, Alexander

---

12. "Un univers homogène de masse constante et de rayon croissant, rendant comte de la vitesse radiale des nébuleuses extra-galactiques," *Annales de la Société Scientifiques de Bruxelles* 47A (1927): 29-39.

Friedman. In his two fundamental papers, published in 1922[13] and 1924,[14] Friedman found a rich class of solutions to Einstein's equations, in which Einstein's static solution and de Sitter's empty solution are special cases. However, he never compared any of his solutions with observational data. Friedman died in 1925, and his papers did not become known in the West until a few years later.

In his paper, Lemaître reproduced only one solution of the Friedman family. It describes a spatially closed universe that initially (from minus time infinity) is in a static Einstein's state, and then starts to expand in a logarithmic way (i.e., when regarded backwards in time, it contracts and asymptotically approaches the Einstein solution). There is a paragraph testifying to the fact that Lemaître was aware of the existence of other solutions.[15] In fact, handwritten notes preserved in the Lemaître archive in Louvain-la-Neuve show that, when preparing this paper, he explicitly computed all Friedman's solutions (with positive space curvature).[16] However, the novelty of Lemaître's paper did not consist in mathematically discussing all solutions to Einstein's equations, but in identifying the solution that remained in best agreement with observational data. And according to his estimates, it is the "logarithmic model" that satisfies this criterion. On the one hand, having no temporal beginning (no initial singularity), it puts no constraints on the age of the universe, and, in this respect, it does not contradict observational data. On the other hand, it explains astronomical measurements of galactic red shifts; in this model they are "a cosmic effect of the expansion of the universe."

If one wants to learn about the inspirations and "private philosophies" of given authors, one should look in their research papers for passing remarks and loose comments made by them "on the margins" of the main stream of their reasoning. The last paragraph of Lemaître's work is exactly of this character. The question asked in this paragraph is natural, but the answer seems rather strange. The question is: If the universe had been in the static state during an infinite period of time, what started its expansion? And the answer runs as follows: "We have seen that the pressure of

13. "Über die Krümmung des Raumes," *Zeitschrift für Physik* 10, no. 1 (1922): 377-86.

14. "Über die Möglichkeit einer Welt mit konstanter negativer Krümmung des Raumes," *Zeitschrift für Physik* 21, no. 1 (1924): 326-32.

15. In Section 5, Lemaître says that other solutions have "a minimum of *R*" (in such situations we today speak about the initial singularity), which makes the age of the universe too short as compared with observational data.

16. See O. Godart and M. Heller, *Cosmology of Lemaître* (Tucson: Pachart, 1985), p. 57.

radiation does work during the expansion. This seems to suggest that the expansion has been set up by the radiation itself. In a static universe light emitted by matter travels around space, comes back to its starting-point, and accumulates indefinitely. It seems that this may be the origin of the velocity of expansion R'/R, which Einstein assumed to be zero and which in our interpretation is observed as the radial velocity of extra-galactic nebulae." The expression R'/R is now called "Hubble's constant," and it describes the velocity of the cosmic expansion.

Dominique Lambert remarks that this explanation is somehow unexpected and in no way implied by the logic of the paper, but that it could be regarded as an echo of Lemaître's old idea that light (radiation) is at the origin of the universe. In the logarithmic model of the universe, there is no absolute beginning (the universe is from eternity in the Einstein static state); there is only the beginning of its present expanding phase, and this beginning is caused by light.

I do not quite agree with Lambert that this explanation is unexpected. There is a place in Lemaître's paper that, in a sense, prepares for it. Both in Einstein's original static universe and in de Sitter's empty universe the pressure p exerted by matter is assumed to be zero (we say today that the equation of state in these models is $p = \emptyset$). In Lemaître's logarithmic model this assumption is maintained, and for a good reason, since in the present universe the pressure is indeed vanishing. However, in section two of Lemaître's paper we read: "Nevertheless it might be necessary to take into account the radiation-pressure of the electromagnetic energy traveling through space; this energy is weak but it is evenly distributed through the whole of space and might afford a notable contribution to the mean energy. We shall thus keep the pressure p in the general equations as the mean radiation-pressure of light, but we shall write $p = \emptyset$ when we discuss the application to astronomy." Lemaître continues: "We denote the density of total energy by ρ, the density of radiation energy by $3p$, and the density of the energy condensed in matter by $\delta = \rho\text{-}3p$." Both these forms of the energy density are taken into account in Lemaître's general formulas. In this way, the space is, as it were, prepared for the remark in the last paragraph of his paper.

The evidence that, when writing his fundamental paper of 1927, Lemaître had in mind his earlier "philosophy of light" is only circumstantial, but it is strengthened if we take into account the evolution of his later views.

5. Primeval Atom

As time passed, Lemaître was more and more immersed in his scientific activities and was, it seems, less and less thinking about his theological inspirations, although it cannot be excluded that they somehow persisted in his subconscious. It is very significant that in his 1927 paper he selected the world model with no temporal beginning. In doing so he evidently preferred scientific reasons (agreement with observational data) over theological motives. However, the problem of the beginning soon became a scientific problem. In the family of all Friedman solutions, models having the initial singularity are "generic." Lemaître's logarithmic solution is a very special exception. The avoidance of the initial singularity is assured in it by a very delicate balance between attracting gravity and a repulsive force represented in the equations by the positive value of the so-called cosmological constant. Lemaître was aware of the fact that any more realistic model of the universe should be represented by a "generic" solution, and, in this way, the problem of the beginning became pressing. The existence of the beginning implied a finite age of the universe, and estimates, based on the recession of galaxies, gave two billion years as the age of the universe. It was too short as compared with the age of some systems of stars and some rocks on earth estimated to have existed for four billion years. For this reason, world models with a beginning were "not wanted."

Lemaître discussed this problem with Einstein, who claimed that the existence of the initial singularity was a byproduct of too high symmetries assumed in constructing Friedman models. He suggested to Lemaître how to deviate from the Friedman symmetries and encouraged him to compute the result.[17] Lemaître did that with no great difficulty.[18] The result was striking: in the class of models obtained, singularities did not disappear. On the contrary, a tendency to their appearance was even stronger. "[T]his indicates — concluded Lemaître — that anisotropy acts in an opposite direction [than the one suspected by Einstein]."

Clearly, a model was needed with a beginning and prolonged history (so that the age of the universe could be sufficiently long). Lemaître took a closer look at all Friedman's world models (at that time he had become

17. Einstein's idea was to compute the world model based on an anisotropic spacetime metric, today classified as Bianchi I metric.

18. G. Lemaître, "L'univers en expansion," *Annales de la Société Scientifique de Bruxelles* 53A (1933): 51-85.

Michael Heller

aware of Friedman's work). It turned out that there is a subclass of models with the required properties. If one assumes a cosmological constant with a positive value a little bigger than that for the Einstein static universe, one obtains world models with the following history: after the beginning (initial singularity), there is a period of rapid expansion and then the expansion slows down to an almost static phase. (By manipulating the value of cosmological constant, one can make the length of this phase as long as one wishes.[19]) Then a third period follows in which expansion accelerates again.

Starting with his 1927 work, Lemaître made his main goal not to study mathematical properties of world models, but rather to construct the model that would best describe the real universe. With the above results he already had a geometric stage for such a model. It was clear to him that this stage had now to be filled in with physical processes, thus changing a "geometric cosmology," developed so far, into the real "physics of the universe." Happily enough, in 1931, Eddington published in *Nature* an article titled "The End of the World: From the Standpoint of Mathematical Physics"[20] in which, basing himself on principles of thermodynamics, he considered the thermal death of the universe. We do not know whether this article suggested to Lemaître the idea, or became only an occasion to make the idea public. The fact is that shortly afterwards, he published in *Nature* a short note, "The Beginning of the World from the Point of View of Quantum Theory,"[21] which contained the program for the famous Primeval Atom hypothesis that he developed later in many of his works. In Lemaître's opinion, principles of thermodynamics, considered by Eddington, should be regarded in the context of quantum theory. In this context, they can be stated as follows: "(1) The energy of constant total amount is distributed in discrete quanta. (2) The number of distinct quanta is ever increasing. If we go back in the course of time, we must find fewer and fewer quanta, until we find all the energy of the universe packed in a few or even in a unique quantum."[22] In his later works, Lemaître called this original blast of energy the Primeval Atom, emphasizing that he meant "atom" in the Greek sense of maximal simplicity rather than in the present mean-

19. The closer the value of the cosmological constant to that for the Einstein static universe, the longer the quasi-static phase.

20. *Supplement to Nature* 3203 (1931): 447-53.

21. *Nature* 127, no. 3210 (1931): 706. Notice an "antiparallelism" with the title of Eddington's article.

22. *Nature* 127, no. 3210 (1931): 706.

38

ing of atomic physics. In Lemaître's view, the initial singularity, present in the corresponding solution to the Einstein equations, provides a "geometric support" for such a picture. Today we call it Big Bang. The present Big Bang theory is very different from Lemaître's Primeval Atom hypothesis, the main difference being that Lemaître's hypothesis is, as we have seen, based on the idea of a disintegration of the primeval quantum of energy, whereas our present theory stems from the application of the current elementary particle physics to the extreme conditions in the very early universe. It was George Gamow who could be regarded as a predecessor of this approach. In fact, Odon Godart, Lemaître's former assistant, suggested to him that he should get in touch with Gamow's group. However, Lemaître refused. He believed that particle physics was not mature enough and possibly would undergo substantial change.[23]

6. The Beginning and Light

The Primeval Atom — or better the primeval quantum of energy — was a radically quantum "object." It did not exist in space and time, since space and time are statistical notions, and multiplicity was born only with disintegration of the Primeval Atom. "The beginning of multiplicity really means the beginning of the very meaning of any notion which involves a great number of individuals. Space and Time are such notions."[24] The Primeval Atom is indeterministic: "From the same beginning, widely different universes could have evolved." Only when the number of particles (the products of disintegration of the Primeval Atom) became large, "the essential indeterminacy became ineffective and was replaced by the practical determinism characteristic for macroscopic phenomena."[25]

Lemaître thinks that the first physical question that arises, when the number of particles is sufficiently large, is "whether the resulting assembly of particles has to be considered as a gas."[26] His answer is negative. In order to be a gas the assembly of particles "must have velocities with a distribu-

---

23. See Godart and Heller, *Cosmology of Lemaître*, p. 133.

24. G. Lemaître, "The Primaeval Atom Hypothesis and the Problem of the Clusters of Galaxies," in *La structure et l'évolution de l'univers*, Onzième Conseil de Physique, Bruxelles, 9-13 juin 1958, Institute International de Physique Solvay, Bruxelles, 1958, pp. 1-25.

25. Lemaître, "The Primaeval Atom Hypothesis," pp. 1-25.

26. G. Lemaître, "Instability in the Expanding Universe and Its Astronomical Implications," *Pontificiae Academiae Scientiarum Scripta Varia* 16 (1958): 475-86.

tion strongly concentrated around a mean velocity of the gas, and distribution around this velocity according to a law not too different from the Maxwellian distribution, which is realized in ordinary gases."[27] Products of the Primeval Atom disintegration behaved differently. They moved "with velocities spreading in every direction with speeds of the same order of magnitude." Consequently, they should be described as "an assembly of corpuscular rays, as corpuscular radiation."[28] Only later, because of collisions, this radiation reached a state of statistical equilibrium and became a gas. So in the beginning there was light.

In this sense, Lemaître could be thought of as the first cosmologist who predicted the existence of the radiation era in the early universe. There is, however, a striking difference between the mechanism producing this radiation as proposed by Lemaître and as proposed in the present standard model of the universe. Lemaître believed that the radiation was a product of disintegration of the Primeval Atom in the nonequilibrium state of early epochs, whereas, in the present world model, it is regarded as due to a local thermal equilibrium "in the beginning." Lemaître was aware of the fact that remnants of the primordial radiation should today be present in the universe and tried to identify them with cosmic rays. At that time — yet in the 1930s — there was no other candidate for this role. This is why he devoted a lot of work and effort to study cosmic rays and their interaction with the earth's atmosphere. He published several research papers in this field.[29]

In the years after the Second World War, the cosmological scene was dominated by the controversy between the Big Bang cosmology and the so-called "steady state" cosmology, propagated by Hermann Bondi, Thomas Gold, and (in a different version) by Fred Hoyle.[30] Hoyle, in particular, was very active in leading a campaign against the Big Bang theory (the name itself "Big Bang" was invented by Hoyle as a contemptuous nickname for cosmologies with the initial singularity). The main assumption of the steady state cosmology was that the universe always presented the same global picture, independently of its expansion. To maintain constant density, matter was assumed to be created out of nothing (out of a "creation

27. Lemaître, "Instability in the Expanding Universe," pp. 475-86.
28. Lemaître, "Instability in the Expanding Universe," pp. 475-86.
29. For a review, see M. Heller, "The Legacy of Lemaître," *Acta Cosmologica* 22, no. 2 (1956): 135-50 (Section 2.6).
30. See H. Kragh, *Cosmology and Controversy* (Princeton: Princeton University Press, 1996), p. 199.

field") at a constant rate. When the steady state cosmology gradually gained greater and greater popularity, Lemaître, highly dissatisfied, gave up doing cosmology and turned to his old passion — numerical calculations.

Only a few days before his death (which occurred on June 20, 1966), Georges Lemaître learned from Odon Godart about the discovery of the microwave background radiation by Penzias and Wilson — and was glad that the idea of the "violent beginning of the universe" has been in this way corroborated.[31]

7. Concluding Remarks

There is no doubt that the idea of the "Primordial Light" was a motive and inspiration for many cosmological works of Georges Lemaître, and that it had its source in the theological considerations of his younger years. During his theology studies in the seminary of Malines, he fostered rather strong "harmonizing" views. His symbolic interpretation of the biblical story of creation provided a basis for such an attitude.

As Lemaître was more and more deeply immersed in scientific works, this harmonizing attitude gradually disappeared, but his interest in the role of light in the early universe remained alive. In his groundbreaking paper of 1927, there is a clear trace of his fascination with light, and the physics of radiation is one of the cornerstones of his Primeval Atom hypothesis. In his subsequent scientific works, he never mentioned any religious or theological ideas as inspirations for his research. And as time passed, he developed a quite radical "separatist" position. Science and religion (or theology) are situated on two different cognitive levels, and even if they use the same words, the meanings attached to them are different.

A good example of this "disjunction" is the concept of beginning. The scientific concept of beginning has nothing to do with the religious idea of beginning, understood as the creation of the universe by God. In one of his unpublished manuscripts,[32] Lemaître writes: "[D]uring the first rapid expansion of the ever expanding universe matter was engaged in super-radioactive activity and emitted the cosmic rays. What happened before?

---

31. See D. Lambert, *Un atome d'universe. La vie et l'oeuvre de Georges Lemaître* (Bruxelles: Lessius, 2000), p. 345.

32. "The Expanding Universe," in M. Heller, *Lemaître, Big Bang and the Quantum Universe: With His Original Manuscript* (Tucson: Pachart, 1996), p. 47.

Before that we have to face the zero value of the radius. . . . We may speak of this event as of a beginning. I do not say a creation. Physically it is a beginning in the sense that if something has happened before, it has no observable influence on the behaviour of the universe, as any feature of matter before this beginning has been completely lost by the extreme contraction at the theoretical zero." This is what Lemaître calls "natural beginning." In his last major cosmological work,[33] Lemaître clarifies the problem in the following way: "As far as I can see, such a theory [i.e., the theory of the expanding universe] remains entirely outside any metaphysical or religious question. It leaves the materialist free to deny any transcendental Being. He may keep, for the bottom of space-time, the same attitude of mind he has been able to adopt for events occurring in non-singular places in space-time."

Why such a shift in Lemaître's views, from a harmonizing tendency in his younger years to strict separatism in later views? I think that there were two main reasons. First, there were accusations frequently made against him that, being a Catholic priest, he used cosmology, especially the problem of the beginning, as a means of propaganda on behalf of a religious worldview. Lemaître wanted to show that this was not the case, that he was an honest scientist who practiced science in strict accordance with scientific methodology. Second, at that time, the ideology of two separate, nonintersecting cognitive planes was a quasi-official doctrine of neo-Thomist philosophy with regard to science-religion interactions, and the University of Louvain was one of the leading centers of this philosophy. During his theological studies Lemaître was trained in such Thomistic philosophy, and during all his life as a professor at Louvain he was certainly exposed to its influences.[34]

Individual views of great scientists are born and die together with them. But their scientific achievements, incorporated into the chain of progress, remain alive and are ready to produce further fruits.

33. G. Lemaître, "The Primaeval Atom Hypothesis," p. 7.
34. One of the leading neo-Thomists, Fernand Renoirte, was his friend.

On the Development of Physical Characteristics Through Interactions

Andrew M. Steane

This chapter is intended to achieve two aims. The first is to present certain thought-provoking aspects of fundamental physics to an audience or readership not familiar with the technical details. The second is to make some tentative suggestions as to how these scientific insights might make an impact on theology. In the first aim I do not say a "nonscientific" audience, because I take it that we are all scientific, in the sense that we recognize the role of science in intellectual life and in human endeavor. Although it is not recognized as such by everyone, science is *part of* — not an adjunct to — the life of faith and the kingdom of God.

Science and theology have a crucial dissimilarity. In science we are "looking down," seeking to understand the patterns of the natural world, something which in principle we have the intellectual capacity to grasp, and which being impersonal makes only limited claims on our will and allegiance. In theology we are "looking up," using our limited intellectual capacity to help clarify knowledge of God — someone we cannot completely comprehend and who makes absolute claims on us. We are also "looking back": interpreting past human experience.[1] It is appropriate for some types of theological statement to be much more tentative than scientific statements — for example, anything concerning abstract ideas of God's relation to time — while others ought to be asserted confidently and faithfully, well beyond their basis in reason alone — such as John's "Beloved, let us love one another, because love is from God."

The symposium that provided the prompt for this chapter has as its theme "Light from Light." The statement referred to, from the Nicene

---

1. See John Behr, "Let There Be Light," in this volume.

Creed, is of course theological. Its meaning is to be grasped by bringing in the discussions that led up to it, and its wider context, such as the New and Old Testament writings, and subsequent reflections and responses. A scientific investigation into physical light as electromagnetic radiation and as a quantum field is almost irrelevant to this. However, it is appropriate for theologians to explore whether or not, or the extent to which, light might serve as a symbol that orients us correctly towards God, or reveals something of God's nature. Such a program will be more helpful if it draws on properties of physical light that make sound physical sense. Otherwise one is in danger of descending into a mere muddle. Therefore I shall begin by saying a few words about physical light — electromagnetic radiation — in the next section.

After thus presenting some aspects of the physics of light, I will turn to the second aim of the chapter. Here the central theme will be the character of physical reality that we learn from quantum physics. This has been and continues to be much discussed.[2] Here I will adopt a particular emphasis, one that I have explored at a more technical and detailed level elsewhere.[3]

Quantum physics reveals that, at a deep level, the physical world is not made of individual well-defined entities that have from the outset well-defined characteristics independently of one another. Rather, physical entities can acquire properties such as mass and charge and velocity through their interactions with one another and with their surroundings. In such a model, in the first instance the world is undefined but full of potential; as time goes on, well-defined subsystems such as particles with well-defined mass and motion can emerge, and the process whereby they acquire properties involves primarily a succession of interactions that establish correlations between one part of physical reality and another. However, these correlations only lead to the world as we experience it when there is a mechanism to prefer one type of correlation above another. This mechanism is subtle and not universally agreed among physicists, but it involves irreversible interactions with a wider environment. This broad-brush summary will be elaborated in Section 2. The main idea I want to work towards is that a *context* or *environment* for physical interactions appears to be crucial to allowing sense to be made of them. Physical entities acquire

2. See, for example, J. C. Polkinghorne, *The Quantum World* (London: Penguin, 1990), for an introduction.

3. See A. M. Steane, "Context, Spacetime Loops and the Interpretation of Quantum Mechanics," *Journal of Physics A: Mathematical and Theoretical* 40 (2007): 3223-43.

their status as recognizable entities with well-defined properties by means of their interactions with one another and with such an environment.

The chapter is laid out as follows. Section 1 is a survey and a celebration of the role of electromagnetic radiation in the physical universe. It is there mostly for enjoyment; it connects only indirectly to the rest of the chapter. However, I hope it may offer ideas as to how a symbolic role for light could be enriched. Section 2 is the main content of the chapter, introducing quantum *entanglement* and what we learn about the character of the world from quantum theory. Section 3 briefly and tentatively discusses the impact these ideas might have on theology.

1. The Electromagnetic Field

It turns out that light — in the broader sense of electromagnetic radiation — plays a larger role in the physical structure of the world than one might guess. Most of us, when we think of light, probably think first of all of the idea of light beaming down, as from the sun, or from a searchlight beam, shining upon the surface of things. However, we also have a sense of "light all around us," the air itself having a hint of luminosity about it, and this is right: the sky is blue because the molecules of the air scatter light to and fro (with greater success in the blue than the red part of the spectrum). The air is filled with light.

This second aspect of light, the way it can permeate the inside of things as well as illuminate the outside of things, corresponds more closely to what we find in physics when we study light in as much detail as we can. What we call "light" is found to be an excitation of a "field," and the "field" permeates all of time and space. It is called the electromagnetic field. I would like to sketch in layman's terms what we mean by this technical language.

Physics currently has, at its foundations, a set of ideas that seem to be here to stay. I don't pretend that these are final or anything like complete — suggestions in popular science books and in some learned articles that we are somehow "near to a final theory" seem to me to be extraordinarily unimaginative, even blinkered. However, some of the big ideas have so much beauty and explanatory power that we suspect they, or something recognizably descended from them, will continue to play a role in future, more complete scientific models.

Among these big ideas are the Second Law of Thermodynamics; the idea of symmetry, and one of its instances: the principle of relativity; the concept of curved spacetime; the concept of quantum amplitudes; and quantum field theory.

The starting point of quantum field theory is an existence statement: "There exists. . . ." The thing that exists is called a quantum field, and the job of the theory is to describe it and draw out the implications for observable phenomena. Among the great discoveries of the twentieth century were the *unifications* where it was found that two such quantum fields could be understood to be different aspects of a single entity. This naturally makes one suspect, or hope, that all such fields could be so combined into a single framework. Such a combination eludes us, but however it might proceed, the fields that it combined would be recognizably the ones we currently know and enjoy.

The electromagnetic field is the easiest one to understand. That does not mean it is straightforward, but it leads the way (and historically led the way) into getting to grips intellectually with the others (the so-called "color" and "weak" fields — and possibly the gravitational field, though this remains to be seen). A field can be thought of as a physical entity, having energy and momentum, but it is part of the basic structure of spacetime. It cannot come and go like a football or a rabbit; it is there everywhere and always. The word "vacuum" refers, in physics, to the character of spacetime when all the fields are in their lowest energy state. "Vacuum" in everyday parlance means "nothing there," but this is not what the study of physics teaches us. The fabric of spacetime is always there, and this fabric is not dull and featureless: it has rich structure.

The principal property of the electromagnetic field is that it can carry "excitations," called photons. When these excitations pass from one particle to another the emitting particle loses energy and suffers a change in motion (the product of its mass and velocity undergoes a change); the absorbing particle gains energy and suffers a change in motion. There are precise equations describing the rate of such events; the rate is related to a property that a particle can possess, called electric charge. The archetypical particle carrying electric charge is the electron.

A remarkable thing about the theory of the electromagnetic field, called *quantum electrodynamics,* is the physical picture it gives of what is going on all around us, within and around the familiar objects of our lives: the chair, the road, the coffee cup. These objects are all built out of electrically charged particles (electrons and quarks). These particles are in motion, and in continuous interaction with the electromagnetic field. According to quantum electrodynamics, or "QED," the electrons and quarks maintain their relative distances in balance by a continuous exchange of photons. Electrical charge is essentially a "propensity to emit or absorb" photons, and emitted photons are more likely to be picked up by a neighboring particle if the neighbor is close. These ideas, simple to sketch but requiring sophisticated mathematics to make precise, describe in full precision the observed "inverse square law" for the size of the force between particles as a function of their separation. In this sense we may say that *light,* in the broader sense of "electromagnetic radiation," permeates the universe not only in the vacuum between objects, but also throughout the interior of objects, enabling them to hold themselves together.

The table before me is full of light. We don't see that light because it is mostly not coming up out of the table, but passing to and fro within it, hidden inside, each photon glimmering just long enough to pass from one particle to another.

I sometimes like to muse on this fact as I walk along the road, enjoying the feeling that if it were not for this dance of energy and light, I would fall through the surface of the road into the interior of planet Earth — or to be more thorough and accurate, my body would dissipate entirely into a vapor of dust, and so would Earth.

Light commonly symbolizes things such as purity, hope, and truth. It has an interesting subtlety compared with other symbols, however, because it is our common experience that light is not so much something we see as *something by which we see.* To a physicist, light can also stand for the "go-between," a messenger by which things come together or are driven apart. It can also express a unity in nature: the light from the Sun is of the same nature as the light that binds our molecules or binds the rocks of planet Earth.

2. Physics and Relationships

The main aim of this chapter is to present certain striking features of quantum physics, especially the idea that physics is very much concerned with, and perhaps purely concerned with *relationships.* By this I mean that in physics we find ourselves chiefly concerned with how one body or entity interacts with or relates to another, rather than with absolute properties of isolated entities. To give the flavor of this idea, consider the simple example of uniform motion, i.e., motion at a constant speed in a fixed direction.

The principle of relativity asserts that there is no way to assign or define velocity in an absolute way: the only meaning that can be attached to the word "velocity" is that of relative velocity of one body with respect to another. In physics we find it is quite sufficient to understand motion purely in terms of relative motion. There is simply no need to introduce an idea of absolute uniform motion: it can never be detected or influence anything.

In quantum physics a broader type of relativity is a central idea, which I will try to describe. It should be noted that when we talk about quantum physics we are not talking about a restricted part of the science of physics. In principle, quantum mechanics is the mathematical "language" that underlies *all* physics (with the possible exception of gravitation). Since nonphysicists sometimes think that quantum mechanics is merely concerned with the very small, it should be emphasized that it is in fact our basic theory of all motion, at whatever scale. To put it another way, we live in a "quantum mechanical" world.

In quantum physics the state of affairs for any given system at any given time is described by means of a mathematical entity called a "state vector" or simply a "quantum state." It is not necessary to understand the details of this mathematical method for my present purposes; the main point is that such a quantum state gives *complete* information about the system in question. This means that in order to know what would happen if the system undergoes any sort of interaction with another, it is sufficient to know the quantum state of each and the nature of the interaction (by contrast, it is not necessary to know, for example, the past history of the systems in question).

To be more specific, suppose we consider a single atom of the element calcium. Such an entity is small enough to enable laboratory experiments to explore the phenomena I am about to discuss in full detail, but large enough to be reasonably tangible and familiar. In many respects, an atom behaves somewhat like a small sphere or ball, but one should include in the picture the fact that most atoms are, like planet Earth, magnetic, and therefore possess a sense of direction. A (singly ionized) calcium atom has a north magnetic pole and a south magnetic pole, and although the magnetic field it produces is exceedingly small, its orientation can be detected by sensitive experiments.

Suppose an atom is prepared with its magnetic north pole pointing upwards (i.e., away from the center of Earth), then the atom is rotated through 180 degrees about a horizontal axis, and then its orientation is measured. It should not surprise us to learn that in such a case the atom will be found at the end to have its magnetic north pole pointing downwards. These simple quantum states of "north pole up" and "north pole down" are denoted by the mathematical notation $|\uparrow\rangle$ and $|\downarrow\rangle$, in which the odd-looking bracket "$|\langle\ldots\rangle$" should be read as announcing "this is a quantum state" and the arrow in the middle describes the orientation of the atom in an obvious manner.

Suppose now we consider two atoms, say one calcium and one beryllium. Let both be prepared with their north poles upwards. The complete quantum state of the pair is then written $|\uparrow\rangle_C |\uparrow\rangle_B$; that is, we simply write the quantum states side by side, with the subscript letter serving to indicate which atom is being described.

Atoms can be in other orientations besides purely up or down, of course. If we begin to rotate an atom from up to down, but stop halfway, then its orientation is horizontal. In quantum theory such a state can also be understood to be an equal combination of "up" and "down," written $(|\uparrow\rangle_C + |\downarrow\rangle_C)$. Here the subscript C reminds us that there is only one atom being described, and the plus sign should be understood to indicate that the state in question is composed of more than one part, in a way similar to that in which a musical chord is composed of more than one note.

The type of quantum state that I would like to focus attention on now is a remarkable type much discussed in the physics community. In the notation I have introduced, it would be written

$$|\uparrow\rangle_C |\uparrow\rangle_B + |\downarrow\rangle_C |\downarrow\rangle_B \tag{1}$$

The reader should understand by this that the state concerns *two* atoms (labeled C and B), and their complete quantum state has contributions from two parts (somewhat like a musical chord), one corresponding to both atoms "up," the other corresponding to both atoms "down."

A state of the form (1) is called an *entangled state,* and the important property it has is that in such a state the two atoms partially lose their individual identities. For, suppose we prepare such a state and then apply a 180-degree rotation to atom C. This will rotate "up" to "down" and "down" to "up" *for atom C alone,* thus producing the transformation:

$$|\uparrow\rangle_C |\uparrow\rangle_B + |\downarrow\rangle_C |\downarrow\rangle_B \rightarrow |\uparrow\rangle_C |\downarrow\rangle_B + |\uparrow\rangle_C |\downarrow\rangle_B \tag{2}$$

But what if, instead of rotating atom C, we took the original state and rotated atom B?

$$|\!\uparrow>_C |\!\uparrow>_B + |\!\downarrow>_C |\!\downarrow>_B \rightarrow |\!\uparrow>_C |\!\downarrow>_B + |\!\downarrow>_C |\!\uparrow>_B \tag{3}$$

If you look carefully at the quantum states on the righthand sides of (2) and (3) you will see that they are composed of precisely the same two parts $|\!\uparrow>_C |\!\downarrow>_B$ and $|\!\downarrow>_C |\!\uparrow>_B$, simply written down in a different order. But just as two notes make the same chord, no matter which note you hear first, this sum of two contributions makes precisely the same quantum state, no matter which is written first. To be precise,

$$|\!\uparrow>_C |\!\downarrow>_B + |\!\uparrow>_C |\!\downarrow>_B = |\!\uparrow>_C |\!\downarrow>_B + |\!\downarrow>_C |\!\uparrow>_B$$

(We are of course familiar with other sums that don't depend on the order, for example, $4 + 6 = 10$ and $6 + 4 = 10$, so $4 + 6 = 6 + 4$.)

Now let us notice what has transpired in the two transformations shown in (2) and (3). We find that in order to go from a *given* initial state to a *given* final state, one can rotate *either* atom. This is truly remarkable and quite different from our everyday experience. Normally a rotation applied to one object gives a quite different state of affairs to a rotation applied to another object. If one has a cup and a bicycle and inverts one of them, then the final situation will depend on which was rotated. In one case one would finish with an upside-down cup and an upright bicycle. In the other, one has an upright cup and an inverted bicycle. In the case of the quantum-entangled state, however, we can have a situation where such apparently different operations produce precisely the same transformation of the complete system.

The best way to describe the properties of a quantum-entangled state is still a matter of debate among physicists. That is to say, there is no doubt about the results of any experiment we might care to invent, but there is debate about how best to put into words what it is that we learn about the physical world from this. It is certain that an entangled state cannot be described as a state of two separate entities with individual properties. Thus it suggests a limit on the extent to which reductionism succeeds as a model of the physical world. It also brings into question whether completely isolated systems can be described in any way at all. For, suppose we take one of the atoms C and B and place it, for the sake of argument, in isolation in outer space, somewhere out beyond the orbit of Pluto. Then what shall we say concerning its magnetic state? Is it oriented away from Earth? or towards it? or in some other direction? The only satisfactory answer appears to be that it has no well-defined orientation in and of itself. The entanglement has ensured that its magnetic state is *correlated with* that of atom B, but neither atom has an orientation of its own. Thus the principle of relativity which earlier we saw applied to relative velocity is now appearing in a new form applied to orientation and magnetism . . . and similar arguments can be made for any property whatsoever.

It turns out that entangled states are very common, and they are associated with another issue called the "quantum measurement problem." The essence of this problem is that the quantum state language can sometimes appear to make bizarre predictions, such as that a cat can be alive and dead simultaneously, in a quantum state involving a vast entanglement of all its particles and all its surroundings, including, for example, ourselves. The $|\uparrow>_C$ state in (1) could refer for example to a living cat, and the $|\uparrow>_B$ state to the brain of a person who looks at the cat and has sense-impressions corresponding to "it purrs and pounces"; the $|\downarrow>_C$ state could refer to a dead cat and $|\downarrow>_B$ to the brain of a person who receives sense-impressions corresponding to "it is still and cold." Then it may be argued that such a joint state is consistent with our experience, in that it describes the correlation between our own physical state and that of the cat. However, it is unable to affirm which eventuality actually transpired. Some physicists, following Hugh Everett,[4] are willing to infer that both eventualities coexist. I believe that this will prove to be a misinterpretation. An alternative, and in my opinion more satisfactory, approach is to argue that the physical world is described by the mathematical language in a less direct manner. The mathematics describes correlations between different parts of spacetime and the particles therein, but the physical world is so configured as to express these correlations in as economic a way as possible. In the case of the cat the outcome is that a physical cat is either alive or dead, but in order to rule out the "both, and" interpretation in favor of this "either, or" interpretation it is necessary to introduce a third party. The third system E interacts with the other two so as to produce the three-party entanglement

$$|\uparrow>_C |\uparrow>_B |\uparrow>_E + |\downarrow>_C |\downarrow>_B |\downarrow>_E$$

We then consider the case that the third system is not itself measurable in intimate detail, but plays the role of a larger environment with respect to which the first two can be described. The mathematical method to do this

4. Hugh Everett, "'Relative State' Formulation of Quantum Mechanics," *Review of Modern Physics* 29 (1957): 454-62.

is called "taking a partial trace"; it yields probabilistic information about the first two systems, C and B. The importance of the third system is that it is able to resolve the quantum measurement problem for the first two, because it exerts a subtle kind of pressure on them. If the environment cannot be manipulated, then the future evolution of C and B is not consistent with the entangled form (1), but it is consistent with the form either $|\uparrow\rangle_C$ $|\uparrow\rangle_B$ or $|\downarrow\rangle_C$ $|\downarrow\rangle_B$. Thus the systems *acquire a well-defined orientation* by a combination of their interaction with each other and their interaction with the wider environment. [For specialists: the basic problem is resolved by obtaining the reduced density matrix, and then imposing the interpretation that this represents a probabilistic mixture composed of separable states, by the hypothesis that the physical dynamics prefers a separable decomposition when it is available.[5]]

The problem with this resolution is that the third party E must itself be a physical system, so could be regarded as part of a larger system. However, the conclusion still stands if E is sufficiently large and complicated that it is not possible to reverse the effects of the interaction it had with C and B. The complete argument therefore has to bring in the issue of irreversibility and the nature of time.

Experts will recognize that I am in part here referring to an aspect of physics in this area called *decoherence*. However, for the avoidance of misunderstanding, I would like to emphasize that decoherence (namely a thermodynamically irreversible process in which off-diagonal elements of a density matrix tend to zero) does not in itself resolve the issue. The crucial point is that physics cannot fundamentally treat systems one at a time, nor in pairs, but only offers, and can only offer, statements about interactions between pairs of entities when a third entity is available to exert a subtle kind of influence that involves both an atemporal and an irreversible component.

3. Discussion

To summarize, developments in physics including relativity and quantum theory have driven us towards a description of the physical world in which physical statements are primarily about relationships, and furthermore there is a process whereby physical entities can both lose their individual-

5. See Steane, "Context, Spacetime Loops," pp. 3223-43.

ity and regain it. Quantum theory offers a mathematical language that can express the idea that an isolated system may be completely undefined, the attempt to assign properties to it meaningless. Physical systems can acquire their own individual properties, and thus a characteristic nature and name, when they interact with one another, as long as there is a third party to provide what amounts to a background or context for these interactions. The reason why we can discuss well-defined properties of well-defined objects in everyday language, "the bag is heavy, the grass is green," and so on, is because of interactions in the past that have resulted in well-defined field excitations called particles, with well-defined properties.

This description, when applied to the cosmos as a whole, leads to an impasse. "Who shall guard the guardians?" or, "Does the cosmos as a whole have an environment?" Statements concerning the whole cosmos should be tentative. We don't fully understand this, but the implication is that in order to have well-defined properties the universe has to be subject to an influence that is not describable in terms of quantum states and quantum mechanics. That does not imply very much about this further influence, but it does imply that we will struggle to understand what its nature may be. Nevertheless, we can do more than merely acknowledge that we don't know everything. We can assert that the natural laws that describe the fundamental workings of the physical world — laws that make an attempt to assign properties to an isolated system, without respect to anything else — are as meaningless as the attempt to talk about absolute velocity.

This type of natural law is intrinsically incapable of describing a completely self-contained cosmos.

Our knowledge of quantum theory as it applies to gravitation and cosmology is, however, either nonexistent or very incomplete, so statements about the cosmos as a whole must be treated with a great deal of caution. On the other hand, our knowledge of how quantum theory applies to small-scale phenomena is very accurate and confident. We can be fairly sure from the latter that relationships are the central business of physics and that the physical world is of such a kind that the properties and character of any one physical thing emerge via its interactions with other things. A rough impression of what this means can be gained by comparison with evolutionary biology and human development. In the former, the "big picture" is of no fixed organism at the outset, but a great potential and an efficient mechanism for exploring ecological niches, which requires and is molded by an environment with the right balance of stability and slow change. The environment is crucial in evolutionary biology: evolution is not simply a story of individual genes or organisms developing independently. In the second example (human development), insofar as human character is molded by nurture rather than genetics, it is molded chiefly by interactions with other people. These comparisons are not intended to be precise; they illustrate in more familiar terms what fundamental physics seems to be saying in abstract terms about the very fabric of physical reality.

The physical insight might fill out a little our understanding of the relationship between the natural world and its Originator, God. The case cannot be made strong enough to rule out completely one belief or another. However, it is possible to say that some beliefs are more coherent with physical evidence than others.

It is reasonable to say that the existence of the physical world should not be taken for granted: it is remarkable and not self-evident that anything should exist. The same can be said of aspects of the world of various degrees of profundity, from the existence of long-lived entities such as stars, to life, to altruism and the ability of some organisms to reflect and to love or hate. It is remarkable and not self-evident that the world should be able to support and express such entities and virtues.

I shall not rehearse here the arguments for and against theism or atheism. It is sufficient to my purpose to note that theism, correctly understood, is coherent with the nature of the physical world as we find it. By "correctly understood" I mean, for example, that the active verb of "creation" should not be understood in a simple-minded way as an event long ago, but as a continual process, more like an orchestra creating music, which is brought into being in the moment of its performance.

As Richard Harries and others have emphasized, the Creator must respect the patterns of the world if it is to be a world, i.e., have its own character and being.[6] There is, and has to be, therefore, some "standing back" of God from the world, but it is a standard intuition of theism that this is nothing like the deistic concept of a mere initiator of a self-contained cosmos. I should like to submit that the physical evidence is not coherent with the latter concept. The physical evidence suggests rather that the Creator brings about the character and being of inanimate physical things not by making them just as they finally are, but by imbuing the world in the first instance with creative potential, and then acting as the ground or context which is needed in order that some specific realization of this potential can

6. Richard Harries, *Questioning Belief* (London: SPCK, 1995).

take place. The word "ground" here is useful because it picks up the association of "ground of our being," but it is important to note that here this role is not *and cannot be* altogether passive. The world is woven from stuff that when left completely alone cannot acquire a character.

In Christian thinking there is a strongly held intuition that God is in the business of realizing people with the capacity to be and to love (and that these are not altogether separate). We learn as parents of our own children that, having provided food and shelter, our role is largely one of example and affirmation. Something like that may be going on at a basic physical level with regard to God and the universe: a continual affirmation. This type of relationship is there whether we welcome it or not. Of course Christians will go further and testify to further aspects, in which God's freedom to mold events is not less than our own, and is enhanced by our cooperation.

Light on Quantum Physics from Experiments with Quanta of Light

Markus Aspelmeyer and Anton Zeilinger

1. Introduction

Which worldview is completely consistent with all possible observations? This question, which seems to be an ultimate challenge to humanity, is an implicit working assumption of science. There, the first goal of devising theories is to explain existing observations and to predict future observations. But the final goal is to "understand" the world in a deep sense. Quantum theory brings us into a peculiar situation: it provides a perfect description of the physical world in the sense that no experiment to date is in conflict with quantum-theoretical predictions. However, some observable quantum phenomena are dramatically inconsistent with our "intuitive" understanding of "how the world should work." In other words, our current worldview does not allow for explaining naturally all observable phenomena.[1] Since there is no obvious need to modify the theory (as it works so perfectly), a change in our epistemology and our ontology might be necessary. Guided by the astonishing results of quantum optics experiments, in what follows we will describe two of the most challenging conceptual difficulties that quantum experiments pose to our current worldview: namely the question of physical realism, and the question of possible intrinsic and fundamental limitations of the explanatory power of physical theories.

---

1. This statement is true irrespective of one's personal preference of interpretation of quantum theory.

2. Physical Realism

The concept of "realism" per se is ill-defined, as witnessed by its evolution in the history of philosophy. In the domain of physics it seems reasonable (at least within classical physics) to introduce the concept of (local) "physical realism," which has to fulfill the following set of assumptions: first, the assumption that the outcome of a measurement on a physical system, say, a particle, reflects properties that the particle carried prior to and independent of the measurement; second, that an external influence on one physical system (A) has no *immediate* effect on another physical system (B).

Intuitively one might think that each measurement process has to obey these two assumptions naturally, or, in other words, that measurements reveal some local elements of physical reality carried by the observed physical system. Take, for example, the polarization of photons, the elementary particles of light. An individual photon can be polarized along a specific direction. We can measure this polarization by passing the photon through a polarizer oriented along this direction, say, the "horizontal" direction, and by placing a photon detector that is sensitive to an individual photon behind the polarizer (Figure 1b). A detector click indicates a successful measurement, i.e., the photon has been found to "be" horizontally polarized. If the photon does not pass the polarizer, it had to be orthogonally polarized, i.e., polarized along the vertical direction. These simple experiments are obviously consistent with physical realism since we find polarization as a local property of the particle. However, our intuition goes wrong when more than one particle gets involved,[2] or when we deal with systems of more than two dimensions.[3]

Quantum theory allows particles to become entangled. In its strongest form, maximally entangled particles are described exclusively by their joint properties. As a consequence, the joint behavior, i.e., the outcome of joint measurements on the system, is no longer a logical sum of the behavior of the individual particles. This essential feature was pointed out in 1935 by Erwin Schrödinger, who coined the technical term "quantum entangle-

2. See J. S. Bell, "On the Einstein-Podolsky-Rosen Paradox," *Physics* 1 (1964): 195; D. Greenberger, M. A. Horne, and A. Zeilinger, "Going Beyond Bell's Theorem," in *Bell's Theorem, Quantum Theory, and Conceptions of the Universe* (Dordrecht: Kluwer, 1989); and D. Greenberger, M. A. Horne, A. Shimony, and A. Zeilinger, "Bell's Theorem Without Inequalities," *American Journal of Physics* 58 (1990): 1131.

3. S. Kochen and E. Specker, "Problem of Hidden Variables in Quantum Mechanics," *Journal of Mathematical Mechanics* 17 (1967): 59.

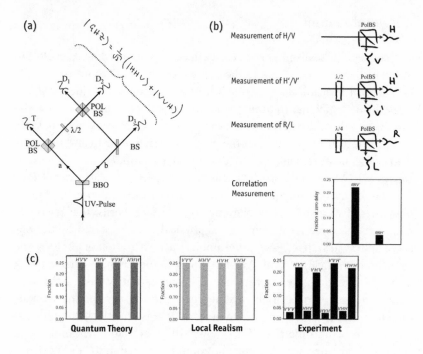

Figure 1: Experimental falsification of (local) physical realism. (a) Generation of a three-particle entangled "GHZ" quantum state in a photon experiment.* A strong pulse of ultraviolet (UV) light creates two pairs of polarization-entangled photon pairs

---

ment."[4] A specifically striking situation arises for three (or more) particles (Figure 1). Let us again consider the polarization property of photons. One specific example where three photons can get maximally entangled is such that one would find all photons polarized along the same direction when measurements are performed along the horizontal/vertical (H/V) direction, but it is principally undefined whether they are all three H or V. The correct quantum-theoretical description of this particular state would be a superposition of these two possible (but complementary) three-photon states. Since no information whatsoever is provided on the measurement outcome of the

4. E. Schrödinger, "Die gegenwärtige Situation in der Quantenmechanik," *Die Natur-wissenschaften* 23 (1935): 807, 823, 844.

$$|\Psi\rangle_{ab} = \frac{1}{\sqrt{2}}(|H\rangle_a|V\rangle_b - |V\rangle_a|H\rangle_b)$$

such that one photon of each pair is emitted along direction a and the other one along direction b. The polarizing beamsplitters in the setup (POL BS) operate such that they transmit horizontally polarized light and they reflect vertically polarized light, while beamsplitters have an equal transmission and reflection probability of 50 percent irrespective of polarization. In this configuration there are only two possibilities to observe a fourfold detection event (i.e., all detectors T, D_1, D_2, and D_3 register a photon at the same time): T registers an H photon and D_1, D_2, and D_3 register photons of polarization H, H, and V, respectively, or that T registers H, and D_1, D_2, and D_3 register V, V, and H, respectively. Since these possibilities are in principle indistinguishable (because of the original two-particle entanglement) we are left with a superposition state, i.e., the wanted GHZ state. (b) Realization of polarization measurements along the three complementary directions in a photon experiment. The bottom graph displays a typical result for measurements on the shown GHZ state. When photons 1 and 2 are found in R polarization (righthand circular), photon 3 is found with certainty (up to experimental errors) in V' polarization and V' can therefore be attributed an "element of physical reality" of photon 3. (c) No consistent set of such elements of reality is possible. The graphs show correlation data as measured experimentally,** which are in direct conflict with the predictions of local realism.

*D. Bouwmeester, J.-W. Pan, M. Daniell, H. Weinfurter, and A. Zeilinger, "Observation of Three-Photon Greenberger-Horne-Zeilinger Entanglement," *Physical Review Letters* 82 (1999): 1345.

**J.-W. Pan, D. Bouwmeester, M. Daniell, H. Weinfurter, and A. Zeilinger, "Experimental Test of Quantum Nonlocality in Three-Photon Greenberger-Horne-Zeilinger Entanglement," *Nature* 403 (2000): 515.

---

individual particle, quantum theory predicts a random outcome (in a series of measurements on equally prepared states) — as is the case for an unpolarized particle. It turns out that the genuine features of this three-particle entangled state can produce an immediate conflict with the concept of local realism, in principle for each individual photon. The idea is the following: specific measurements on two of the three particles allow us to predict with certainty the property of the third particle. For example, the measurement outcome on two of the particles that were measured, say, along the ±45 degree direction of polarization (H'/V' in Figure 1), allows us to predict with certainty the outcome of a polarization measurement along the left/right circular direction. Consequently, this particular predicted property qualifies as a local realistic property of the individual particle. Since the same holds for any two of the three particles, one can find four sets of correlation measurements that provide a contradicting set of "local realistic" properties of the individual particles. While one set of measurements will predict one property, say, left circularly polarized, another set will predict the exact opposite. It is therefore impossible to assign a consistent set of predefined local properties to each individual particle such that all possible correlation measurements can be explained based on these local realistic pre-assumptions. The quantum-theoretical predictions for three entangled particles are hence in direct conflict with the very idea that any measurement reveals some local property of the particle, i.e., in direct conflict with local realism.

This particular incompatibility theorem for local realism is known as GHZ theorem after Greenberger, Horne, and Zeilinger, who suggested it in 1989.[5] It is a stronger version of the Bell theorem (after John Bell, who suggested it in 1964).[6] Of particular conceptual significance is the fact that while Bell in his argument needs the possibility of prediction with certainty to derive his incompatibility theorem for statistical correlations, the GHZ argument shows that such "predictions with certainty" are intrinsically inconsistent.

Experiments that would reveal these inconsistencies of local realism go back to the early 1970s and involve tests of Bell's theorem in two-particle experiments.[7] In all (but one) cases, the experimental outcome was in conflict with the prediction of any possible local realistic theory. Since the late 1990s it has also become possible to entangle three and more photons,[8] and a first test of the direct conflict of local realism via the GHZ theorem was performed in 2000.[9] (See Figure 1.) Of course, to be conclusive, such experi-

5. See Greenberger et al., "Bell's Theorem Without Inequalities"; and Kochen and Specker, "Problem of Hidden Variables in Quantum Mechanics."

6. Bell, "On the Einstein-Podolsky-Rosen Paradox."

7. See S. J. Freedman and J. F. Clauser, "Experimental Test of Local Hidden-Variable Theories," *Physical Review Letters* 28 (1972): 938; A. Aspect, J. Dalibard, and G. Roger, "Experimental Test of Bell's Inequalities Using Time-Varying Analyzers," *Physical Review Letters* 49 (1982): 1804; G. Weihs, T. Jennewein, C. Simon, H. Weinfurter, and A. Zeilinger, "Violation of Bell's Inequality Under Strict Einstein Locality Conditions," *Physical Review Letters* 81 (1998): 5039; and M. A. Rowe, D. Kielpinski, V. Meyer, C. A. Sackett, W. M. Itano, C. Monroe, and D. J. Wineland, "Experimental Violation of a Bell's Inequality with Efficient Detection," *Nature* 409 (2001): 791.

8. Bouwmeester et al., "Observation of Three-Photon Greenberger-Horne-Zeilinger Entanglement."

9. Pan et al., "Experimental Test of Quantum Nonlocality in Three-Photon Greenberger-Horne-Zeilinger Entanglement."

ments have to be performed under conditions that allow for a strict test of the underlying assumptions. There are still some loopholes in existing experiments. To close these loopholes is an impressive experimental challenge, which we expect to be met in the not-too-distant future.

The described experiments are in clear conflict with our intuitive notion of local realism. In order to be consistent with observable phenomena, we have to revise this intuition. But what should one give up? Only the notion of locality? Most likely this would be in direct conflict with Einstein's theory of special relativity, which pre-assumes locality in some sense. Also, Leggett has recently suggested a first incompatibility theorem for an intuitive class of nonlocal realistic theories,[10] which allowed their falsification in recent experiments.[11] The notion of realism? But what does it mean to give up physical realism? Before we try to provide a possible answer to this problem let us address a second, related, intellectual challenge of quantum theory: the so-called measurement problem.

3. The Measurement Problem

Quantum theory provides a complete description of a physical system (to be precise: of all possible measurement results). Formally, it treats possible states of a physical system as independent vectors in a complex vector (Hilbert) space. From this we can calculate the probabilities for all possible measurement outcomes of a given experiment. Interestingly, in most cases quantum theory does not provide us with predictions with certainty (i.e., with probability equal to unity) for a measurement outcome but only with probabilities. While quantum theory does not single out a specific measurement outcome from the whole spectrum of possible results according to the probabilistic prediction, the fact that any actual experiment *has* a definite result is also referred to as the measurement problem. In other

10. A. J. Leggett, "Nonlocal Hidden-Variable Theories and Quantum Mechanics: An Incompatibility Theorem," *Foundations of Physics* 33 (2003): 1469.

11. See S. Gröblacher, T. Paterek, R. Kaltenbaek, C. Brukner, M. Zukowski, M. Aspelmeyer, and A. Zeilinger, "An Experimental Test of Non-Local Realism," *Nature* 446 (2007): 871; T. Paterek, A. Fedrizzi, S. Gröblacher, T. Jennewein, M. Zukowski, M. Aspelmeyer, and A. Zeilinger, "Experimental Test of Nonlocal Realistic Theories Without the Rotational Symmetry Assumption," *Physical Review Letters* 99 (2007): 210406; and C. Branciard, A. Ling, N. Gisin, C. Kurtsiefer, A. Lamas-Linares, and V. Scarani, "Experimental Falsification of Leggett's Nonlocal Variable Model," *Physical Review Letters* 99 (2007): 210407.

Markus Aspelmeyer and Anton Zeilinger

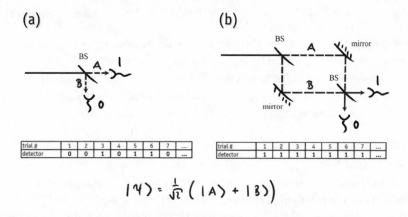

$$| \Psi \rangle = \tfrac{1}{\sqrt{2}} \left(| A \rangle + | B \rangle \right)$$

Figure 2: A variant of the measurement problem. (a) A photon behind a symmetric beamsplitter (BS) is in a superposition state as described by the wavefunction below. Photon detectors placed in the output port of the BS will find a perfect random sequence of detection events, in accordance with quantum-theoretical predictions. Where does the measurement occur? (b) When recombining the paths on a second BS, the resulting measurement outcome (a deterministic sequence of detection events) is incompatible with the assumption that the photon took a specific path A or B after the first BS.

---

words, quantum theory cannot provide a causal explanation of the specific detection event observed in the experiment. The measurement outcome is not itself a part of the explanatory framework of quantum theory.

Let us consider the following simple experiment (Figure 2): a single photon is impinging on a 50-50 beamsplitter, typically realized by a half-silvered mirror, from which it can be reflected or transmitted. The beamsplitter is chosen such that a beam of many photons would be approximately split in half, i.e., one would find approximately half of the photons in the transmitted port and the remaining ones in the reflected port of the beamsplitter. We now focus on the situation of a single photon. If we place photon detectors in both the transmission and reflection port, A and B, of the beamsplitter, which of the two detectors will register a photon? All we know about the situation is in the wavefunction, which here comprises a superposition of two vectors: one for the photon in the reflected arm (and subsequently detected by A) and one for the photon in the transmitted arm (and detected by B), or

$$|\Psi\rangle_{ab} = \frac{1}{\sqrt{2}}|A\rangle + \frac{1}{\sqrt{2}}|B\rangle$$

The probability for either detection event to occur is given by the square of its prefactor in the wavefunction, i.e., detector A or B will each register a photon with a probability of

$$|\frac{1}{\sqrt{2}}|^2 = \frac{1}{2}$$

If we repeat the experiment many times we will find a perfectly random sequence of detector clicks of A and B, respectively (Figure 2a). Alas, we cannot predict which of the two detectors is going to fire in an individual run and hence the problem of quantum theory with "measurements."

The superposition state $|\Psi\rangle$ emphatically implies that no "measurement" occurred, i.e., the particle "is" not in one definite output port of the beamsplitter, before the particle is actually registered in the detector. How can this be confirmed? We can perform another experiment to test if the state of the photon is indeed correctly described by the superposition state $|\Psi\rangle$. To do that we recombine the two possible photon paths on a second beamsplitter (in a way that the two paths between the beamsplitters have the same length) and we move the particle detectors to its output ports (Figure 2b). If the particle were "measured" and would follow a definite path after the first beamsplitter, it would also enter the second beamsplitter via a well-defined input port, and we are left with the previous experiment: a particle hitting a beamsplitter will be equally likely found in one of the two output ports. The actual experimental observation, however, is completely different. If we keep the path lengths between the beamsplitters stable, we will always find the particle in the same output port of the second beamsplitter, never in the other one! This observation contradicts directly the assumption that each particle had a definite, though unknown, position all the way between the two beamsplitters. It is in fact only the registered measurement outcome that leaves the particle irreversibly in one of its two possible states. As long as no measurement occurs the system cannot be said to be exclusively in either of its two possible states. It is, colloquially speaking, as if both states were "equally real" at the same time — which obviously (again) contradicts our notion of realism.

It is an essential feature of quantum physics that this argument carries through for every quantum system, irrespective of its size, complexity, or mass. Every complete quantum-physical description only contains superpositions of states of possible measurement outcomes. This observation is also at the heart of Schrödinger's cat paradox.[12] In this well-known example, Schrödinger constructs what he calls a "burlesque" situation in which a cat could "exist" in superposition of being "alive" and "dead." The amazing developments in the field of quantum physics are now enabling first experimental attempts to investigate such highly counterintuitive macroscopic superposition states.[13]

4. Conclusion

The obvious question is how to resolve these paradoxes. How can we obtain a consistent epistemology of the physical world that also incorporates the lessons from quantum physics such as the failure of local realism and the impossibility of explaining the individual measurement outcome?

We start with the plausible working assumption that each physical theory provides us with some fundamental insight into the working principles of the physical world and hence describes the world "as it is." In our view, the elements of the specific formalism can in principle be rather disconnected from "reality," as long as the predictions of the theory refer to observable events (in the sense of irreversible, intersubjective occurrences) in the physical world.[14] This is consistent with Bohr's view that (quantum) physics should be treated as a description of possible observations within the physical world, which does not necessarily imply a deeper meaning of the formalism. For the case of quantum theory, these events are the measurement outcomes. One immediate lesson to learn from quantum theory — without invoking any additional interpretation of the formalism such as the ontological status of the state vector(s) — is that a description of these events has to contain an intrinsically probabilistic element. In that sense, quantum theory is "about" probabilities (of measurement outcomes). It is for this reason that it cannot provide a complete description of the kind one would expect from a more naïve point of view, in which, for example, each "event" can be predicted with certainty.

12. Schrödinger, "Die gegenwärtige Situation in der Quantenmechanik."
13. See A. J. Leggett, "Testing the Limits of Quantum Mechanics: Motivation, State of Play, Prospects," *Journal of Physics: Condensed Matter* 14 (2002): R415; and M. Arndt, M. Aspelmeyer, and A. Zeilinger, "How to Extend Quantum Experiments," *Fortschritte der Physik* 57 (2009): 1153.
14. This is a much weaker "correspondence axiom" than the one of Einstein, in which each element of a physical theory has to correspond to an element of physical reality.

Another important point concerns the fact that the picture that the world exists in all its properties independent of us, independent of the kinds of observations we perform, is simply wrong. We are not just passive observers. The Austrian physicist Wolfgang Pauli expressed it by saying that the picture of an observer who is detached from the world does not work anymore. A detached observer would be just like a person in a theater watching a play taking place on stage. The question of whether or not he watches the stage or whether he looks down on the floor does not at all change what happens on stage. We have learned that the observer has a significant influence through his choice of the measurement instruments, through his decision about which kind of quantity to measure. The point is that his measurement instruments don't just influence or change the observed systems. That would still be accepted in some way. But we have learned that the choice of measurement instrument decides which property of a quantum system can become reality. In our little example, it depends on whether the observer positions the two-photon detectors just behind the first beamsplitter or behind the second, which then decides whether the path taken between the beamsplitters can become physical reality. So which quality, which feature can become reality is the experimenter's choice, and the specific individual result for the quality chosen is then in general random, i.e., nature's choice.

A further intrinsic feature of every physical theory is that it cannot explain by principle those elements of the theory that are pre-assumed for establishing the formalism. Such "enabling conditions" in the Kantian sense are necessary for each descriptive framework. In other words: a theory can only be consistent, but not fully self-referential. For example, Newtonian physics can deterministically describe the dynamics of point masses in spacetime without being able to explain by principle the origin of either mass or spacetime, or the direction of time. Quantum theory predicts the probabilities of measurement outcomes, but the measurement itself, i.e., the fact that a physical system will irreversibly end up in one definite state (of the measurement apparatus), is not described by the theory. It is a necessarily predefined concept to which the theory refers. Because quantum theory is about probabilities of measurement outcomes, the "fact" of the measurement outcome is not part of the theory and hence beyond its explanatory power. In that view the measurement paradox arises as a natural consequence of quantum theory as a physical theory.[15]

15. We conjecture that one should be able to construct similar paradoxes, for example, for the direction of time in the Newtonian case.

We would finally like to raise the question: Can the formalism of quantum theory be a necessary consequence that can be derived from a more general set of physically plausible principles? Zeilinger and Brukner have shown in a series of papers that some of the essential aspects of quantum theory can be recovered if one assumes that the information content of a physical system is finite.[16] For example, a two-level quantum system, such as a polarized photon, would carry exactly one bit of information. This conjecture certainly contradicts our notion of classical physical realism, after which the measurement result of all possible measurements should already be specified prior to the measurement (the information content of a classical system would therefore be infinite). On the other hand, the finiteness of information reflects in a very genuine way the actual situation of a quantum measurement. For a two-dimensional system, a measurement resembles one single question with two possible answers, yes or no, which can be encoded in exactly one bit. Higher-dimensional systems allow for measurements with more, but still a finite number of yes/no measurement outcomes. The quantization of information therefore seems to be a necessary consequence of (quantum) measurements. In this "information approach," intrinsic randomness occurs when the system contains less information than is necessary to provide definite answers to a given set of measurements, and all features of entanglement are reproduced when the full information content is encoded only in joint properties of systems. It is worth mentioning on the side that the concept of information about correlations contains also an intrinsic "nonlocal" feature, as the change in my knowledge about one system can instantaneously change the state of my knowledge about another system (as no physical mechanism is involved).

In conclusion, we are left with measurement outcomes as the only entities with ontological meaning, as they are irreversible (classical) events on whose occurrence everybody can agree on. Since they belong to the necessary preconditions for building the quantum-theoretical formalism, they themselves cannot be part of the explanatory framework of quantum theory. From that point of view there is no measurement problem. The

16. See A. Zeilinger, "A Foundational Principle for Quantum Mechanics," *Foundations of Physics* 29 (1999): 631; C. Brukner and A. Zeilinger, "Young's Experiment and the Finiteness of Information," *Philosophical Transactions of the Royal Society of London A* 360 (2002): 1061; and C. Brukner and A. Zeilinger, "Information and Fundamental Elements of the Structure of Quantum Theory," in *Time, Quantum, Information*, ed. L. Castell and O. Ischebeck (Berlin: Springer-Verlag, 2003).

"disappearance" of physical realism on the other hand is linked to the fact that we can choose one specific "framework" for our observation, but another choice can provide results that are inconsistent (from a physical realist's point of view) with the previous one. In that sense quantum theory provides us with a necessary openness of the world: first, a complete description of the physical world in one universal framework is in principle impossible because the explanatory power of every theory is bounded by its pre-assumed concepts and entities.[17] Second, there is always the freedom of choice of the experimenter as to which property should become a "physical reality." Maybe the answer to a new epistemology lies in incorporating this eminent role of the observer via the concept of information, as was briefly sketched above. Future work both in theory and in experiment will have to show that this approach carries through to a full reconstruction of quantum theory — and therefore to a more profound understanding of our world.

17. This reasoning leads to the immediate conclusion that a "wavefunction of the universe" is a meaningless (because logically impossible) concept.

Studies of the Velocity of Light and Causality

Robert W. Boyd

In recent years, the physics community has come to realize that studies of the properties of light can be used to address deep questions that lie at the foundations of physics. In this contribution, we concentrate on the relation between measurements of the velocity of light and the principle of causality.

In detail, in this contribution we first review some recent experimental studies that show the velocity of light can be significantly modified through use of nonlinear optical effects. Under certain circumstances, light pulses are observed to propagate with velocities that exceed the velocity of light in vacuum *c*. We then review theoretical arguments showing that the principle of causality limits the maximum velocity with which signals can be transmitted to the velocity of light in vacuum. This apparent contradiction is resolved by arguing that the velocity at which the peak of a pulse moves through a material (known as the group velocity) is not the same as the velocity at which information is transmitted through a material. Finally, we speculate on what it would mean to live in a universe in which the principle of causality could be violated. One broad conclusion to be drawn from work of this sort is that studies of the prop-

I gratefully thank Professor Charles H. Townes for his skillful mentoring early in my career and for arranging for me to be invited to participate in this symposium. I also thank Professor Marlan O. Scully for numerous scientific discussions on the topic area of this article. I am particularly grateful to Michelle Malcuit and Wayne Tompkin for their help in preparing Figure 1. I am grateful to the U.S. National Science Foundation for their support of the scientific investigations that form the substance of this chapter. Finally, I thank the John Templeton Foundation for their support, which has allowed me to cast my research in this broader context.

erties of light can shed insight on questions of a fundamental and philosophical nature.

1. Nonlinear Optics and the Control of the Velocity of Light

Let us begin by making some introductory comments regarding the research field known as nonlinear optics. The name of this field arises from the fact that it involves effects that arise when the light source (almost always a laser light source) is so intense that the linear superposition principle breaks down. In these situations, it is no longer true that two different beams of light act independently. If two light beams intersect in an appropriate material, each beam can influence the propagation of the other. This interaction is known as light-by-light scattering,[1] although the descriptor light-from-light would be equally appropriate. It has been predicted that this interaction can take place even in vacuum by means of relativistic quantum effects,[2] although this effect has never been observed experimentally. However, light-by-light scattering is routinely observed in the nonlinear response of optical materials. One example from my own laboratory of such behavior is shown in Figure 1. In this example, two laser beams intersect inside a nonlinear material and interact in such a way that two additional light beams are created. In terms of simple equations, we can explain the phenomenon of light-by-light scattering by means of the intensity dependence of the refractive index of common materials according to the relation

$$n = n_0 + n_2\, I, \tag{1}$$

where n_0 is the usual value of the refractive index experienced by weak light fields, I is the intensity of the strong light field, and n_2 is a quantity known as the nonlinear refractive index.

Over the past several years, the present author has been engaged in research aimed at making use of nonlinear optical methods to control the velocity with which light pulses pass through optical materials. It is useful to distinguish two different velocities of light: the phase velocity given by

1. See R. Y. Chiao, P. L. Kelley, and E. Garmire, "Stimulated Four-Photon Interaction and Its Influence on Stimulated Rayleigh-Wing Scattering," *Physical Review Letters* 17 (1966): 1158.

2. See H. Euler and B. Kockel, "Über die Streuung von Licht an Licht nach der Diracschen Theorie," *Naturwissenschaft* 23 (1935): 246.

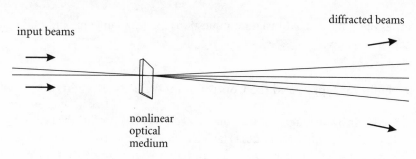

input beams

diffracted beams

nonlinear
optical
medium

Figure 1: The nonlinear-optical process of light-by-light scattering. Here two intersecting light beams excite the process, and two additional light beams are created. For this reason, the process could equally well be described as the generation of light from light.

$$v_p = c/n \qquad (2)$$

and the group velocity given by

$$v_g = c/n_g \text{ where } n_g = n + \omega \frac{dn}{dw} \qquad (3)$$

In these equations c is the velocity of light in vacuum and ω is the frequency of the light. The phase velocity describes the velocity at which the wavefronts of a light wave move through a material, whereas the group velocity gives the velocity at which the point of maximum intensity of a pulse of light moves through a material. Other workers and I have found that through use of nonlinear optical methods we can exercise great control over the group velocity of light.[3] One sometimes speaks figuratively of "slow light" under circumstances such that $v_g \ll c$,[4] "fast light" for $v_g > c$,[5] and "backward light" when v_g is negative.[6] An example of laboratory data

3. R. W. Boyd and D. J. Gauthier, "Controlling the Velocity of Light Pulses," *Science* 326, no. 5956 (2009): 1074.

4. See L. V. Hau, S. E. Harris, Z. Dutton, and C. Behroozi, "Light Speed Reduction to 17 Metres per Second in an Ultracold Atomic Gas," *Nature* 397 (1999): 594; and M. M. Kash, V. A. Sautenkov, A. S. Zibrov, L. Hollberg, G. R. Welch, M. D. Lukin, Y. Rostovtsev, E. S. Fry, and M. O. Scully, "Ultraslow Group Velocity and Enhanced Nonlinear Optical Effects in a Coherently Driven Hot Atomic Gas," *Physical Review Letters* 82 (1999): 5529.

5. See L. J. Wang, A. Kuzmich, and A. Dogariu, "Gain-Assisted Superluminal Light Propagation," *Nature* 406 (2000): 277; and M. D. Stenner, D. J. Gauthier, and M. A. Neifeld, "The Speed of Information in a 'Fast-Light' Optical Medium," *Nature* 425 (2003): 695.

6. See G. M. Gehring, A. Schweinsberg, C. Barsi, N. Kostinski, and R. W. Boyd, "Obser-

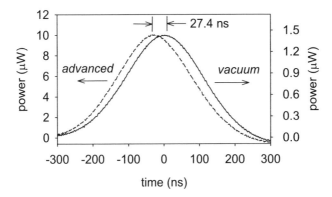

Figure 2: Fast-light pulse propagation. Temporal evolution of a 263.4-ns-long (full width at half maximum) pulse propagating through a laser-pumped potassium vapor (dashed line) and through vacuum (solid line).[7]

showing superluminal propagation is given in Figure 2. The phenomenon of backwards light is especially intriguing, as it entails the motion of a pulse of light in the "wrong" direction through an optical material. But such behavior has actually been observed experimentally, as illustrated in Figure 3.

2. Connection Between the Velocity of Light and Causality

As we mentioned above, recent research has shown that it is possible to find situations in which pulses of light can propagate with velocities greater than the velocity of light in vacuum c or even with negative group velocities. Such behavior is certainly counterintuitive. But from a more formal point of view, these results are disturbing in that at first glance they seem to be at odds with some well-established features of the special theory of relativity. In particular, a direct consequence of the special theory of relativity is that the transmission of information at a speed greater than the velocity of light in vacuum would allow one to violate the principle of causality. In this section we examine this point in some detail. We first examine why super-

vation of Backward Pulse Propagation Through a Medium with Negative Group Velocity," *Science* 312 (2006): 895.

7. See Stenner, Gauthier, and Neifeld, "The Speed of Information in a 'Fast-Light' Optical Medium."

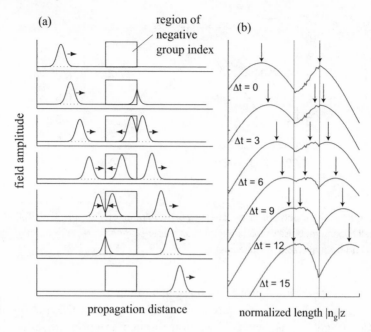

Figure 3: Conceptual prediction (a) and experimental results (b) showing the backwards propagation of the peak of a light pulse.[8]

luminal transmission of information would lead to a violation of causality. We also take a careful look at what one means by causality, and conclude with some remarks as to why none of the experiments reported to date imply a violation of causality.

Relation Between Superluminality and Causality

Let us begin by investigating why superluminal velocities can imply a violation of causality.[9] It can be shown by means of simple Lorentz transformations that if there is some reference frame in which party A can transmit information to party B with a velocity that exceeds the velocity of light in vacuum c, then there will exist some other reference frame in which the

---

8. See Gehring et al., "Observation of Backward Pulse Propagation Through a Medium with Negative Group Velocity."

9. See P. W. Milonni, *Fast Light, Slow Light, and Left-Handed Light* (Bristol, UK: Institute of Physics Publishing, 2005).

information reaches B before it leaves A. In the following discussion, we will use the term "superluminal transfer of information" to describe this sort of situation. The concept of causality is often assumed to be a cornerstone of physical theory, and thus the proof just described is often taken to imply the impossibility of superluminal transfer of information.

What Is Causality?

The concept of causality has several related meanings within science and philosophy. In general terms, one often says that event A cannot possibly cause event B to occur if event A occurs after event B. Thus the concept of causality is closely linked with that of the unidirectional flow of time and with the concept of simultaneity. That is, two events are either simultaneous, or else one event occurs after the other. Also, time always flows in one direction. People get older as time progresses, not younger, etc. If events A and B occur at the same point in space, then causality is well described in these terms.

Distant Causality and Clock Synchronization

If events A and B occur at different points in space, then the concepts of simultaneity and causality need to be refined. We need to ask what it means for two events to be simultaneous if they occur at different points in space. Discussion of this point goes back at least to the golden age of Greece, and of course took on a new life in terms of discussions of the theory of relativity. Much of the current discussion has dealt with the concept of clock synchronization. That is, how does one ensure that two clocks at different points in space read the "same" time? Of course, if the two clocks are in relative motion, then it is not possible to synchronize them, because of the effect known as time dilation. But even if the two clocks are at rest with respect to one another, one needs to describe in detail just how one would go about synchronizing them. One approach, due originally to Eddington,[10] is to transport one clock to the location of the other, set them both to register the same time, and then move the clock back to the original position. In doing so, it is crucial that the clock be moved sufficiently slowly that time dila-

10. A. S. Eddington, *The Mathematical Theory of Relativity* (Cambridge: Cambridge University Press, 1923).

tion effects do not affect the synchronization. The other approach, due to Einstein,[11] is to send a light signal from A to B and back again, perhaps by reflection with a mirror. B sets its clock when the pulse arrives, and A sets its clock at the midpoint between the moment that the pulse was sent and the moment at which it returns. In this manner, clocks at different points can be synchronized, and one can thereby meaningfully speak of which of two distant events occurs first and could possibly influence the other event.

St. Augustine's Treatment of Distant Simultaneity

As a historical footnote, we note that Einstein's protocol for clock synchronization was actually anticipated approximately 1500 years earlier by St. Augustine.[12] As related by Jammer,[13] it appears that St. Augustine was interested in this issue because he wanted to develop arguments suited to challenging the validity of the practice of astrology. Augustine argued that if two babies were born at exactly the same moment of time, then they would be "astrologically identical." If one baby grew up to be more successful than the other, it would imply that astrological forces did not play a crucial role in human development. To formulate his argument, Augustine needed to show how one could demonstrate that two babies were actually born at the same moment. He suggested that a runner be placed at the home of each expectant mother, and that as soon a baby was born the runner at that house would begin running at a fixed speed toward the house of the other mother. If the two runners crossed en route, the exact spot at which they crossed would be noted. At some later time the distance from this spot to each of the homes would be measured to high accuracy, and if the distances were found to be equal it would be concluded that the babies were born at the same moment.

Einstein Causality

Another definition of causality is that which emerges from Einstein's special theory of relativity. One begins by considering events that are de-

11. A. Einstein, *Relativity: The Special and the General Theory* (New York: Gramercy, 1988).

12. St. Augustine, *Confessions,* book 7, chapter 6 (ca. CE 397).

13. M. Jammer, *Concepts of Simultaneity* (Baltimore: Johns Hopkins University Press, 2006).

scribed by their locations in a four-dimensional space known as Minkowski space. A two-dimensional cut through Minkowski space is shown in Figure 4. An event occurring at point A could be influenced by event E, because there is time for a light signal from E to reach point A. But an event at B cannot be influenced by event E, because there is not time for a signal from E to reach B. It should be noted that if signals could propagate faster than the speed of light in vacuum, it would be possible for E to influence B. Similarly, an event occurring at point C can influence E, but an event occurring at point D cannot. The Minkowski diagram thus presents a simple graphical picture for understanding the relation between superluminality and causality.

Why Do Superluminal Group Velocities Not Imply Violations of Causality?

We have argued above that recent experiments have demonstrated that the peak of an optical pulse can propagate with a velocity that exceeds the velocity of light in vacuum. We have also argued that superluminal transfer of information would imply a violation of the principle of causality, a principle that is considered to be a cornerstone of our understanding of nature. What is the resolution of this apparent paradox?

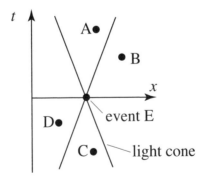

Figure 4: Illustration of Einstein causality. The light cone is associated with an event occurring at spacetime position E. If E is at the origin of the coordinate system, the light cone is given by the relation $|x| = ct$. Points within the light cone, such as point A, can be causally related to event E. Points outside of the light cone, such as point B, cannot be influenced by event E. Events A and E are said to be time-like separated, whereas events such as B and E are said to be space-like separated.

Robert W. Boyd

One important consideration is that there is more than one way to define the "velocity of light." It now appears as if there are at least six different ways to define the velocity of light, depending on what properties of the light field are under consideration.[14] Most crucial to the issues under consideration here is that the peak of a light pulse propagates at a velocity known as the group velocity, whereas the information content of a light pulse propagates at a velocity known as the information velocity. The group velocity is given by Eq. (3). It is not quite so clear how to define the information velocity, although for certain technical reasons it is often taken to be equal to the velocity of light in vacuum c.

These issues are illustrated conceptually in Figure 5. The information content of a pulse is contained in the "front" of the pulse. The front heralds the fact that the remainder of the pulse has been emitted and will arrive shortly. The actual arrival of the peak of the pulse adds no information beyond that contained in a brief time window surrounding the front of the pulse. This figure also tries to show that while the peak of the pulse can attempt to catch up to the pulse front, it can never overtake it. But how do we know that this conclusion is correct? Formal mathematical proofs have been given, but these proofs necessarily are based on the assumption that no disturbance can propagate faster than the velocity of light in vacuum. Perhaps more intuition comes out of analysis such as that shown in Figure 6. Here we have performed a numerical evaluation of the equations that govern the propagation of light pulses through material media.[15] These results show why it is impossible to advance a pulse by more than approximately two pulse widths. When the propagation distance is chosen to be too large, the pulse does not experience increased advancement. Rather it breaks up into multiple sub-pulses with no additional advancement.

Speculations on Causality Violation

Let us now turn our attention to the much more speculative topic of whether it could be possible to violate the principle of causality and what the implications of such a violation would be.

14. See Milonni, *Fast Light, Slow Light, and Left-Handed Light,* and R. Smith, "The Velocities of Light," *American Journal of Physics* 38, no. 8 (1970): 978.
15. See R. W. Boyd and P. Narum, "Slow and Fast Light: Fundamental Limitations," *Journal of Modern Optics* 54 (2007): 2403.

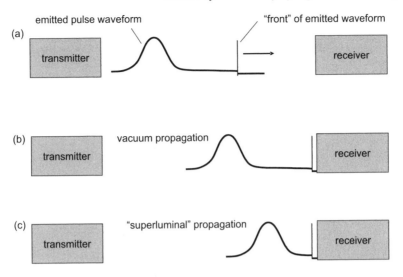

Figure 5: (a) Any real pulse has a "front," the first moment in time at which the intensity becomes nonzero. (b) For propagation through vacuum, the time interval between the front and the peak of the pulse remains fixed. (c) In "superluminal" propagation experiments, the peak of the pulse moves at a superluminal velocity, but the front of the pulse moves as c. Since the information content of the pulse is contained in the front, no information is transmitted at a velocity exceeding c.[16]

We comment first that there has been serious scientific speculation about the possible existence of faster-than-light particles known as tachyons.[17] Such particles seem not to be strictly forbidden by established laws of physics. Einstein's special theory of relativity implies that it is impossible to accelerate a normal, slower-than-light particle to a velocity exceeding c. But it does not prohibit the existence of particles whose velocity has always exceeded c. Tachyons, if they exist, could serve as the carriers of faster-than-light information.

From a different point of view, it is interesting to think about what it would mean to live in a world that was acausal. So much of our intuition is based on the idea of causality and the forward flow of time that it is not clear just what it would mean to live in an acausal world. For example, it

16. See D. J. Gauthier and R. W. Boyd, "Fast Light, Slow Light and Optical Precursors: What Does It All Mean?" *Photonics Spectra* (January 2007): 82.

17. See G. Feinberg, "Possibility of Faster-Than-Light Particles," *Physics Review* 159 (1967): 1089.

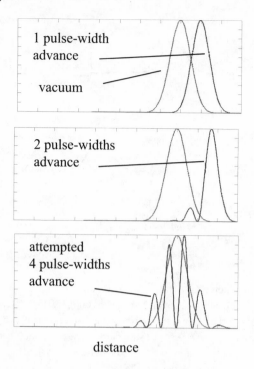

distance

Figure 6: Example of why arbitrarily large pulse advancements are not possible. In all situations that we have tested in numerical simulations,[18] a light pulse breaks up into many individual components when propagating through large distances of a fast-light material.

might seem very desirable if something I could do today would "undo" a mistake that I made in the past. For example, it might seem desirable to be able to undo the traffic accident I had last year. But where would that leave the auto mechanic who fixed my car? How would his life be modified if something I did today could cause his income of a year ago to suddenly disappear?

It is not clear whether a demonstration of the violation of the principle of causality would require "only" a complete reformulation of the laws of physics. Or would the rules of logic need to be modified as well?

Another speculative idea is that causality actually can be violated in our present world, but only at very small time and distance scales. At these

18. Boyd and Narum, "Slow and Fast Light."

time and distance scales, time would perhaps not flow in a unidirectional sense. Physical processes could depend on the time as averaged over both positive and negative values. Such a possibility could allow the existence of new physical processes on a microscopic scale, while preserving causality on a more human time and distance scale.

There has also been speculation that, in the cosmological expansion of the universe, different regions were created in which different physical laws are valid. Then perhaps causality is preserved in our region of the universe but not in others. The fact that causality is preserved in our region of the universe is then perhaps a consequence of some anthropic principle, in the sense that human life as we know it perhaps could not have developed in regions of the universe that did not preserve causality.

3. Summary

Recent experiments have shown that under specialized circumstances pulses of light can be made to propagate at speeds that appear to exceed the velocity of light in vacuum. However, a crucial distinction must be made between the velocity with which the peak of the pulse moves (the group velocity) and the velocity with which the information content of the pulse moves (the information velocity). Our conclusion is that the group velocity can exceed c, whereas the information velocity cannot. No experiment performed to date has given evidence of superluminal values of the information velocity, and thus no causality violation is implied by any laboratory results currently available. Nonetheless, it is intriguing to speculate what it would mean if evidence of noncausal processes could be identified in nature.

Light in the Beginning

Marco Bersanelli

1. Introduction

Since ancient times, human beings have speculated about the nature of celestial bodies and have become deeply attracted by their stable luminosity and by the regularity of their motion. The powerful shining of the Sun provided heat and light for their environment, as well as for all creatures on which their lives depended. Light from the sky was clearly recognized as an element essential to human existence. The Moon, the stars, and the planets glowing in the dark nights of pretechnological eras were the subject of deep wonder and surely an incentive to develop a vivid imagination. The height of the sky was evidently beyond any possible human reach. In various prescientific civilizations, heavenly bodies were perceived as pertaining to a level of reality superior to our human existence, and they were often worshiped as gods and supernatural entities. In ancient Greece, celestial bodies were seen as formed by incorruptible matter, eternally revolving in their perfect circular orbits. Their light was thought to originate from an element, the ether, inherently different from any earthly material. This dual vision of the universe, encoded in the Aristotelian distinction between the sublunar and the superlunar realms, resisted change for nearly two millennia.

When Galileo turned his telescope to the sky in 1609, for the first time he captured light with a power exceeding that of the human eye. Immediately, new details became visible, opening up an uninterrupted chain of astronomical conquests in the following four centuries. Since then, technology has provided amazing instruments capable of gathering and detecting very faint sources (more than 100 million times fainter than those seen by

Galileo) and of analyzing their light in great detail, leading to enormous progress in our understanding of the cosmos.

Even today, however, everything we know about the universe comes from light we receive from very distant objects,[1] essentially unreachable by us. Just as for those ancient peoples, astronomical distances are simply too large for any direct exploration — except for our very immediate neighborhood. Indeed, we have visited the Moon and sent spacecraft to Mars and to other selected locations in our solar system, but no direct investigation is possible or, for the time being, even conceivable at interstellar distances — not to speak of the extragalactic scale, which appears as an expanse of space extending for billions of light years in all directions. We sit at an immobile point in the universe, surrounded by an inaccessible vastness that reveals itself through the light we receive. As English physicist Sir William Bragg noted, "light brings us news of the universe."[2]

2. Brilliant Insight from the "Dark" Ages

The great philosophers in ancient Greece recognized the importance of light in nature. Aristotle identified light-giving fire as one of the four elements that constitute the world, and Pythagoras placed a cosmic fire at the center of the universe. Aristarchus of Samos (310–c. 230 BCE) imagined his heliocentric system, probably recognizing the unique nature of the Sun as a majestic source of light and measuring its size with ingenious methods. In the Middle Ages, the Christian culture conferred an even more central status on light in nature, as it was perceived as a privileged sign of God's presence. The beauty of light in its diverse manifestations, its power of enabling our eyes to see, its apparently instantaneous velocity, all the properties that make light indispensable for human life, led medieval scholars to consider that no natural form other than light could be a better vestige of the Creator. The emphasis on light was sustained by the combined heritages from the Greek and the Judaic traditions. Indeed the Bible is full of passages in which light acts as a protagonist. In the Old Testament, light as a natural element is appreciated in its beauty and warmth: "Light is sweet,

1. Noteworthy exceptions are astrophysical studies based on the detection of cosmic rays and, very recently, the new field of gravitational waves. However, even these techniques are based on a passive observation that gathers information reaching us rather than on active exploration.

2. William Bragg, *The Universe of Light* (London: Bell, 1933), p. 1.

and it pleases the eyes to see the sun" (Eccles. 11:7). In addition, and more important, it is repeatedly proposed as an image of God's wisdom and power: "Send out your light and your truth" (Ps. 43:3); "You are dressed in glory and splendor, you are covered in light like a cloak" (Ps. 104:1-2). Light is also the divine gift to human beings enabling them to live and to discern the truth: "Give light to my eyes, or I will sleep in death" (Ps. 13:3). "You, O LORD, keep my lamp burning; my God turns my darkness into light" (Ps. 18:28). In the New Testament, light becomes the preferred image to indicate the divine nature of Jesus Christ: "The true light that gives light to every man was coming into the world" (John 1:9).

In medieval culture, light was indeed the supreme substance. It is not surprising, therefore, that cosmological discussions of that time retained light as the distinctive, fundamental element. We shall now revisit two eloquent examples.

A Luminous Beginning: Robert Grosseteste

Robert Grosseteste (1175-1253) was an English Franciscan theologian and a scholastic philosopher, who became chancellor of Oxford University and then Bishop of Lincoln. He was a true pioneer of the scientific method, and proposed a theory of knowledge based on an experimental approach.[3] Alistair Crombie[4] described Grosseteste as "the real founder of the tradition of scientific thought in mediaeval Oxford, and in some ways, of the modern English intellectual tradition." Grosseteste mastered astronomy, mathematics, and physics, but he was especially devoted to the study of optics. In 2009, on the occasion of the Galilean Year, his groundbreaking insight on the use of lenses for optical observation received renewed attention. In his treatise on rainbows, the *De iride*, we find remarkable anticipations of the concept of the optical telescope. He writes: "This part of optics, when well understood, shows us how we may make things a very long distance off appear as if placed very close, and large near things appear very small, and how we may make small things placed at a distance appear any size we want, so that it may be possible for us to read the smallest letters at incredible distances, or to count sand, or seed, or any sort of minute objects."[5]

3. Morris Bishop, *The Middle Ages* (Boston: Houghton Mifflin, 2001), p. 254.
4. Alistair Cameron Crombie, *Science, Optics, and Music in Medieval and Early Modern Thought* (London: Hambledon Press, 1990).
5. Robert Grosseteste, *De iride*, in *Die philosophische Werke der Robert Grosseteste*, ed. Ludwig Baur (Münster: Aschendorff, 1912), p. 74.

Perhaps less known, but not less interesting, are Grosseteste's ideas on cosmology, which he developed in the years 1220-30 in three works: the *De luce* and *De motu corporali et luce,* and the *Hexameron.* Grosseteste's central idea was the fundamental character of light in nature, an assumption that led him to develop a cosmogony entirely based on light.[6] In the *De luce* he writes: "Light is more exalted and of a nobler and of a more excellent essence than all corporeal things. It has, moreover, greater similarity than all bodies to the forms that exist apart from matter, namely, the intelligences." In the *Hexameron,* he notes that when the Creator generated light in the beginning and dispersed the darkness, sadness was dissolved and every creature was full of joy. In his vision, light is beautiful in itself because its nature is the simplest and it has maximal proportion in itself.[7] He also claimed that light, among all corporeal creatures, is the clearest manifestation, in an analogical sense, of the unity and trinity of God. For this reason, he suggested, "God began His work of the six days starting with the creation of light itself, whose dignity is so high."[8]

In the *De luce,* Grosseteste proposes that light is the source of every corporeity in nature:

> The first corporeal form which some call corporeity is in my opinion light. For light of its very nature diffuses itself in every direction in such a way that a point of light will produce instantaneously a sphere of light of any size whatsoever, unless some opaque object stands in the way. Now the extension of matter in three dimensions is a necessary concomitant of corporeity, and this despite the fact that both corporeity and matter are in themselves simple substances lacking all dimension. . . . Corporeity, therefore, is either light itself or the agent which . . . introduces dimensions into matter in virtue of its participation in light, and acts through the power of this same light.

Interestingly, in Grosseteste's vision, light is of a more fundamental nature than space ("dimension") itself: physical space is understood as a contingent reality, emerging as a consequence of the expansive property of light.

When he pondered the origin of the universe, he surely had in mind

6. Francesco Agnoli, *La filosofia della luce: dal big bang alle cattedrali* (Tavagnacco: Edizioni Segno, 2001).

7. See L. Miccoli, "Two Thirteenth-Century Theories of Light: Robert Grosseteste and St. Bonaventure," *Semiotica* 136 (2001): 69-84,

8. Robert Grosseteste, *On the Six Days of Creation: A Translation of the Hexaëmeron,* trans. C. F. J. Martin (Oxford: Oxford University Press, 1996), p. 198.

the opening verses of Genesis: "And God said, 'Let there be light,' and there was light. God saw that the light was good, and he separated the light from the darkness" (Gen. 1:3). In the biblical tradition light was the first element to be created, just after the setting of the cosmos ("heaven and earth"). Interestingly, in the biblical account light is first created as a pure element in the universe and "separated from darkness." Only later, in the "third day," the light-emitting bodies — the Sun, the Moon, and the stars — were created (Gen. 1:14-16).

In the *De luce,* Grosseteste describes the formation of the universe entirely based on the properties of a primordial light. His aim was not to examine the standard model, the Aristotelian-Ptolemaic system, but rather to provide an account of its formation, coherent with the Genesis account, and supported by a believable natural description. In his picture, the universe was first created in the form of a single point of light ("genus body"), which instantaneously propagated itself into an expanding sphere, thereby giving rise to spatial dimensions. Matter is dragged by the expanding light, thus forming regions of lower and higher density. The first diffusion produced the outermost sphere (the sphere of the fixed stars) in which matter is maximally rarefied: "Thus light, which is the first form created . . . spread itself out uniformly in every direction. In this way it proceeded in the beginning of time to extend matter which it could not leave behind, by drawing it out along with itself into a mass the size of the material universe."[9] Grosseteste calls the outer sphere "first body" or "firmament," using the same word as in Genesis.

At this point, every part of the outer sphere of the firmament becomes a source of light propagating back towards the center. Matter is again involved in the process of expansion and contraction of light, whereby producing other regions of higher and lower density, from which the second sphere (i.e., that of Saturn) was formed:

> When the first body, which is the firmament, has in this way been completely actualized, it diffuses its light from every part of itself to the centre of the universe. For since light is the perfection of the first body and naturally multiplies itself from the first body, it is necessarily diffused to the centre of the universe. . . . This light expanded and brought together

9. Robert Grosseteste, *De luce,* in Baur, ed., *Die Philosophischen Werke des Robert Grosseteste.* See http://evans-experientialism.freewebspace.com/grosseteste.htm). *De luce* has been translated into English by Clare C. Riedl. See *Robert Grosseteste on Light* (Milwaukee: Marquette University Press, 1978).

from the first body towards the centre of the universe, gathered together the mass existing below the first body . . . the inner parts came to be more dense and the outer parts more rarefied . . . thus in the outermost parts of the mass in question, the second sphere came into being.[10]

Similarly, by means of light emanating inwards from the second sphere, the third sphere was created, then the fourth, and so on. In this way, all the Aristotelian orbs, including those of the four elements, were generated. In Grosseteste's remarkable account, matter and light appear complementary to each other, with matter having a limitative role and light acting by its "natural appetite" to self-multiplication and expansion.

The works of Grosseteste were likely known by Dante Alighieri (1265-1321) when he started his monumental work, the *Divine Comedy,* about seventy years later.

Light at the Boundary: Dante Alighieri

Light is the fundamental scenic element in the *Divina Commedia.* Dante not only uses light as a metaphor of divine presence, but also in doing so he very carefully describes its natural properties, often exhibiting the skill of an acute naturalistic observer. For example, in *Purgatorio* XXV, we find a beautiful description of the rainbow that goes as follows:

> And even as the air, when full of rain,
> By alien rays that are therein reflected,
> With divers colours shows itself adorned.[11]

Here, in the same *terzina,* Dante not only gives a poetic rendering of the rainbow (the air that shows itself adorned with colors), but he also gives a synthetic but accurate description of the physical phenomenon that is producing the observed effect. This is done according to the most convincing natural explanation available at the time, i.e., by reflection of the solar light ("alien rays") in the droplets of moist ("air full of rain"). There is no sharp division here between aesthetics and science, between the de-

10. Grosseteste, *De luce.*

11. Dante, *Purgatorio,* XXV, 91-93. The translation of passages from Dante's *Divine Comedy* comes from Henry Wadsworth Longfellow. An online version of his translation is sponsored by Columbia University's Institute for Learning Technology.

Marco Bersanelli

scription of the physical phenomenon and its metaphoric purpose. In *Purgatorio* XV, Dante goes as far as giving a quantitative description of the law of refraction:

> As when from off the water, or a mirror,
> The sunbeam leaps unto the opposite side,
> Ascending upward in the selfsame measure
> That it descends, and deviates as far
> From falling of a stone in line direct,
> As demonstrate experiment and art.[12]

In the last part of the *Paradiso*, at the apex of his journey towards the divine vision, God himself is represented in the form of light. The scene takes us to Canto XXVIII, when Dante and Beatrice reach the *Primum Mobile* and cross the boundary between the physical universe *("il mondo sensibile")*[13] and the Empyrean. The Empyrean, the heaven inhabited by God, is described as a place of pure light that encircles the entire physical universe:

> Within a circle light and love embrace it,
> Even as this doth the others, and that precinct
> He who encircles it alone controls.[14]

Here "it" refers to the *Primum Mobile,* an extremely uniform sphere ("Its parts . . . are all so uniform, I cannot say / which Beatrice selected for my place") encompassing the sphere of the fixed stars. Thus the Empyrean is described as the ultimate sky made of "light and love" surrounding the entire universe. And when he and Beatrice cross the boundary, these are the words that Beatrice uses to introduce Dante to the heavenly realm:

> . . . We from the greatest body
> Have issued to the heaven that is pure light;
> Light intellectual replete with love,
> Love of true good replete with ecstasy,
> Ecstasy that transcendeth every sweetness.[15]

12. Dante, *Purgatorio,* XV, 16-21.
13. Dante, *Paradiso,* XXVIII, 49.
14. Dante, *Paradiso,* XXVII, 112-14.
15. Dante, *Paradiso,* XXX, 37-42.

Again, the Empyrean is "the heaven that is pure light" *("ciel ch'é pura luce"),* a light that is a manifestation of ultimate love and characterizes the home of the divine. At the beginning of Canto XXVIII, Dante is looking at his beloved Beatrice when he sees a light reflected in her eyes ("looking into those fair eyes, / Of which Love made the springs to ensnare me"), just as the light of a candle is reflected in a mirror ("As in a looking-glass a taper's flame / He sees who from behind is lighted by it"). It is an extraordinary poetic intuition that Dante experiences his first vision of God as a reflection in the eyes of Beatrice: only subsequently he turns and looks directly to the ultimate object of his desire. And what does he see?

> A point beheld I, that was raying out
> Light so acute, the sight which it enkindles
> Must close perforce before such great acuteness.
> And whatsoever star seems smallest here
> Would seem to be a moon, if placed beside it,
> As one star with another star is placed.[16]

God is represented as an infinitely sharp and bright point of light. It is the light emanating from the very presence of God, center of the cosmos and king of the Empyrean — a light so intense that human sight could not resist its brightness, and so tiny in extent that a star would appear as large as the Moon in comparison. The divine Point is then described as the center of a system of nine luminous circles inhabited by the angelic beings, mirroring the structure of the physical universe. The luminosity and the speed at which the angelic spheres revolve around the Point are greater the closer they are to the divine light.

In some passages the Empyrean is represented in the usual fashion, as an all-encompassing sphere of light surrounding the *Primum Mobile* and thus the whole physical universe;[17] in other passages it is rendered as a separated world, like "another universe,"[18] mirroring the space of the planetary spheres, with God as the vivid infinitesimal Point at its center.[19] How can the Empyrean and the divine Point be both at the center and the edge of the universe? In Canto XXX, in the very same verse Dante states that it is both simultaneously:

16. Dante, *Paradiso,* XXVIII, 13-21.
17. Dante, *Paradiso,* II, 112-14; XXVII, 109-14.
18. Dante, *Paradiso* XXVIII, 71.
19. Dante, *Paradiso,* XXVIII, 16-39.

    . . . the Triumph, which for ever
    Plays round about the point that vanquished me,
    Seeming enclosed by what itself encloses.[20]

These peculiar yet careful descriptions have triggered the suggestion, first made in 1925 by German mathematician Andreas Speiser,[21] that Dante might have imagined a geometry based on what today we call a 3-sphere or hypersphere, i.e., the three-dimensional analogue of a familiar spherical surface: under this assumption, all these apparent contradictions are readily resolved.[22] In an ordinary 2-sphere, concentric circles at increasing distances from a given point grow larger and larger, but past the equator they become smaller and converge to the antipodal point. Dante's spheres are arranged just like that, in one more dimension.

In the cosmic landscape of the *Divina Commedia* light is a fundamental ingredient both as a physical component and as a metaphoric image. Similarly, in the imaginative cosmogony of Grosseteste, light plays a uniquely fundamental role. As we shall see, some of the intuitions proposed by both authors turn out to have remarkable resonances when compared to the cosmic picture developed by modern science.

3. Glow on the Modern Universe

Light Revolutions

Since the times of Dante and Grosseteste, physicists have learned a great deal about the properties of light. Fundamental discoveries have paved the way to an immense variety of applications that have changed profoundly our way of living. The wave nature of light is beautifully encoded in Maxwell's equations, whose solutions indicate that light propagation is set by very rapid oscillations of electrical and magnetic fields. Light waves are characterized by a wavelength that equals the speed of light divided by its frequency. Light's speed in a vacuum (299,792.458 kilometers per second)

---

20. Dante, *Paradiso*, XXX, 10-12.
21. A. Speiser, *Klassiche Stücke der Mathematik* (Zürich: Orel Füssli, 1925).
22. For further discussion on this point, see M. A. Peterson, "Dante and the 3-sphere," *American Journal of Physics* 47 (1979): 1031-35; William Egginton, "On Dante, Hyperspheres, and the Curvature of the Medieval Cosmos," *Journal of the History of Ideas* 60 (1999): 195-216.

is known to be a constant of nature as predicted by Einstein's theory of relativity, and it is the limiting velocity in nature. Its enormous, yet finite, value stems from a combination of two constants that characterize the properties of an electrical and a magnetic field in a vacuum. The discovery of the electromagnetic nature of light suddenly revolutionized the very concept of "light," extending its domain well beyond the tiny range of wavelengths (~0.39 to 0.75 micrometers) accessible to our eyes: in the new, generalized sense light's wavelengths range from kilometers to billionths of a centimeter. A second major revolution concerning the nature of light took place in the beginning of twentieth century, when Max Planck and Albert Einstein showed that light can transfer energy only as a multiple of a small, discrete quantity. In this view, light behaves like a stream of particles rather than a continuous wave. Each photon, the particle of light, has an energy proportional to the frequency. The double nature of light as a particle and as a wave set off quantum mechanics, and revealed for the first time the mysterious nature of the microscopic world.

Astronomers have enthusiastically followed these two "light revolutions"; first, by extending their observations of celestial objects beyond the traditional range of visible light; and, second, by exploiting the particle-and-wave nature of light to design a variety of telescopes and detectors capable of gathering photons of greatly different energies. Today astronomical observations, from the ground or from space, are routinely carried out in a wavelength range spanning some fourteen orders of magnitude, from radio waves to gamma rays.

Photons propagating in a vacuum never vanish, but as soon as they are detected they instantly disappear. Like the marathon athlete, the photons we receive from space travel for a very long time to bring their message to its destination, ready to sacrifice themselves. They may have traveled for billions of years before reaching us here and now. Light, while an extremely fast messenger, is not instantaneous as Grosseteste believed. At the speed of 300,000 kilometers per second, light takes a few million years to reach us from nearby galaxies, and over 10 billion years from the most distant ones. Interestingly, therefore, light allows us to gather information not only from distant regions of space, but also from past epochs of cosmic history: the farther away we look into space, the deeper into the past we see. This has profound implications for our understanding of the universe.

Marco Bersanelli

Primordial Light

In 1922 Edwin Hubble noticed a faint point of light in a photographic plate of M31, the Andromeda spiral nebula. The time variation of the light of that barely distinguishable star turned out to be typical of a class of variable stars, named Cepheids, that allow astronomers to estimate their intrinsic luminosity, and therefore to calculate their distance. Hubble estimated the distance of M31 ~2 million light years.[23] It was by far the largest distance ever measured, well outside the Milky Way: it was the first leap into extragalactic space. Nowadays, astrophysicists can study galaxies that are thousands of times more distant than our neighbor M31. Systematic galaxy surveys, such as the Sloan Digital Sky Survey (SDSS)[24] or the 2dF Redshift Galaxy Survey (2dFRGS),[25] have mapped hundreds of thousands of galaxies, measuring for each of them the location in the celestial sphere and their distance from us. Hence, we can build accurate three-dimensional charts of significant samples of the universe and measure the statistical distribution of matter in deep space. Current data show that matter tends to clump in clusters, sometimes containing thousands of galaxies; clusters also form long filaments intertwined by huge voids; however, on the very largest scales, greater than 10 Mpc,[26] the distribution is relatively uniform. Future space missions currently under study[27] are planned to perform all-sky spectroscopic surveys of more than 500 million galaxies, dramatically improving our understanding of the dynamics and large-scale distribution of matter in the universe.

The Hubble Space Telescope (HST) has provided us with the deepest optical images to date. The "Hubble Ultra Deep Field" image,[28] taken with

23. Currently the distance to the Andromeda galaxy is measured to be (784 ± 21) kpc = $(2.556 \pm 69) \times 10^6$ light years. See K. Z. Stanek and P. M. Garnavich, "Distance to M31 with the Hubble Space Telescope and HIPPARCOS Red Clump," *Astrophysical Journal* 503 (1998), letters 131.

24. D. G. York et al., "The Sloan Digital Sky Survey: Technical Summary," *Astronomical Journal* 120 (2000): 1579.

25. See, e.g., W. J. Percival et al., "Parameter Constraints for Flat Cosmologies from Cosmic Microwave Background and 2dFGRS Power Spectra," *Monthly Notices of the Royal Astronomical Society* 337 (2002): 1068-80; references therein.

26. A megaparsec (Mpc) is 10^6 parsec (pc). The parsec (1 pc = 3.26 light years = 3.086 × 10^{16} m) is a standard distance unit in astronomy, defined as the distance from which the angle subtended by the average radius of Earth's orbit around the Sun is 1 armin.

27. See EUCLID proposal, submitted to ESA Cosmic Vision program (www.esa.int).

28. S. V. W. Beckwith et al., "The Hubble Ultra Deep Field," *Astronomical Journal* 132 (2006): 1729-55.

the Advanced Camera for Surveys, shows nearly 10,000 galaxies in a sky area equivalent to only 1.5 percent of the full Moon. In this image, we see some of the farthest known galaxies, whose light has traveled for some 13 billion years before hitting the HST mirrors. Those far sources belonged to our universe when it was in its youth, at an age of < 1 billion years — less than 10 percent of its present age. Because of cosmic expansion, at that time the universe was about ten times smaller than today and galaxies were closer to each by the same factor.

Can we receive light from anything farther away than those very distant galaxies? Or, which is the same, can we look farther back towards our cosmic origins? The answer, surprisingly, is yes. The clue lies under our eyes, and it was there even in the eyes of prehistoric observers to see: the dark background of the sky. Ancient astronomers wondered about the nature of stars and planets, but apparently it was not until Kepler that the significance of the diffuse darkness of the night sky was realized.[29] What is that black veil we see every night beyond the stars, and that we still see in the deepest HST images? Today we know that the dark background is not completely lightless, but it glows with a very soft, diffuse luminosity reaching us from an epoch preceding the very formation of galaxies. These prodigious fossil photons, named cosmic microwave background (CMB),[30] are the remnant of the initial, hot state of the universe. The CMB was serendipitously discovered[31] in 1965 by Arno Penzias and Robert Wilson, and has since become a rich goldmine of cosmological information. The CMB photons were released when the expansion of the universe cooled the temperature below 3000 K and allowed the first atoms to form from previously separated electrons and light nuclei. This took place when the universe was 380,000 years old, only 0.003 percent of its present age. As charged particles joined to form neutral atoms, suddenly the universe became transparent to light. At that time, the photons' wavelength was ~0.5-1μm, i.e., in the visible to near-infrared. If a human observer had witnessed that dramatic moment, he would have seen a blaze of (visible) light flood-

---

29. The darkness of the night sky, which became known as the Olbers paradox, has cosmological significance, since it rules out a static infinite universe. A full account is given in Edward Harrison, *Darkness at Night: A Riddle of the Universe* (Cambridge, MA: Harvard University Press, 1987).

30. The word "microwave" reflects the fact that the radiation spectral range, as observed today, is in the millimeter-microwave range.

31. A. Penzias and R. Wilson, "A Measurement of Excess Antenna Temperature at 4080 Mc/s," *Astrophysical Journal* 142 (1965): 419-21.

ing uniformly from all directions.[32] That light has traveled to us, and we now see it in the background of the sky. Why then do we see a dark sky? The reason is that billions of years of cosmic expansion have since stretched the wavelength of the ancient photons by a factor ~1000, shifting them into the microwave range (with wavelengths of a few millimeters), where the corresponding photon energy is extremely low and invisible to our eyes.

The CMB was not emitted by any particular source but was released by the universe itself in its infancy, when photons decoupled from matter. It is the first light in the universe. We do not see it coming from any particular point in space, but rather as a uniform bath of light reaching us from all directions. Despite the enormous number of galaxies, the voids between them are huge and the universe is essentially empty. Therefore the cosmic photons traveled rather undisturbed in their 13.7 billion years' journey, and they bring to us a remarkably faithful view of the early universe.

The sea of relic radiation fills every cubic centimeter of the universe with about 500 photons moving in all directions. Its spectrum is pure blackbody, with a temperature[33] of 2.725 ± 0.002 K. While extremely cold, the CMB photons are everywhere and their total energy far exceeds that of light produced by all other sources in the universe. Data taken by many observatories, most of which are in space, show that the 95 percent of the total luminous energy in the universe is contained in the CMB. The remaining 5 percent comes from radiation emitted by all galaxies since their formation, and is approximately evenly distributed across the visible and infrared. X-ray radiation and gamma radiation contribute to only around 0.01 percent and radio background to only one millionth of the energy of the entire electromagnetic spectrum. What is the contribution of light to the overall matter-energy budget of the universe? In the present cosmic epoch, the energy density of photons (essentially the CMB) is only a tiny fraction, about 0.2 percent, of the energy density of matter. But if we go back to the first 1500 years or so of cosmic history, the universe was completely dominated by photons. As in Grosseteste's scenario, the universe started up as an expanse of nearly pure light.

32. The transition from an opaque to a transparent universe corresponds to a redshift range $\Delta z \sim 100$, or a time interval $\Delta t \sim 2 \times 10^4$ yr. Although abrupt in cosmic terms, it's a bit long on the human scale: our cosmic witness would need a long life to tell us that story!

33. In the radio and microwave range it is usual to specify intensity in terms of equivalent blackbody temperature.

Then, as time went on, cosmic expansion changed the balance in favor of matter.[34]

The region of spacetime from where we see the CMB photons emerge is called "last scattering surface": almost as a modern version of the ancient *Primum Mobile,* it is a sort of cosmic photosphere encompassing the whole universe accessible to our observation. How far and how big is the last scattering surface? The answer requires care. Because space expands, its distance calculated at the present epoch is about three times larger than the 13.7 billion light years we would expect in a nonexpanding universe.[35] So we receive CMB photons from a sphere of material that "today" surrounds us 42 billion light years away. However, when those photons were emitted, the radius of the last scattering surface was 1100 times smaller than it is today, or only 38 million light years (nothing compared to the present cosmological scale). Paradoxically, therefore, even though it appears to us as an ultimate background in all directions, the last scattering surface is much smaller than the space occupied by galaxies and clusters of galaxies it contains! The CMB brings us the image of a small, ancient universe. Looking up at the sky in any direction literally means looking towards a single spacetime point at the origin of the universe.[36] This picture has surprising similarity with Dante's hyperspherical space. In fact, topologically it is exactly the same,[37] the main difference being that in the modern universe we deal with spacetime, while in Dante's case the curvature was only spatial.

Surrounded by Radiance

An observer with no peculiar motion in expanding space would see the same CMB temperature in all directions with high precision. Just as in

---

34. This is because radiation scales with the expansion factor as R^{-4}, while matter scales as R^{-3}.

35. Tamara M. Davis and Charles H. Lineweaver, "Expanding Confusion: Common Misconceptions of Cosmological Horizons and the Superluminal Expansion of the Universe," *Publications of the Astronomical Society of Australia* 21 (2004): 97-109.

36. R. Osserman, *Poetry of the Universe* (New York: Anchor Books, 1995); H.-R. Patapievici, *Gli occhi di Beatrice* (Milan: Mondadori, 2004); M. Bersanelli, "Dalla cosmologia contemporanea echi di antiche domande," *Marcianum* 4 (2008): 401-45.

37. The shape of the light cone in relativistic cosmology at cosmic age t_0 in the Euclidean space is given by a function $x_i(t) = (t^{2/3} - t)$. This is a closed surface, with a water-drop-like profile in 2-d, topologically equivalent to a 3-sphere.

Dante's description of the *Primum Mobile,* the ultimate sphere of last scatter is extremely uniform. Because of the motion of our rest frame with respect to the last scattering surface, we do observe a ~0.1 percent asymmetry in the CMB with 180° angular scale. This so-called dipole anisotropy[38] is interpreted as a Doppler shift, and indicates that we move at the speed of ~600 km/s due to the effect of local gravitational fields at galactic and extragalactic scales. Remarkably, we can also detect a second-order dipole modulation due to Earth's yearly revolution around the Sun: a brilliant confirmation of the theories of Aristarchus and Copernicus!

The last scattering surface represents a physical obstacle to direct observation into earlier cosmic epochs: beyond that limit, the universe was hot and dense enough to make space completely opaque to light.[39] Nonetheless, by observing in detail the properties of the CMB we can learn a great deal of what happened back in the first 380,000 years of cosmic infancy.[40] As cosmologists had predicted from theory, we now know that the uniformity of the CMB is not complete. In 1992, NASA's COBE satellite discovered small deviations from isotropy[41] at a level of 0.001 percent at all angular scales larger than seven degrees. The groundbreaking discovery of these "anisotropies" triggered more ambitious projects. The WMAP satellite,[42] launched by NASA in 2000, has provided full-sky maps of the fluc-

38. E. K. Conklin, "Velocity of the Earth with Respect to the Cosmic Background Radiation," *Nature* 222 (1969): 971-72; P. S. Henry, "Isotropy of the 3 K Background," *Nature* 231 (1971): 516-18; G. F. Smoot, M. V. Gorenstein, and R. A. Muller, "Detection of Anisotropy in the Cosmic Blackbody Radiation," *Physical Review Letters* 39 (1977): 898-901.

39. In principle, we could *direct* information from epochs preceding the last scattering surface, but here light would be an inadequate messenger. As mentioned, the universe before the epoch of recombination was opaque to photons. However, in some far future, perhaps we might become able to detect low-energy cosmic neutrinos, which easily cross the hot plasma unimpeded and reach us directly from a universe only 1 second old. And if someday, in an even farther future, primordial gravitational waves could be detected, these would get us a direct signature from the inflation era.

40. Wayne Hu and Scott Dodelson, "Cosmic Microwave Background Anisotropies," *Annual Review of Astronomy and Astrophysics* 40 (2002): 171; M. Bersanelli, D. Maino, and A. Mennella, "Anisotropies of the Cosmic Microwave Background," *La Rivista del Nuovo Cimento* 9 (2002): 1-82.

41. http://lambda.gsfc.nasa.gov/product/cobe. The discovery of CMB temperature anisotropies and the high-precision measurement of the CMB frequency spectrum obtained by the COBE satellite in 1992 brought the 2006 Nobel Prize for Physics to George Smoot and John Mather. See G. F. Smoot et al., *Astrophysical Journal* 396 (1992): letters 1; J. C. Mather et al., *Astrophysical Journal* 420 (1994): 439.

42. http://map.gsfc.nasa.gov/ C. Bennett et al., "First-Year Wilkinson Microwave Ani-

tuations with subdegree angular resolution and improved sensitivity. In 2009 the European Space Agency (ESA) launched Planck,[43] a third-generation satellite dedicated to the CMB, designed to push the frontier of observational cosmology a step further.

The anisotropy of the cosmic light encodes a wealth of cosmological secrets. In fact, precision measurements of the CMB provide one of the sharpest tools to precisely ascertain the age, composition, and geometry of the universe, to test theories about its origin, and to investigate the nature of mysterious dark matter and dark energy components that we believe dominate the present universe.

On angular scales smaller than ~1 degree, the first evidence is revealed of the universe becoming a structured and ordered reality. The observed fluctuations are due to well-understood physical processes. Primordial density perturbations propagate in the primordial mixture of light and matter (the so-called photon-baryon fluid) as sound waves that influence the intensity of photons emerging from different regions of the last scattering surface. This process is analogous to reconstructing the assembly of a musical instrument by carefully listening to its sounds, even though the universe is turning out to be a highly remarkable instrument whose music is accompanied by several special coincidences that are crying out for an explanation.[44] Not too differently from the density-and-rarefaction process imagined by Grosseteste, these sound waves are the seeds of cosmic structure. By studying the statistics of bright and cold spots in the CMB, we can infer the precise amount of the various components of mass-energy density in the universe.

Fluctuations on scales greater than ~1 degree might represent the most primordial cosmic objects accessible to our observation. They offer a visual glimpse, although *indirect,* of the universe when it was less than a tril-

---

sotropy Probe (WMAP): Observations: Preliminary Maps and Basic Results," *Astrophysical Journal Supplement Series* 148 (2003): 1-27. G. Hinshaw et al., "Three-Year Wilkinson Microwave Anisotropy Probe (WMAP): Observations: Temperature Analysis," *Astrophysical Journal Supplement Series* 170 (2007): 288.

43. Planck (http://www.esa.int/Planck) is a project of the European Space Agency — ESA — with instruments provided by two scientific consortia funded by ESA member states (in particular the lead countries: France and Italy) with contributions from NASA (USA), and telescope reflectors provided in a collaboration between ESA and a scientific consortium led and funded by Denmark.

44. Wayne Hu and Martin White, "The Cosmic Symphony," *Scientific American,* February 2004, pp. 44-53.

lionth of a second old. According to the currently favored scenario, anisotropies at those scales display primordial quantum fluctuations amplified to macroscopic sizes by an exponential expansion that occurred in the first 10^{-35} seconds, called inflation. The inflation scenario, introduced in the early 1980s,[45] offers at present the best explanation for a number of puzzling problems, such as the high isotropy of regions outside causal contact and the nearly flat geometry of space, and it provides a physical mechanism for the origin of primordial fluctuations.

At present, our best chance to test observationally the physics of inflation is through high-precision measurements of the polarization of the CMB.[46] In addition to temperature anisotropies, the primordial photons carry wonderful information via their polarization anisotropy, i.e., the variations of the prevalent plane of oscillation of the electric and magnetic fields in different regions in the sky. The CMB is only weakly polarized, and the signal is only a few millionths of a Kelvin: precise measurements represent a major challenge for experimentalists. But the information conveyed carries extremely important indicators of the processes that occurred in the initial moments, at energies far greater than any other conceivable experiment can test. By studying the polarization of the fossil light, we may be able to determine the energy scale at which the initial fluctuations were generated.

Planck: The New Frontier

Following the COBE and WMAP space missions, the Planck satellite represents the new frontier in the field. Unlike most observatories, which look at a large number of discrete celestial sources, Planck and its predecessor CMB missions observe a single, peculiar object: the whole sky. Planck was successfully launched from Kourou, French Guiana, on May 14, 2009, at 10:12 (local time). The mission[47] was designed to extract all the cosmological information encoded in the CMB temperature anisotropies, with accuracy limited by intrinsic astrophysical confusion rather than by instru-

45. Alan H. Guth, *The Inflationary Universe: The Quest for a New Theory of Cosmic Origins* (Reading, MA: Addison-Wesley, 1997).

46. Latham A. Boyle, Paul J. Steinhardt, and Neil Turok, "Inflationary Predictions for Scalar and Tensor Fluctuations Reconsidered," *Physical Review Letters* 96 (2006): 111-301.

47. J. Tauber et al., "Planck Pre-launch Status: The Planck Mission," *Astronomy and Astrophysics* 520 (September-October 2010): A4, 1-22.

ment noise. Furthermore, Planck will push polarization measurements well beyond previous results. The instruments and observing strategy are devised to reach an unprecedented combination of angular resolution (up to a tenth of a degree), sky coverage (100 percent), wavelength coverage (from 10 to 0.3 millimeters), sensitivity (one part in a million), and calibration accuracy (better than 0.5 percent). Never before has the first light of the universe been imaged with such accuracy. This will lead Planck to achieve a wealth of innovative results including new, accurate estimates of the cosmological parameters that describe the geometry, dynamics, and matter-energy content of the universe, as well as bring a first quantitative test of the inflation scenario.

Thanks to a happy coincidence of nature, the maximum of the blackbody spectrum of the CMB lies close to a minimum of the combined microwave emission of our galaxy and extragalactic sources. In the wavelength interval between three to four millimeters, the signals that we receive from the microwave sky apart from the galactic plane are dominated by the old CMB photons. But even in this most transparent of all windows, galactic and extragalactic sources of "foreground radiation" contribute to the photons to a degree of several percent. In order to recognize this astrophysical "contaminant" and to eliminate it, CMB experiments are designed such that measurements are taken at several wavelengths in order to detect noncosmological components by means of their divergent spectra. In the case of Planck, the target sensitivity requires highly accurate measurement of the foreground sources and this in turn requires that the measurements be made within a wide wavelength range. Planck images the sky in nine frequency bands covering the entire spectrum relevant for the primordial light. This way, the Planck maps will also represent a superb dataset for galactic and extragalactic astrophysics.

Up to now, no single technology can reach the required performances in the entire Planck frequency range. For this reason, two complementary instruments were developed and integrated, exploiting state-of-the-art radiometric[48] and bolometric[49] detectors in their best windows of operation. The two instruments share the focal plane of a single telescope, an off-axis dual reflector Gregorian system with 1.5m aperture. The combina-

48. M. Bersanelli et al., "Planck Pre-launch Status: Design and Description of the Low Frequency Instrument," *Astronomy and Astrophysics* 520 (September-October 2010): A1, 1-21.

49. J.-M. Lamarre et al., "Planck Pre-launch Status: The High Frequency Instrument, from Specification to Performance," *Astronomy and Astrophysics* 520 (September-October 2010): A9, 1-20.

tion of the instruments will allow Planck to reveal about fifteen times more information on the CMB than is currently available from WMAP.[50] Planck is currently observing the sky from an orbit at about 1.5 million kilometers away from Earth. The ambitious performance of the Planck instruments were successfully verified on sophisticated ground tests before launch, and are now wonderfully confirmed by the ongoing in-flight survey. The first results are expected in 2012.

4. Conclusion

There are essentially two kinds of light in the universe: light generated by all sources in the universe and light released by the universe itself at the beginning of cosmic history. Photons of the second type, the CMB, today still permeate all space and carry the bulk of luminous energy in the universe. Furthermore, if we go back about 13.7 billion years in cosmic history, we find that the energy of CMB photons dominated by far the entire matter-energy budget. The early universe was essentially constituted by light, and the CMB we see today is just the fossil remnant of that initial glow.

A necessary condition for the formation of galaxies, stars, planets, and eventually of complex systems is the onset of acoustic waves, i.e., over-densities and rarefactions in the mixture of light and matter in the early hot plasma. Today we see the details of these processes encoded in the fine properties of the CMB. When space became transparent, at a cosmic age of about 380,000 years, light traveled freely and today we can take a snapshot of the embryos of forming structures in the details of the CMB. Today our telescopes are able to measure with exquisite precision the anisotropy and polarization of the first light and allow cosmologists to gain extraordinary physical insight on the evolution, composition, and geometry of the universe, on the origin of cosmic structures, and possibly on the physics of inflation in the very early universe. New results are expected soon from the ongoing survey of the Planck satellite.

The CMB photons reach us from the last scattering surface, the region of spacetime where they last scattered with matter. We see this surface as an all-encompassing, external, cosmic photosphere embracing our entire observable universe; however, paradoxically, because of cosmic expansion,

50. In terms of the angular scales (or multipoles), which are detected with a signal-to-noise ratio larger than unity.

that surface is actually much smaller than the regions of space that it contains. Furthermore, the curvature of spacetime in the expanding universe means that wherever we look in the depth of the sky, beyond stars and galaxies, we look back towards the same point into the primordial universe.

We noted some remarkable analogies between the role of light in the modern cosmological scenario and in Grosseteste's and Dante's conjectures. Science tells us that the early universe was a place of light, just as Grosseteste had imagined. The sound waves of light-and-matter fluid in the early hot plasma are strikingly similar to the rarefactions and overdensities driving Grosseteste's light-based cosmogony. We also noted a similitude between the spacetime geometry of the expanding universe and the structure of Dante's light-filled Empyrean. While intriguing, these analogies should not be misunderstood. Our medieval authors had no physical or quantitative argument to support their ideas, and their cosmic sketches were based almost entirely on imagination. Their intuitions were not primarily founded on observational data, which they lacked, and they could not verify their principles by experiment.[51] It would be a mistake, therefore, to treat their cosmological ideas as scientific theories in the modern sense of the term. Nonetheless, it is notable that their open-minded thinking, their enthusiasm in searching for beautiful, symmetric, and coherent explanations of the universe enabled them, just as it happened to some great thinkers of ancient Greece,[52] to foreshadow natural scenarios that modern science was destined to confirm on a scientific basis.

There is one more difference between them and us. Dante and Grosseteste treated light as a key element in nature, but for them light was also, *at the same time,* a privileged sign of the Creator. Can a modern scientist, acquainted with what cosmology and physics have discovered, still appreciate light as a sign of the Mystery? Is there anything left of light, apart from what science has been (or will be) able to tell? Somehow, we modern scientists have difficulty in going beyond the physical mechanism that sci-

51. It is true that, as we noted, both Dante and Grosseteste attributed much importance to observations of natural phenomena, and in both of them we can see premonitions of the rational attitude that three centuries later would result in the explosion of modern science.

52. We can mention, for example, the intuition of the atomic structure of matter by Democritus (ca. 460–ca. 370 BCE); or the idea, dating from pre-Socratic times and persisting throughout the Middle Ages, of the definition of a few fundamental elements (Earth, Water, Air, Fire, and Ether) out of which every other material reality is constituted. Also in these cases, modern science has shown the basic correctness of these ideas, in spite of the fact that the ancient authors could not be supported by experimental evidence.

ence itself can unveil. It is often believed that, as science advances with its ability to "explain" the observed phenomena, it supersedes any further dimension that the phenomena themselves may convey. So, for example, once we have a good physical theory of light, its aesthetic or metaphysical values may appear to be obsolete. But Dante and Grosseteste show that this reduction is not necessary. For them, their knowledge of physical properties of light, though rudimentary, was felt as a motive for an even more passionate and richer appreciation of light as a metaphor of God. Their ingenious works demonstrate that achieving a good scientific explanation is by no means an obstacle to maintaining deeper levels of meaning that light, or other physical reality, may communicate and inspire. Indeed, if we were to follow their attitude, how beautiful a sign of the creator we would contemplate today in the presence of light in the universe, as it emerges from modern cosmology!

PART TWO

"Light from Light": The Divine Light Reflected in and by the Son and the Holy Spirit

Gerald O'Collins, S.J.

Only a few miles from where the Templeton Foundation symposium met in Istanbul (April 2009) is the museum of Chora, with its glorious fresco of the "Anastasis." In a pure white robe Jesus has descended into the netherworld. He has battered down the gates of Hades and is pulling Adam and Eve out of their tombs. To the left, kings wait for their deliverance and so too does Cain on the right. The fresco pictures Jesus himself within a luminous frame ornamented with stars. In his vision of Jesus, the artist has built luminosity into this fresco. The victorious Jesus is the light of the netherworld.

The glorious Jesus ascends, rather than descends, in the astonishing resurrection painted by Matthias Grünewald on the Isenheimer altarpiece (1512-16), which is now kept in Colmar (France). Pictured as scarlet and gold and with his arms lifted in ceremonial grace, Jesus rises into the sun and is himself the sun. The other figures are not saints of old but soldiers posted to guard his tomb; they are now crushed with the wind of his ascent as he rushes upwards. His face has become like light itself; he seems pure luminosity as he scatters starlike sparkles into the sky. The heavens have been transfigured by his new brilliance; the earth, it seems, must either accept this brightness or lapse into decay. Viewers look with awe at this vision of his transformed humanity, gazing at what they hope to become in him. As with the Chora fresco, this work mirrors forth in art what faith believes.

Surprisingly, none of the Easter narratives in the Gospels depict the risen Jesus in a glorious, luminous form. The closest they approach to doing so is through a kind of "stand-in," the "angel of the Lord," who descended from heaven, rolled away the stone closing the tomb of Jesus, and sat down on the stone. "His face," Matthew adds, "shone like lightning" and "his garments were white as snow" (Matt. 28:2-3). Yet this is not said of the risen Jesus himself, neither when he met "Mary Magdalene and the other Mary" (Matt. 28:9-10) nor when he kept a rendezvous with "the eleven disciples" on a mountain in Galilee (Matt. 28:16-20).

The Book of Acts introduces light, when it three times tells the story of Paul's encounter on the road to Damascus. Since in the Lukan scheme the risen Jesus had already "been taken up into heaven" (Acts 1:9-11) to sit "at the right hand of God" (Acts 2:33-35), his meeting with Paul did not exhibit the everyday, earthly traits of the Easter appearances in Luke 24 and Acts 1. Paul experienced a "light from heaven" that suddenly flashed about him (Acts 9:3), and was qualified in the second account as "a great light from heaven" (Acts 22:6) and in the third account as "brighter than the brilliant sun" (Acts 26:13). It was from the light of God that the gloriously risen Christ came to meet Paul on the Damascus road.

What Acts implies, the Letter to the Hebrews states more explicitly when it calls the incarnate Son "the radiance of God's glory" and "the imprint of his very being/substance" (Heb. 1:3). Here the language of the New Testament comes closest to the Nicene Creed of 325 and its confession of Christ as "Light from Light."[1]

In this chapter I want to do four things: (1) recall some major themes about light from the Hebrew Bible; (2) sketch the New Testament recognition of Jesus as "the light of the world" (John 8:12); (3) retrieve some relevant material from the Christian tradition about Christ and the Holy Spirit as light; and (4) signal some links between my presentation of the Holy

---

1. When commenting on this verse, Origen (d. around 254) adopted a term that would enter the Nicene Creed, *homoousios* (one in being, of the same being) with the Father: "What else are we to suppose the eternal Light is but God the Father, who never so was that, while he was the Light, his Splendour (Heb. 1:3) was not present with him? Light without splendour is unthinkable. But if this is true, there never was [a time] when the Son was not the Son. He will not be, however, as we have described the eternal Light, unborn (lest we seem to introduce two principles of light), but, as it were, the Splendour of the unbegotten Light, with that very Light as his beginning and source, born of it indeed, but there was not [a time] when he was not. . . . Thus Wisdom, too, since it proceeds from God, is generated out of the divine substance itself. Under the figure of a bodily outflow, nevertheless, it too is thus called 'a sort of clean and pure outflow of omnipotent Glory' (Wis. 7:25). Both these similes manifestly show the community of substance between Son and Father. For an outflow seems *homoousios*: that is to say, of one substance with that body of which it is the outflow or exhalation" (*In Hebr.*, fragment 24.359; trans. J. Quasten, *Patrology*, vol. 2 [Utrecht: Spectrum Publishers, 1953], p. 78; trans. slightly emended).

Trinity as the ultimate mystery of light and some other chapters in this book — above all, the one by Kathryn Tanner.

1. The Hebrew Bible

The Israelites knew nothing about the speed of light (see chapter by Robert Boyd) and the "counterintuitive properties" of the "wave/particle duality" (see chapters by John Polkinghorne and Andrew Steane). Yet they could hardly have valued light more highly.[2] The psalmist pictures God as surrounded by radiant light: "Lord GOD, how great you are, clothed in majesty and glory, wrapped in light as in a robe" (Ps. 104:1-2). God's "countenance is light" (Ps. 89:15). God is described as "shining forth": "out of Zion, the perfection of beauty, God shines forth" (Ps. 50:1-2). The psalmist prays that the Lord would "shine forth" (Ps. 80:1; 94:1) and manifest himself. Repeatedly the divine manifestations or theophanies show God surrounded by light, fire, and flashes of lightning. It is in a "burning bush" that God reveals himself to Moses (Exod. 3:1-6).

In biblical imagery "light" comes across as thoroughly interconnected with "glory," or the splendor/radiance of the divine presence. One can describe "glory *(kabod)* as the light streaming from God and thus as the glory that makes its home in the Temple (Ps. 26:8). Hence the psalmist yearns to gaze on God in the sanctuary and see the divine power and glory (Ps. 63:2). The "glory of the Lord" visibly manifests and expresses the divine presence, the overwhelming power and majesty that settles on Mt. Sinai (Exod. 24:16), appears at the Tent of Meeting (Num. 14:10; 16:19), fills the tabernacle (Exod. 40:34-35), and eventually permeates the Temple built by Solomon (1 Kings 8:10-13). "Glory," for all intents and purposes, designates the divine reality.

At the time of the Babylonian exile, the prophet Ezekiel lamented the departure of the Lord's glory from the Temple (10:1-22; 11:22-25), and yearned for the divine glory to return to the restored Temple (43:2-5; 44:4). Within the Temple a seven-branched lampstand symbolized the divine glory and presence. Hanukkah, the Feast of the Dedication of the Temple, was the Feast of Lights.

---

2. See S. M. Lewis, "Light and Darkness," in *The New Interpreter's Dictionary of the Bible,* vol. 3 (Nashville: Abingdon, 2008), pp. 662-64; C. C. Newman, "Glory, Glorify," in *The New Interpreter's Dictionary of the Bible,* vol. 2 (Nashville: Abingdon, 2007), pp. 576-80. *The Anchor Bible Dictionary,* 6 vols. (New York: Doubleday, 1992), carries no entry on either "light" or "glory."

Gerald O'Collins, S.J.

Human beings, while they cannot see the deity as such, can perceive the glory that symbolizes God's presence. Moses is granted a fleeting glimpse of God's "glory" (Exod. 33:18-23). This visible divine glory serves as a kind of envelope for the unearthly bright light that, paradoxically, veils God's being. One of the New Testament's pastoral letters expresses this conviction: "God dwells in unapproachable light; him no one has ever seen or can ever see" (1 Tim. 6:16). A screen of light hides God, who is utterly holy and beyond human perception. God remains an invisible figure. "Light" articulates and symbolizes this divine otherness and holiness.

Besides associating light and glory with the divine presence, the Scriptures represent God as the *creator of light* (Isa. 45:6-7). Even before making the heavenly luminaries (Gen. 1:3-5, 14-18), in the primal chaos and darkness God spoke and created light ("let there be light"). "Immediately and without resistance," light "filled the world," which had been "flooded by chaos."[3] By starting the work of creation with the creative command "let there be light," God shows — within the scheme of the Book of Genesis — that light is the most basic, general, and even perfect manifestation of the divine reality and operations. From among all the gifts through which God creates and then blesses creatures, light, the firstborn of creation, proves the most sublime: a power provided for the benefit of human beings and their world. By creating light, God "makes possible the basic cycle of time and order." The separation of light and darkness "sets in motion the march and rhythm of time."[4] In this presentation of creation, "time takes precedence over space . . . creation does not begin with the division of space, but with the division of night and day as the basis of time."[5]

A classic hymn goes beyond what the text of Genesis explicitly says to associate each of the three persons of the Trinity with the decree "let there be light." This hymn, "God, Whose Almighty Word," helps worshipers to appreciate how the sublime creation of light is due not only to

3. G. von Rad, *Genesis: A Commentary,* trans. J. H. Marks, rev. ed. (London: SCM Press, 1972), p. 51. As David Jones has pointed out to me, St. Augustine of Hippo (d. 430) suggests that the angels were created when God said, "let there be light" (*The City of God,* 11.9). The angels are illuminated by God, the eternal light, who is all wisdom, understanding, and love. The angels participate in this light, which brings them understanding. It is in this sense, according to Augustine, that angels are beings of light.

4. C. Westermann, *Genesis 1–11: A Commentary,* trans. J. J. Scullion (London: SPCK, 1984), p. 112.

5. Westermann, *Genesis 1–11,* p. 114.

the Word of God but also to the Father Almighty and to the Holy Spirit.[6]

Created by God, light not only symbolizes God but is also an image of divine salvation and deliverance. Where darkness symbolizes illness (especially, blindness), death, and the forces of evil, light symbolizes life, health, and the presence of God. Yet, as Metropolitan Kallistos Ware notes, through a *coincidentia oppositorum* of the light/darkness symbolism, God is also revealed in "mingled light and darkness" or in "divine darkness." David Brown prefers to talk of the symbols of light and darkness being "subverted."

The biblical expression "seeing the light" amounts to "being alive." We can unpack the expression "the light of life" as "the light which is life and the source of life" (Eccles. 11:7; Ps. 49:19; Job 3:20). When the divine light shines on human beings, they experience "liveliness" and happiness. That is the sense of "in/by your light we see light" (Ps. 36:9). When the psalmist prays "show us the light of your face" (Ps. 4:6), he is asking for the grace to see/experience happiness.

"The commandment of the LORD," the psalmist knows, "is pure and gives light to the eyes" (Ps. 19:8). The longest psalm celebrates the Torah or Law of God: "Your word is a lamp to my feet, a light on my path" (Ps. 119:105; see 119:139). This is a light that brings and even embodies order and salvation. The righteous experience God's light as their saving guide: "the LORD is my light and my salvation" (Ps. 27:1). The king knows how the Lord is his "lamp," the God who "lights up my darkness" (Ps. 18:28).

Through the gift of God, Jerusalem is a zone of light in the surrounding darkness: "Arise, shine; for your *light* has come, and the *glory* of the LORD has risen upon you. Though darkness covers the earth and dark night the nations, on you the LORD shines and over you his *glory* will appear; nations will journey towards your *light* and kings to your radiance" (Isa. 60:1-3). By twice setting "light" and "glory" in parallelism, this passage implies a functional identity between the glory of God and the light of God.

These pages should suffice to illustrate some of the rich ways in which the Hebrew Bible associates God with light and the divine gift of light to creatures. The First Letter of John will firmly bring together the key Old Testament themes on light by declaring: "God is light and in him there is

---

6. John Marrriot wrote the text of "Let there be light" (first published in 1825); the tune is taken from an eighteenth-century Italian hymn.

no darkness" (1 John 1:5).[7] What then of the New Testament and its part in initiating talk about Christ as "Light from Light"?

2. The New Testament

The first New Testament writer, St. Paul, draws on Genesis to express the way the divine light (or its equivalent, the divine glory) has been revealed in Jesus Christ: "God who said, 'out of darkness let *light* shine,' has caused his *light* to shine in our hearts, to give the *light* of the knowledge of God's *glory* in the face of Jesus Christ" (2 Cor. 4:6). Two verses earlier Paul writes of seeing "the *light* of the Gospel of the *glory* of Christ" (2 Cor. 4:4). We could well detect here a genitive of identity: "the light of the Gospel" that is "the glory of Christ." The Second Letter to the Corinthians (written around 57 CE) anticipates the theme that Jesus was/is the divine light — a statement that years later will emerge fully in John's Gospel and the Book of Revelation.

Naturally Paul adopts the language of light when exhorting his addressees: "You are all children of light, children of the day. We do not belong to night and darkness. We must not sleep like the rest, but keep awake and sober" (1 Thess. 5:5-6). "Darkness" constitutes sin and evil, while the "enlightenment" brought by faith means turning from such darkness to walk in the light. A few years later the apostle exhorts the Christians of Rome: "It is far on in the night; day is near. Let us therefore throw off the deeds of darkness and put on the armor of light. . . . Let Christ himself be the armor that you wear" (Rom. 13:12, 14). The kingdom of the Son of God, so Paul (or one of his followers) assures readers, is a domain of light (Col. 1:12-13).

Turning to the Gospels, we find Matthew interpreting the ministry of Jesus to fulfill a passage in the prophet Isaiah: "the people that lived in darkness saw a great light, and on those who lived in the land and shadow of death a light dawned" (Matt. 4:16). In Luke's Gospel the hymn of Zechariah adopts similar language on the occasion of the birth of Jesus' precursor, John the Baptist: "by the tender compassion of our God the dawn from on high will break upon us, to shine on those who sit in darkness and un-

---

7. Martin Luther called light "the best figure or representation of the Divine Majesty" in his *Lectures on Genesis;* see *Luther's Works,* ed. J. Pelikan, vol. 2 (St. Louis: Concordia, 1960), p. 247.

der the shadow of death" (Luke 1:78-9). When Jesus was born, "the glory of the Lord shone" around the shepherds (Luke 2:9). On the occasion of the Christ Child being presented in the Temple, old Simeon said: "my eyes have seen the salvation you have prepared in the presence of all nations: a light that will bring revelation to the Gentiles and glory to your people Israel" (Luke 2:30-32).

According to the Synoptic Gospels, the ministry of Jesus featured an episode on a high mountain when, in the presence of Peter, James, and John, Jesus was "transfigured" and his clothes became "dazzling white" (Mark 9:2-8) — in the "light of Tabor," as John Behr's chapter explains. Matthew introduces more luminosity into the scene, by stating that the face of Jesus "shone like the sun" and the cloud that overshadowed the three disciples was "bright" (Matt. 17:1-8). Luke goes further by saying that the disciples saw "the glory" of Christ and of the two heavenly companions who had appeared with him, Moses and Elijah: "they appeared in glory and were speaking of his departure which he was about to accomplish in Jerusalem" — a clear indication that the glory of the transfiguration should be understood as a preview of the glory to come with the crucifixion and resurrection (Luke 9:28-36). Luke thinks of glory as preeminently associated with the post-resurrection situation of Jesus: by rising from the dead, he enters into his glory (Luke 24:26).

Further New Testament witnesses share the same scheme. What is apparently a quotation from an early Christian hymn celebrates the risen Christ as "taken up into glory" (1 Tim. 3:16). The Letter to the Hebrews likewise speaks of the "glory" that characterizes the crucified and exalted Son (2:7, 9; 3:3; 13:21) and that will be the goal of the people he leads (2:10). First Peter adopts a similar pattern: "God raised him [Jesus] from the dead and gave him glory" (1:21; see 1:11).

Other New Testament authors follow the same scheme by speaking in terms of the "glory" that belongs to the risen and exalted Christ, enthroned now and to come at the end: "our Lord Jesus Christ reigns in glory" (James 2:1); "we wait for the blessed hope, the appearing of the glory of our great God and Savior Jesus Christ" (Titus 2:13). Since Christ embodies and fully expresses the glory of God, "the Glory of God" might serve as a title for him. Jesus is "the Glory of God," just as he is elsewhere called "the Mystery of God" (Col. 2:2).

Right from its prologue, John's Gospel differs by simply identifying Jesus (under the title of the Word) and not the Torah as "the Light" (John 1:4-5, 7), and announcing: "the true light, which enlightens everyone, was coming into the world" (John 1:9).[8] He is the "genuine source of illumination, universal in its scope, enlightening every person."[9] The prologue climaxes with one of the most famous and cherished claims made in the New Testament. In Jesus divine glory was present from the beginning for those who had eyes to see it: "the Word became flesh, and made his home among us. We saw his glory, such glory as befits the only Son of the Father" (John 1:14).[10] God is invisible ("no one has ever seen God" — John 1:18), but the incarnate Son of God is visible and revealed as "the light of the world" (John 9:5) and the "glory of God." "Walking in the light" means seeing the "signs" of his divine "glory" (e.g., John 2:11), believing that Jesus is the unique revelation of the invisible God and so, through this faith, enjoying "the light of life" (John 8:12; 12:46).

Light and water imagery distinguished the Jewish Feast of Booths (or Tabernacles) held in the Temple: in particular, four large "menorahs" or lampstands were set up in the Court of the Women and provided light for celebrants to dance through the night. Present on the last and greatest day of this festival, Jesus disclosed that in his person he embodied what the festival celebrated in its light and water imagery (John 7:37-9). He has replaced the significance of the Feast of the Booths; he is the light illuminating not merely the Temple and Jerusalem but also the whole world (John 8:12).

Unlike the other three Gospels, John sees the whole of Jesus' life as manifesting his divine glory.[11] During the public ministry seven "signs" reveal this glory: from the miracle at Cana (John 2:11) to the raising of Lazarus (John 11:4, 40). Since the entire mission of Jesus is suffused in glory, it would make little sense to include an account of the transfiguration as a *preview* of his future glory. The glory manifested right through the ministry of Jesus reaches its climax at his crucifixion and resurrection. What could seem the depth of deadly humiliation is in fact "the hour" or supreme manifestation of his glory (John 12:23; 13:31-32; 17:1). The divine glory that the Son enjoyed in his Father's presence "before the world ex-

8. This verse could be translated: "he was the true light that enlightens everyone coming into the world." On the opposition of light and darkness that we find in John's Gospel and 1 John, see G. Strecker, *The Johannine Letters*, trans. L. M. Maloney (Minneapolis: Fortress, 1996), pp. 26-28.

9. A. T. Lincoln, *The Gospel According to John* (London: Continuum, 2005), p. 101.

10. Lincoln comments: "faith finds in Jesus the glory of the divine presence" (*John*, p. 105).

11. Lincoln, *John*, pp. 66-68, 104-5.

isted" has also distinguished the Son's mission on earth and led to the glory that he will share forever with his Father (John 17:4-5, 24).

Before leaving John's Gospel, we should note that it associates not only "light" and "glory" with Christ but also beauty. As commentators have often observed, the "good *(kalos)*" shepherd is equivalently the "beautiful shepherd" (John 10:14).

Finally, the Book of Revelation opens with a vision of the exalted Christ among seven lampstands of gold, his eyes flaming like fire and his face shining "like the sun at full strength" (Rev. 1:13-16). The book finishes with a vision of the New Jerusalem, a city that did not need the sun or the moon to shine on it, "for the glory of God gave it light, and its lamp was the Lamb" (Rev. 21:23; see 22:5). Then the glorious Jesus himself speaks: "I am the bright star of dawn" (Rev. 22:16).

3. Bible Survey Conclusions and Questions

When we survey the sweep of biblical testimony to light, we face two startling developments. The first is the shift from Genesis to 1 John. When saying, "let there be light," God creates the most sublime gift for many further beings that then will be created in their turn. Yet light is "other" than God and totally dependent upon God for its existence. Nevertheless, "let there be light" will move beyond providing an image for understanding God's creative act to providing an image about God himself. In a metaphorical statement 1 John makes the simple identification: "God is light, and in him there is no darkness at all" (1 John 1:5). The least we can say is that for 1 John light is a most basic and perfect manifestation of the divine reality. This statement can hardly be intended to define strictly God's essence, any more than the other (and related) statement that "God is love" (1 John 4:8, 16). Rather the author wishes to describe something of the nature of God. Georg Strecker comments: "As light is the source of all illumination, so God is the source of all that makes human life bright. God's being light means the fulfilment of meaning in human life, to which, in the eschaton, God gives a basis, a measure, and a goal. If God is understood as 'light,' this means that God is acknowledged as the giver of eschatological salvation."[12] Add too what Metropolitan Kallistos Ware observes in his chapter: darkness is never used positively by John or any other New Testament author to symbolize God.

12. Strecker, *Johannine Letters,* pp. 25-26.

The second striking development in the biblical story of revelation comes with Jesus himself being identified in John's Gospel as "the light of the world." This provides a starting point for the eventual emergence of the creedal confession of him as "Light from Light."

In retrieving the biblical data about light, I have also paid attention to the closely related theme of "glory." Without being strict synonyms, "light" and "glory" also overlap with "beauty."[13] For Paul to say that he had seen "the glory of God in the face of Christ" was close to saying that he had seen "the beauty of God in the face of Christ." For 1 John to declare "God is light" was close to declaring that "God is beauty."

In *The Glory of God* Hans Urs von Balthasar (1905-88) would bring firmly together "light" and "beauty": "The light of God, which is the simplest of all light . . . is also original beauty." Balthasar reaches for an even stronger qualifier, "absolute" rather than simply "original": "as the absolute light" God is also "absolute beauty." He then introduces a further adjective ("eternal") to express the Incarnation in terms of beauty: "God's eternal beauty becomes a man."[14] Balthasar does not say this, but his language suggests enlarging the Creed to confess Christ as "Light from Light," "Glory from Glory," and "Beauty from Beauty."

Balthasar's reflections could encourage (1) examining the post–New Testament tradition and establishing to what extent earlier and later Christian thinkers have associated the light, glory, and beauty of God. (2) Another line of research could lead us to trace the symbolism of light in the Christian liturgy: the Paschal Candle at the Easter Vigil and the "sol invictus (unconquered sun)" at Christmas and the Epiphany.[15] Yet again one might move beyond the New Testament to investigate (3) the metaphysics of light according to neo-Platonists, Augustine (see the chapter by Robert Dodaro), other Church Fathers, theologians of the Middle Ages (see the chapter by Kathryn Tanner), and modern theologians (see the chapter by George Hunsinger). Or one could fruitfully examine (4) the theme of light according to Christian mysticism down through the centu-

---

13. Light was to form an essential part of the classical account of beauty offered by Thomas Aquinas (d. 1274) in his *Summa theologiae*, 1.39.8: *integritas sive perfectio* (integrity or perfection), *proportio sive consonantia* (proportion or harmony), and *claritas* (splendour).

14. H. U. von Balthasar, *The Glory of the Lord: A Theological Aesthetics*, trans. A. Louth and others, vol. 2 (San Francisco: Ignatius, 1984), pp. 129, 132, 134.

15. See J. Ratzinger, "Licht," in *Handbuch theologischer Grundbegriffe*, ed. H. Fries, vol. 2 (Munich: Kösel-Verlag, 1963), pp. 44-54.

ries, both Western[16] and Eastern. Hesychasm was an Eastern tradition of mystical prayer that reached its full expression with St. Gregory Palamas (d. 1359) and others in the fourteenth century. Hesychasts hoped to reach through God's grace and unceasing prayer a vision of the Divine Light, which they believed to be identical with the Light that surrounded Christ at his transfiguration.[17] In a *tour de force,* the chapter in this book by Metropolitan Kallistos Ware takes readers through the complementary themes of light and darkness, as found in the mystical theology of the Greek Fathers, down to Palamas.

Rather than pursue any forms of these four attractive options,[18] I want to explore some of the Christian answers to the question: To what extent is the ultimate mystery of God, the Holy Trinity, to be understood as a or rather *the* mystery of light? Positive replies to that question entail recognizing the full and true divinity of Christ; otherwise he could not be "Light from Light." They also entail associating light with the Holy Spirit and acknowledging the Spirit to be not only "the Life-giver" but also "the Light-giver."

The New Testament repeatedly links the Holy Spirit with *life* (e.g., Rom. 8:1-17) and with *truth:* "the Spirit of truth" will guide Christ's followers "into all truth" (John 16:13). Further, all the manifestations of the Spirit, according to Paul, reach their climax with *love* (1 Cor. 12:31–13:13); through the Holy Spirit, God's love "floods the hearts" of believers (Rom. 5:5).

Direct links of the Holy Spirit with "glory" and "light" are less apparent. While often linking "glory" to the Father and the Son, the New Testament does so only once in the case of the Spirit: "the Spirit of glory" rests upon believers (1 Pet. 4:14). Where Mark reports John the Baptist as saying of the "mightier one" to come after him that "he will baptize you with the Holy Spirit," Matthew and Luke add a significant phrase: "He will baptize you with the Holy Spirit *and with fire*" (Matt. 3:11; Luke 3:16). In the event neither Mark nor Matthew reports any coming of the Holy Spirit, as does Luke (Luke 24:49; Acts 1:8; 2:1-4), who also includes a reference to the "fiery" Spirit (Acts 2:3, 19). Matthew will include a mandate to baptize "in the name of the Father, and of the Son, *and of the Holy Spirit*" (Matt. 28:19).

16. Here an essential guide would be B. McGinn, *The Presence of God: A History of Western Mysticism,* 4 vols. (New York: Crossroad, 1991-2006).

17. See, e.g., J. Meyendorff, *St. Gregory Palamas and Orthodox Spirituality* (Crestwood, NY: St. Vladimir's Seminary Press, 1974).

18. A further option would be to compare and contrast the light of God in the Christian tradition with what we find in the mystical experiences of Hindus, Jews, Muslims, and followers of other world religions.

Matthew may understand being "baptized with fire" to be the judgment facing those who fail to respond appropriately to the call for repentance (Matt. 7:19; 13:40, 42, 50; 18:9) when the Son of Man comes to judge all people (Matt. 25:41). Luke clearly refers being "baptized with fire" to the fire of the Spirit at Pentecost. The outpouring of the Spirit at Pentecost involved the Spirit being manifested not only by a strong wind but also by "flames like tongues of fire" (Acts 2:2-3). Thus the New Testament provided some platform, albeit a limited one, from which to link the Holy Spirit with "glory" and "light."

Let us take up first some of the developments that led to Christ being confessed as "Light from Light." We can then turn to the road that led to the Spirit being acknowledged as Light-giver and completing a vision of the Trinity as the ultimate mystery of light.

4. Christ as Light from Light: The Road to Nicaea

A verse from the Letter to the Hebrews made a key contribution to the development towards "Light from Light": "He [the Son] is the radiance *(apaugasma)* of God's glory *(doxa)*, the stamp/imprint *(charactēr)* of God's very being/substance *(hypostasis)*" (Heb. 1:3). How does this verse — in particular, its first part — represent the Son's relationship to God (the Father)?[19] From a grammatical point of view, two possibilities open up: either "the Son *actively* radiates divine glory 'out from' God" or "he more *passively* reflects 'back' divine glory, like a mirror."[20] Does he radiate or reflect God's glory? Craig Koester points out that we face a similar "ambiguity in Wisdom 7:25-26, where *apaugasma* is used alongside 'emanation' *(aporroia)* and 'mirror.'" Apropos of *apaugasma* in Hebrews 1:3, the ancient and many modern commentaries prefer the active meaning. But, as Koester rightly points out, "the text does not deal primarily with God's relationship with the Son. The Son is the one through whom God's power and presence are brought into the realm of human experience."[21] From the second century of the Christian era, however, the relationship of Father and Son became paramount for theological reflection. In the run-up to the

19. On this section, see J. Pelikan, *The Light of the World: A Basic Image in Early Christian Thought* (New York: Harper & Brothers, 1962). While attending primarily to Athanasius of Alexandria, Pelikan ranges further and provides extensive bibliographical material.

20. C. R. Koester, *Hebrews* (New York: Doubleday, 2001), pp. 179-80.

21. Koester, *Hebrews*, p. 180.

First Council of Nicaea (325), the contributions of St. Justin Martyr (d. around 165), Tertullian (d. around 220), and Origen (d. around 254) guided thinking about the Son's being "Light from Light."

In his *Dialogue with Trypho* Justin explained that "God has begotten of himself a rational Power," which the Scriptures called by various titles: "sometimes the *Glory* of the Lord, at other times Son, or Wisdom, or Angel, or God, or Lord, or Word" (6.1; see 61.3). To interpret the generation of the Word, Justin appealed to the sun sending forth its rays or a fire kindling other fires. Just as in these analogies, the begetting of the Son did not mean an "amputation, as if the essence *(ousia)* of the Father were divided" (*Dialogue* 128.3, 4). Here Justin raised a question that was to be much debated in the fourth century, the consubstantiality of the Father and the Son (or Word) in sharing the same substance, essence, or *ousia*. By that time, thanks to Tertullian, Origen, and others, Justin's image of "Light from Light" had entered the official creed of the church.

Justin himself, as Jaroslav Pelikan points out, took the image "to mean that as fire could be ignited from fire without diminishing that from which it was taken, so the Son was derived from the Father without loss in the deity of the Father. Here the accent was not so much upon the coessentiality of the Father and the Son as upon the inviolability of the Father despite the generation of the Son." In the fourth century Athanasius was to recognize that "the image of fire kindled from fire suggested that the new fire or firebrand was something external to the old, created and wrought by it but separate from it." If "light from light" was to express the confession that Christ was "true God from true God," "it had to be disengaged from the image of fire from fire."[22]

Some decades after Justin, Tertullian in his *Adversus Praxean* wanted to show how God is a differentiated, triune unity; the divine substance is extended, with the Son and the Spirit sharing in it and being distinct persons, yet without being separated. He introduced three "material" analogies: a root producing a shoot and fruit; a spring issuing into a river and a canal; the sun producing a ray and the point of focus of a ray. "God," he wrote, "produced the Word . . . as a root produces the shoot, a spring the river, the sun a ray. . . . The Spirit makes the third from God [the Father] and the Son, as the fruit from the shoot is the third from the tree, the canal

---

22. Pelikan, *Light of the World,* p. 58. On the contribution to this development that came from Dionysius of Alexandria in the third century, see Pelikan, *Light of the World,* pp. 58-59.

from the river the third from the source, the point of focus of a ray the third from the sun. But none of these is divorced from the origin from which it derives its own properties. Thus the Trinity derives from the Father by continuous and connected steps" (8). The three analogies maintain that the Son and the Spirit are distinct from the Father as individual persons but they are not other in substance from the Father. The Son and the Spirit remain derived from the Father without a real separation taking place. The three divine persons are linked through dynamic relationships of origin that do not separate them. For our purposes we see here light (namely, the light of the sun as understood by the science of Tertullian's day) being one of the three analogies used to present the origin of the Son and the Spirit from the Father. In particular, just as the sunbeam, while it extends the substance of the sun, remains one in substance with the sun and yet differs from it, so too the Son remains one in substance with the Father and yet is distinct from the Father.

I have already quoted a famous fragment from Origen's commentary on Hebrews, in which he related Hebrews 1:3 to the question of the eternal existence of the Son (text in note 1). There is only one principle of divine Light, with the Father as the eternal, unbegotten Light, and the Son as the eternal, begotten, or generated Splendor of that Light. In this fragment Origen prepared the terminology to be used at the First Council of Nicaea about the Son: not only "Light from Light" but also "there never was when he was not" and his being *homoousios* with the Father or sharing his essential reality *(ousia)*. One should add that this clearly stated doctrine of "consubstantiality," or "community of substance," between the Father and the Son may owe something to the translation by Rufinus of Aquileia (d. 411). We do not have Origen's original Greek text but only the Latin version that Rufinus made long after the Council of Nicaea had become accepted orthodoxy.[23]

Prompted not only by Hebrews 1:3 but also by Colossians 1:15 (Christ as "the image of the invisible God") and Wisdom 7:25-26 (Wisdom as "the pure outflow" of God's glory), Origen repeatedly portrayed the Word/Son as eternally reflecting God's glory and light. "There is," he wrote, "an eternal and everlasting begetting, as brightness/radiance is begotten from light." Since God is light (1 John 1:5), the Son is "the brightness/radiance of this light, proceeding from the God without separation, as brightness/ra-

23. See J. N. D. Kelly, *Early Christian Doctrines*, 5th ed. (London: A. & C. Black, 1977), p. 130.

diance from light."[24] God could never be without the radiance of his glorious light.

5. The Council of Nicaea and Its Aftermath

"Light from Light" was one of the ways in which the Nicene Creed took a stand against Arius and his followers to confess that the Son, while begotten by and derived from the Father, shares the same Godhead, is co-eternal with the Father, and is not a creature made in time. He is eternally begotten from the Father and enjoys essential divinity (and not merely participated "divinity"), because the Godhead has been fully communicated to him. As originated from the Father, the divinity of the Son is identical with that of the Father. Hence the Son should be called "God from God," "Light from Light," "true God from true God" and "of one being/substance *(homoousios)* with the Father."

St. Athanasius of Alexandria (d. 373), who attended the Council as a deacon and secretary of his bishop, Alexander of Alexandria (d. 328), summed up years later the central motivation behind the stand taken against Arius: "The Word could never have divinized us if he were merely divine by participation and were not himself the essential Godhead, the Father's veritable image" (*De Synodis*, 51). To put this in equivalent terms, it took the natural Son of God to make human beings the adopted children of God, who are "divinized" by participation.[25]

A classic defender of the Nicene Creed, Athanasius repeatedly introduced "his favourite analogy of the light and its brightness, which, while distinguishable as two, are one and the same substance."[26] The derivation of the Son (the Radiance) from the Father (the Light), far from implying any Arian-style subordination, conveys their unity and equality. Athanasius declared the Son to be "the Radiance" and the Father to be "the Light" (*Contra Arianos*, 2.41). Echoing even more clearly Hebrews 1:3,

24. *De Principiis*, 1.2.5 and 7; trans. G. W. Butterworth (London: SPCK, 1936), pp. 18, 20.

25. In the aftermath of the Council of Nicaea, St. Ambrose of Milan used extensively the imagery of light in his Trinitarian theology; see R. Morgan, *The Imagery of Light in St. Ambrose's Theology* (Melbourne: Carmelite Monastery, 1998).

26. Kelly, *Early Christian Doctrines*, p. 245; see Athanasius, *Contra Arianos*, 3.11; *De Decretis Nicaenae Synodi*, 23-24. In *De Sententia Dionysii* Athanasius wrote: "if anyone . . . dares to separate the radiance from the light and say that the radiance is of another essence, let him join Arius in his insanity" (24).

Athanasius stated: "He [the Son] is the very stamp of the nature of the Father and light from light and the true image of the essence of the Father" (*Contra Arianos*, 1.9). Where the Letter to the Hebrews called the Son "the Radiance" of the Father, this meant, according to Athanasius, "that the radiance cannot be separated from the light but is proper to it by nature and co-exists with it" (*Epistola ad episcopos Aegypti et Libyae*, 13). The co-eternity of Father and Son follows. God, Athanasius wrote, "can never be without his Word, any more than the light can cease to shine" (*Contra Arianos*, 2.32). Or, more concisely, "He who is light, was he ever not radiant?" (*Contra Arianos*, 1.24; see 1.13, 25).

Arius had little to say about the Holy Spirit, and correspondingly, the Council of Nicaea simply confessed, "we believe in the Holy Spirit," and left it at that. Right from New Testament times the liturgy (for instance, baptism "in the name of the Father, and of the Son, and of the Holy Spirit") and the doxology ("glory be to the Father with *(meta)* the Son, together with *(sun)* the Holy Spirit") expressed or at least implied a "high" view of the Spirit's identity. Prior to the fourth century such Christian thinkers as Tertullian and Origen had initiated theological reflection on the Spirit. But from around 360 CE, various groups (often lumped together under the name of "Pneumatomachians") began challenging the truly divine status of the Holy Spirit. These challenges prompted St. Basil of Caesarea (d. 379), St. Gregory of Nyssa (d. around 395), and others to reflect seriously and at length on the Spirit as sharing the divine substance/essence (being "consubstantial") with the Father and the Son. The First Council of Constantinople (381) developed at length the third article of the Nicene Creed in expressing the divinity of the Spirit, the "Lord" and "Life-giver" who is worshiped and glorified together with the Father and the Son.[27]

Those who championed the Holy Spirit followed Tertullian (see above) in applying the language of light. Basil declared that the Holy Spirit shines on believers and illuminates them like the sun (*On the Holy Spirit*, 26.61). Gregory of Nazianzus called the Spirit "Life and Life-giver, Light and Light-giver" (*Oration on Pentecost*, 9). St. Cyril of Jerusalem (d. 386) described the work of the Spirit as "the true Enlightener," who brings "beams of light and knowledge" to "enlighten the mind" (*Catechetical Lectures*, 16.16). But, in the event, the Council of Constantinople inserted in the Nicene Creed a recognition of the Holy Spirit as "Life-giver" but not as "Light-giver."

27. See G. O'Collins, *The Tripersonal God* (Mahwah, NJ: Paulist, 1999), pp. 123-25, 128-34.

By acknowledging the Holy Spirit to be "of one being/substance *(homoousios)* with the Father," Basil and the other Cappadocians faced the challenge of distinguishing between the Son and the Holy Spirit in a way that showed they are not divine "Siblings." The Father does not have two Sons. What differentiates the mode of origin of the Son from that of the Spirit? The distinction between the divine persons is grounded in their origin (in the case of the second and third) and in their mutual relations. The difference between two verbs proved vital: the Son is generated by the Father, whereas the Spirit "proceeds" from the Father (see John 15:26), with the Son somehow involved in this "procession." Gregory of Nyssa wrote of the Spirit proceeding "out of" the Father and receiving "of/from" the Son, and of the Spirit proceeding out of the Father through the Son.[28] In terms of our central topic, he used the analogy of a torch imparting its light first to another torch and then through it to a third.[29]

6. From Eriugena to Dante

To complete this sketch of the Holy Trinity as a mystery of light, we can cite some further witnesses up to Dante. First, John Scotus Eriugena (d. around 877) described the inner life and the outer activity of the Trinity in terms of light. In the opening chapter of his *Commentary on the Celestial Hierarchy* by Dionysius the Pseudo-Areopagite, he wrote of the threefold light of the Trinity: "the first and intimate light *(lumen primum et intimum)*" of the Father, "the true light *(lumen verum)*" of the Son, and "the gifted light *(lumen donativum)*" of the Spirit. This threefold light pervades the universe, "shining in all things that exist, in order that all might be brought back into the love and knowledge of its beauty *(splendens in omnibus que sunt, ut in amorem et cognitionem pulchritudinis sue convertantur omnia)*."[30]

The spiritual experiences of St. Symeon the New Theologian (d. 1022) featured the breaking in of light that he identified as the "light of the Holy Spirit." This led him to introduce his hymns with a prayer to the Spirit: "Come, true Light" and "Come, Light that never ends." Yves Congar writes: "Symeon's mystical experience was above all an experience of light and an

28. *Contra Macedonianos,* 2; 10, 12, 24. See O'Collins, *Tripersonal God,* pp. 138-41.
29. *Contra Eunomium,* 1.42.
30. Quoted by McGinn, *Presence of God,* vol. 2, p. 103.

experience of the Spirit."[31] One might sum up Symeon's message as "the Spirit is light."

The "Golden Sequence" for Pentecost, "Veni Sancte Spiritus," almost certainly written by an Archbishop of Canterbury, Stephen Langton (d. 1128), calls the Spirit "lux beatissima" (most blessed Light) and prays, "veni, lumen cordium" (come, Light of hearts).

Like Eriugena, St. Hildegard of Bingen (d. 1179) depicted not merely the Holy Spirit but the whole Trinity as the divine mystery of light. She wrote of a vision of a bright human figure (the Son) surrounded by light that is both white (the Father) and red (the Spirit) (*Scivias*, 22).

The greatest of all medieval poets, Dante Alighieri (d. 1321), lent his weight to such visions of the Trinity as the mystery of light. At the end of his *Paradiso*, Dante envisions God as utterly active, with "spinning" or "circling" symbolizing the completely actualized divine perfection: "in the profound and clear ground of lofty light there appeared to me three spinnings (circlings) of three colors and of the same extent. The One seemed reflected in the Other as rainbow by rainbow,[32] and the Third seemed fire breathed forth equally from the One and the Other" (Canto XXXIII, 115-20). Dante's "luminous" picture of the Trinity as rainbow/rainbow/fire is, however, "shaded" or "subverted" by an intense vision of God as light that forces the poet to close his eyes in wonder (see the chapter by David Brown). Let me pass to some concluding reflections on the Holy Trinity as the ultimate mystery of light and do so in dialogue with Kathryn Tanner's chapter.

7. Conclusion

Over and above those whom I cited from the Christian tradition, Tanner has added further voices who witnessed to the Trinity as mystery of light: Gregory of Nyssa, Hilary of Poitiers, Augustine, John of Damascus, Thomas Aquinas, and Bonaventure. What I have expounded corresponds largely to the first theme she develops: the imagery of light as providing

---

31. Y. Congar, *I Believe in the Holy Spirit*, trans. D. Smith, vol. 1 (London: Geoffrey Chapman, 1983), p. 96; see also the chapter by John Behr in the present volume.

32. Dante followed Revelation 4:1-11 in associating the image of a rainbow with God. There the rainbow around the throne evokes the glory of God, while some precious stones (jasper, cornelian, and emerald) intensify the light and reflect the unapproachable brightness/glory that surrounds God.

analogies for the relationships between the three persons of the Trinity. She has gone further by drawing our attention to some limits in the analogy of light: for instance, that it may give the impression of the divine persons not being sufficiently distinct.

Her second and third themes take up the value and limits of the light analogy when expounding, respectively, the creative work of God and the divine presence in the world. It is only briefly and in passing that I touched on two themes, and did so mainly in my final section, "Eriugena to Dante."

Light may be the most basic, general, and even perfect manifestation of the divine reality and operations (in creation and in the divine presence to all creatures). But, as Tanner rightly illustrates, we need to note the limits as well as the values in the perceived properties of light as a theological analogy.

Across many traditions God is experienced in light and as light. Using here the language of light seems thoroughly intercultural. Yet, strictly speaking, light is an impersonal analogy, unlike the analogies of "word" and "love" that have long been pressed into service when speaking of the Trinity and their relations.

In his superb hymn "How Wonderful the Three-in-One," Brian Wren does speak of the Trinity's "energies of dancing light," but the emphasis falls on "the communing love in shared delight." Wren draws above all on Richard of St. Victor (d. 1173) to develop the personal analogy of "Lover, Beloved and Equal Friend."[33]

---

33. See O'Collins, *Tripersonal God,* pp. 202-3.

The Use of Perceived Properties of Light as a Theological Analogy

Kathryn E. Tanner

The perceived properties of light provide analogies for three main topics in Christian theology, in particular during the patristic and medieval periods: (1) the relationships between the persons of the Trinity; (2) God's creation of the world; and (3) God's presence within the world. This chapter sketches how and why these analogies work (and fail to work), with the intention of enabling discussion as to whether current scientific understandings of the properties of light support or undermine such analogies.

1. The Light Analogy for the Trinity

The most common analogy with light in Trinitarian theology likens the relationships between first, second, and third persons of the Trinity to relationships between a source of light, an emanating ray of light, and the radiance surrounding the ray. Light imagery is more commonly used to characterize the relationship between the first and second persons of the Trinity, following the "light from light" language of the Nicene Creed. But the Holy Spirit is also associated with light, in particular because it provides us with illumination. Thus, John of Damascus can talk this way about the three persons of the Trinity and their action on us: "It is just the same as in the case of the sun from which come both the ray and the radiance (for the sun itself is the source of both the ray and the radiance), and it is through the ray that the radiance is imparted to us, and it is the radiance itself by which we are lightened and in which we participate."[1]

1. John of Damascus, *Exposition of the Orthodox Faith,* 8; in *Nicene and Post-Nicene Christian Fathers* (hereafter NPNF), vol. 9, p. 11.

The analogy with light is supposed to make clear the following.

(1) The first person of the Trinity is the source of the other two. (2) The other two derive their substance from the first.

(3) They thereby share the same substance with the first — not merely generically in the way two human beings share a common nature but, specifically, in the way a son might be the "spitting image" of his father.

(4) Each reproduces the whole of the first (except for the property of being the source of the other two). Thus, in close parallel to the famous dictum of Athanasius that "the same things are said of the Son, which are said of the Father, except his being said to be Father,"[2] the ray of light is all that its source is; the only difference is that it is not itself that source.

(5) The whole of the others, not simply part of them, is derived from the first; they get all that they are from the first, rather than simply some modification of what they already are. Thus (if one puts the last two points together), "the body of the sun is expressly imaged by the whole disc that surrounds it . . . and . . . the radiance of light sheds its brilliance from the whole of the sun's disc."[3]

(6) This production of them does not involve any partition, division, or diminution of the source. As Hilary of Poitiers wrote, "God is born from God, as light from light, which pours itself forth without self-diminution, giving what it has, yet having what it gave."[4] Indeed, the first person of the Trinity does not lose anything in producing the others; it remains just as it is.

(7) Consequently, all that the first person of the Trinity is can be seen in the others, and all that they are in it. "'I in the Father and the Father in me.' For the Son is in the Father . . . because the whole being of the Son is proper to the Father's essence; as radiance from light . . . [and] the Father is in the Son since the Son is what is from the Father and proper to him, as in the radiance the sun."[5]

(8) What the first person of the Trinity communicates to the others is proper to those others: i.e., they are also by nature divine in themselves (and not simply divine by derivation). The second person of the Trinity, for example, is itself light from what is light.

(9) The productive causality of the first person is instantaneous, with-

---

2. *Against the Arians,* 3.4; NPNF, vol. 4, p. 395.
3. Gregory of Nyssa, *Against Eunomius,* 3.1; NPNF, vol. 5, p. 202.
4. Hilary of Poitiers, *On the Trinity,* 6; NPNF, vol. 9, p. 101.
5. Athanasius, *Against the Arians,* 3.3; NPNF, vol. 4, p. 395.

out the need for intermediaries, and therefore effortless, like the emission of light.

(10) The first person is necessarily productive of the others — that is, simply as a consequence of its being what it is — in the way a light-generating source necessarily emits light.

(11) There is no spatial gap or temporal interval between the first person of the Trinity and the others. They always exist together. There was no time when the first person of the Trinity existed and the others did not; thus, "the Son's generation is eternal and everlasting, just as the radiance is continually generated from the light."[6] Likewise, they are in no way spatially separable from one another but are indivisibly united. The three cannot then exist or operate independently of their relationships with one another. In the case of the relationship between the first and second persons of the Trinity, just as the radiance of the sun and what issues from a fountain "always exist with those things from which they are," so the Son is inseparably and "ever coexistent" with the Father.[7]

Putting together the last few points about the first person's generation of the second person, one can say "that none may think of the [divine] offspring [the second person] humanly. . . . [Scripture] also calls him word, wisdom, and radiance; to teach us that the generation was impassible, and eternal and worthy of God."[8]

(12) The persons of the Trinity are co-implicative in the way a source of light implies a ray, and a ray implies a source of light; or in the way a ray implies radiance, and radiance implies the ray it surrounds.

(13) While co-implicative, the positions of the persons of the Trinity in relationship to one another are not reversible: the first person as source never takes on the position of something produced, or what is produced the position of its source. What receives light may go on to illuminate the source, but the source thereby receives back only what it gave.

Generally speaking, light imagery does a good job of conveying the unity between the persons of the Trinity — unity by way of a single source, sameness of substance, and indivisibility. Thus, Athanasius can say: "the Saints . . . all preach of [the second person of the Trinity] as radiance, thereby to signify his being from the essence, proper and indivisible, and

6. G. L. Prestige, *God in Patristic Thought* (London: SPCK, 1959), p. 154; see Origen, *On First Principles* 1.2.4; Ante-Nicene Christian Library, vol. 10, p. 22.

7. Athanasius, *Against the Arians*, 1.27; NPNF, vol. 4, p. 322.

8. Athanasius, *Against the Arians*, 1.28; NPNF, vol. 4, p. 323.

his oneness with the Father."[9] Elsewhere he writes, "No one would say that they are two lights, but sun and radiance [are] two, yet one, the light from the sun enlightening in its radiance all things."[10]

The imagery can, however, suggest that the other two persons of the Trinity are merely properties or powers of the first person, that the other two have no proper subsistence in and of themselves, and that therefore there is only one person properly speaking in the Trinity — the first.[11] Gregory of Nazianzus wrote, "I thought of the sun and a ray and light. But . . . there was a fear . . . lest we should . . . deny personality to the others, and make them only powers of God, existing in him and not personal. For neither the ray nor the light is another sun, but they are effulgences from the sun, and qualities of his essence."[12] The primary dis-analogy, therefore, with the relationship between a source of light and light is that "whereas light possesses no proper subsistence of its own, distinct from that of the fire, the Son is a perfect subsistence, inseparable from the Father's subsistence."[13] Or, in another way of making the same point, the imagery suggests the persons of the Trinity are not sufficiently distinct from one another. They blur into one another. It is not clear where the one begins and the other ends, because of the continuous character of the way in which light and radiance stream from a light source. The dimming of the light as it streams away from a light source can rather easily, moreover, suggest a lessening of it — -the light gets weaker as it streams farther from the source — thereby implying the inequality of the other two persons in relation to the first. So Gregory of Nazianzus writes: "Apollinarius . . . did not preserve the power of the Godhead. For to make the Trinity consist of great, greater, and greatest, as of light, ray, and sun, the Spirit and the Son and the Father (as is clearly stated in his writings) is a ladder of Godhead not leading to heaven, but down from heaven."[14]

In order to make clear that the unity of light does not imply some confusion of the persons into one, some propose the analogy of three overlapping sources of light. Even if the Trinity is one, it is nevertheless made up

9. Athanasius, *Defence of the Nicene Definition*, 5.23; NPNF, vol. 4, p. 165.

10. Athanasius, *Against the Arians*, 3.4; NPNF, vol. 4, p. 395.

11. Prestige, *God in Patristic Thought*, p. 290.

12. Gregory of Nazianzus, *Fifth Theological Oration: On the Spirit*, 32; in E. R. Hardy, *Christology of the Later Fathers* (Philadelphia: Westminster, 1954; hereafter CLF), pp. 213-14.

13. John of Damascus, *Exposition of the Orthodox Faith*, 8; NPNF, vol. 9, p. 9; see also p. 8.

14. Gregory of Nazianzus, *Letter to Cledonius* (*Epistle* 101); CLF, p. 223.

of three distinct persons in much the way light might be indistinguishably one, despite its coming from three distinct sources. The distinct sources of light are joined to one another and throw off therefore a single combined ray of light. In the words of John of Damascus, "[the persons of the Trinity] are made one not so as to commingle, but so as to cleave to each other. . . . It is just like three suns cleaving to each other without separation and giving out light mingled and conjoined into one."[15] The important point about light here (i.e., the advantage it has over other physical analogies) is the way different streams of light, distinguished by their sources, can nevertheless perfectly mingle in the same space by being superimposed upon one another.[16] They remain distinguishable (in thought) but coinhere in operations that are perfectly coextensive and coterminous.

2. The Light Analogy for Creation

In order to distinguish (a) God's creation of the world from (b) relations of origin within the Trinity, theologians sometimes try to limit use of light imagery (or any terms of material efflux or biological generation) to the latter case. The second person of the Trinity comes out of the first like light from light but the world does not. God makes the world — the analogy is often with a human artisan — rather than generating the world out of its own substance in the way light imagery suggests. The world cannot derive from God's very substance, since, in sharp contrast to the three persons of the Trinity, the world and God do not have even a generic nature in common; the world is nothing like God, certainly not God's equal in the way the different persons of the Trinity are equally divine. In the early church in particular, the primary reason for restricting in this way light imagery to relations of origin within the Trinity was to make clear the sharp divide between the other two persons of the Trinity and creatures, when this was a matter under dispute.

Indeed, various dis-analogies with light imagery are stressed in accounts of God's creation of the world: for instance, in Thomas Aquinas's account of creation, where an artisan analogy is favored and God is said to create the world through will and knowledge.[17] Besides suggesting a

---

15. John of Damascus, *Exposition of the Orthodox Faith*, 8; NPNF, vol. 9, p. 11.

16. See S. A. McKinion, *Words, Imagery and the Mystery of Christ: A Reconstruction of Cyril of Alexandria's Christology* (Leiden/Boston: Brill, 2000), p. 67.

17. See Thomas Aquinas, *Summa Theologiae* (hereafter ST), 1a. 14.8; 1a 19. 4; 1a 45. 6.

shared nature between God and the world, light imagery, it is charged, would restrict the scope of God's creative agency to what is most like itself. In contrast to "artisan causes," which choose from among a variety of ideas what it is they would like to construct, light can give rise only to light. A diverse world could not therefore be the creation of God, if God were to create the world in the way a light-emitting source gives rise to light. Some other cause would have to intervene to produce what is not like God; and therefore God would not be the creator of all that exists.

Moreover, God is not required to create the world in the way a light-generating source must give off light. Were that the case, God could create only a world that was itself necessary and eternal. This would further restrict the scope of God's creative agency: God could not be the Creator of the contingent or the transitory. The world might imply the existence of the creator upon whom it depends, but, unlike what light imagery implies, God could exist without the world. The world and God are not co-implicative in the way the persons of the Trinity, or a source of light and the light it emits, are.

Thomas Aquinas, however, sees some use in light imagery for understanding God's creation of the world.[18] For example, God's creation of the world extends to everything that exists in the way the light of the sun covers everything. Indeed, light imagery becomes pertinent in every respect in which God's creative activity is similar to intra-Trinitarian forms of generation. Thus, like the first person's producing the others, God's creation of the world is effortless, without the need for means or any intervening process. Light imagery conveys this much better than artisan imagery does. An artisan uses tools and expends effort to rework or reshape existing materials, but a light source produces light at once without the apparent need for presupposed materials or external aids. Produced from nothing preceding it, the whole of the world, not just part of it, is created by God in the way the whole of a ray of light is emitted by a light source. Like a light-emitting source but unlike a human artisan, God does not have to take any additional action to bring about what God intends; God already is everything that is necessary to produce created effects. What God needs to do to create the world is what God already is, and therefore one finds neither movement from potential to actual, nor difference between intention and act, in God's decision to create the world. If God intended to create the world, God always had that intention; if God wants the world to come into existence and go out of existence, that very intention is sufficient to bring

18. See Thomas Aquinas, ST 1a 19.4.1.

about the desired effect in just the manner in which God intends it to occur. Gregory of Nyssa makes the latter point well, using light imagery:
"The [Genesis] account [of creation] allows no thought of anything between the purpose and the action, but just as the light shines together with
the kindling of the flame, coming from it and shining simultaneous with it,
in the same way, while the existence of things created is the work of the divine will, yet it does not come after the decision in second place."[19] Because God expends no effort, God is not diminished by creating the world;
light imagery again becomes pertinent to make that point. And so on.

Analogies with light are strongest in theologies of creation, like that of
Bonaventure, where the self-diffusiveness of God's goodness is the predominant and consistent stress. Because God already contains everything good
in the most perfect, unified, and superabundant fashion imaginable, the
goodness of God naturally diffuses itself like light, not simply in the exact
duplications that make up the Trinity, but in all the limited, multiple, imperfect versions of divine goodness that constitute the created world. Aquinas admits as much: all forms of created goodness flow from the divine that
contains them all within itself in an incomparably excellent fashion, just as
the sun spreads its light and heat in generating things different from itself.[20]
Even if, as Bonaventure argues, the divine necessarily diffuses itself in the
way a light source necessarily gives off light, this is nonetheless a free act of
self-diffusion where creation is concerned, because the Trinity is already itself a fully and perfected realized form of divine self-diffusion. God needs
nothing that would be gained by creating the world. Moreover — contrary
to what Thomas suggests — natural causes like light need not be limited in
their effects, any more than intentional agents are: "Just as you see that a ray
of light entering through a window is colored in different ways according to
the different colors of the various parts, so the divine ray shines forth in
each and every creature in different ways and in different properties."[21]

3. The Light Analogy and the Presence of God

Finally, the way that divinity itself becomes present within created things
can draw on the analogy of light's illuminating powers. As Augustine says

19. Gregory of Nyssa, *Answer to Eunomius' Second Book,* 109; NPNF, vol. 5, p. 273.
20. ST 1a 19.4.1.
21. Bonaventure, *Collations on the Six Days,* 12. 14; *Works of Bonaventure,* vol. 5, trans.
Jose van Vinck (Patterson, NJ: St. Anthony Guild, 1970), p. 179.

in the *City of God,* it is "quite appropriate to speak of the illumination of the immaterial soul by the immaterial light of the simple Wisdom of God, in terms of the illumination of the material atmosphere by material light."[22] In both cases, the light remains other than the one illuminated by it and is not (and does not become) its own inherent property. We remain dependent on God's giving God's self to us in the way air remains dependent on the shining sun for its illumination: when the sun sets, the air has no capacity of its own to remain bright.

Like the sun, which retains its purity however degraded the material it lights up, God is not contaminated by contact with and intimate presence to sinful or corrupt creatures. The distance between God's majesty and our finite and sinful condition no more prevents God's bridging the gap immediately and effortlessly, any more than the sun's geographical distance keeps its light from reaching us at once. Like the light of the sun, God's light remains just as it is, undiminished and undivided no matter how many partake of it. The whole of God's light, moreover, is distributed equally and at the same time to everything, with differences in its effect on various creatures being a function of their different capacities to receive it, just as the whole of the sun shines in the same way on everything and is received differently depending, say, on the tarnished or brilliant character of the surfaces that exist to reflect it. Gregory of Nyssa sums up many of these ideas in a single, complex passage:

> When he [the psalmist] saw the rays of the sun reaching from such heights even to ourselves he began to believe, by means of such phenomena, that the intelligible energies of God did not fail to descend from the heights of Deity even to each one of us; for if a single luminary can occupy everything alike that lies beneath it with the power of light, and, more than that, can, while distributing itself to all who participate in it, remain whole for each one yet undivided, how much more shall the Creator of that luminary become "all in all" as the Apostle [Paul] says, and come to each giving as much of himself as its substratum can receive.[23]

22. Augustine, *The City of God,* book XI, chapter 10, trans. H. Bettenson (New York: Penguin, 1972), p. 442.

23. NPNF, p. 378; trans. from V. E. F. Harrison, *Grace and Human Freedom according to St. Gregory of Nyssa* (Lewiston, NY: Edwin Mellen, 1992), p. 108.

Kathryn E. Tanner

4. Conclusion

These then are three ways in which patristic and medieval theologians draw on the analogy of light to illuminate the relationships between the persons of the Trinity, God's creation of the world, and God's presence within the world. They developed the analogy on the basis of the perceived properties of light. To what extent might modern scientific knowledge of light affect these theological reflections? For possible answers one should turn to the chapters that make up the first part of this book and to those by Brown and Dodaro below.

Light and Darkness in the Mystical Theology of the Greek Fathers

Kallistos Ware, Metropolitan of Diokleia

In your light we see light.

Psalm 36:9

He made darkness his secret place.

Psalm 18:11

The darkness and light to you are both alike.

Psalm 139:12

Prologue: A Tale of Two Hills

To express the reality of the divine-human encounter, saints and theologians have habitually employed the contrasting yet interdependent images of light and darkness. This is the case alike in Christianity, both Eastern and Western, and in other faiths. As might be expected, on the whole it is the image of divine light that prevails, but on significant occasions it is counterbalanced and deepened by that of divine darkness.[1]

---

1. For the main evidence, consult the relevant articles in the *Dictionnaire de spiritualité:* "Illumination," vol. 7 (1970), pp. 1330-67; "Lumière," vol. 9 (1976), pp. 1142-83; "Nuit (Ténèbre)," vol. 11 (1981), pp. 519-25. For a classic statement of the Orthodox viewpoint, see Vladimir Lossky, "Darkness and Light in the Knowledge of God," in Lossky, *In the Image and Likeness of God* (Crestwood, NY: St. Vladimir's Seminary Press, 1974), pp. 31-43; cf. (in the same volume), "The Theology of Light in the Thought of St. Gregory Palamas," pp. 45-69.

Within the Christian tradition, there are two outstanding moments in Scripture when the presence of God is associated in the first place with darkness, and in the second with light. In the Old Testament, Moses meets the Lord in darkness on the summit of Mt. Sinai: "Moses entered the thick darkness where God was" (Exod. 20:21; cf. Deut. 5:22). In the Greek Septuagint version, the word used here for "thick darkness" is *gnophos*, rather than the more familiar term *skotos*. Complementing the Old Testament encounter of Moses with God in darkness, there is in the New Testament the Transfiguration of Christ on Mt. Tabor, when he appears before the three chosen disciples in dazzling light (Matt. 17:1-8; Mark 9:2-8; Luke 9:28-36).[2] It is significant that Moses, who in the Old Covenant had met God in darkness, was also present at Christ's Transfiguration in light. This is a point emphasized in the hymnography of the Orthodox Church:

> You appeared to Moses both on the Mountain of the Law and on Tabor: of old in darkness, but now in the unapproachable light of the Godhead.[3]

Taking up these two primary moments, the Greek Fathers make extensive use of the imagery of both Sinai and Tabor. In the Great Canon of St. Andrew of Crete (c. 660-740), for example, the aim of contemplation *(theoria)* is to attain "the innermost darkness": "so shall you reach by contemplation the innermost darkness, and gain great merchandise."[4] On the other hand, for St. Gregory Palamas (1296-1359), Archbishop of Thessalonica, the fullness of contemplation takes the form of a vision of divine light. Such is the way in which, for example, he interprets the experience that St. Paul underwent when he was "caught up to the third heaven" (2 Cor. 12:2):

> This most joyful reality which ravished Paul, and which made his intellect depart in ecstasy outside all created things and caused it to return wholly into itself — this he saw as light, a light of revelation indeed, yet one that did not reveal to him the material objects of sense-perception.

2. See especially John McGuckin, *The Transfiguration of Christ in Scripture and Tradition* (Lewiston, NY: Edwin Mellen, 1986); Andreas Andreopoulos, *Metamorphosis: The Transfiguration in Byzantine Theology and Iconography* (Crestwood, NY: St. Vladimir's Seminary Press, 2005).

3. *The Festal Menaion*, trans. Mother Mary and Archimandrite Kallistos Ware (London: Faber, 1969), p. 483.

4. *The Lenten Triodion*, trans. Mother Mary and Archimandrite Kallistos Ware (London/Boston: Faber, 1978), p. 391.

It was a light without limits below or above or to the sides. He saw no limit whatever to the light that appeared to him, but it was like a sun infinitely brighter and larger than the universe; and he himself stood in the midst of it, having become nothing but eye. Such, more or less, was his vision.[5]

Palamas displays here an apophatic caution typical of the Christian East. He does not claim to offer an exact account of the experience that the Apostle himself had found it impossible to describe, but he merely says, "Such, more or less . . ."

Images and symbols are polyvalent, and this is certainly the case with the notions of light and darkness. These terms can be used on at least four different levels that it is important to distinguish, even though at times the levels may overlap. In regard to light, the levels are these:

1. The light may be physical and created; a light, that is to say, which is perceived outwardly by the senses. Thus, in the opening chapter of Genesis, when it is stated that on the first day of creation "God said, 'Let there be light'; and there was light . . . and God separated the light from the darkness" (Gen. 1:3-4), presumably the light mentioned here is a physical light, part of the material creation, even though at this stage there was no sun.

2. The word "light" may be understood in a metaphorical or figurative sense, as in the phrases "Your word is . . . a light to my path" (Ps. 119:105), "You are the light of the world" (Matt. 5:14), "the light of knowledge" (2 Cor. 4:6), or "children of light" (Eph. 5:8). When used metaphorically, the word "light" bears almost always a positive sense.

3. Some writers speak, as we shall note in due course, about a "light of the intellect *(nous)*" that is perceived, not with the physical eyes, but inwardly. These authors are evidently referring to a specific experience, and are not simply using the word "light" in a metaphorical way; yet at the same time the light in question is not divine but created.

4. There is finally the light seen by the three disciples at the Transfiguration on Mt. Tabor. According to the understanding of the Orthodox Church, the light of Tabor is not physical or created, but is spiritual, uncreated and divine. At the same time it is not a metaphorical light

5. *Triads in Defence of the Holy Hesychasts* I, 3, 21; ed. J. Meyendorff, *Spicilegium Sacrum Lovaniense*, vols. 30-31 (Louvain, 1959), pp. 155-57.

but a genuinely existent reality. It is, indeed, nothing less than a manifestation of the eternal and infinite energies of God. This understanding of the light of Tabor goes back at least to the second century. Clement of Alexandria (c. 150–c. 215) maintains that, when the apostles beheld the light of the Transfiguration, this was not through the normal power of sense-perception, for "that light has no kinship or affinity with this flesh of ours," and so physical eyes cannot see the light of the Transfiguration unless strengthened by divine grace.[6] While the scriptural account says that Christ's face shone "like the sun" (Matt. 17:2), St. John Chrysostom (c. 347-407) goes further than this, asserting that it shone not merely "like" but "more than" the sun.[7] It was, says St. Gregory of Nazianzus (329-89), a light "too fierce for human eyes";[8] according to St. Maximus the Confessor (c. 580-662), it was a light that "transcends the operation of the senses."[9] The hymnography for the Feast of the Transfiguration (August 6) confirms this, terming the light of Tabor "non-material," "everlasting," "infinite," "a glory brighter than light."[10] Similarly, the light of which Palamas speaks in the passage cited above is not merely a physical or material light (level 1), nor yet is it metaphorical (level 2), but he is evidently referring to a definite spiritual experience that is on his understanding not subjective but objective, a true "light of revelation." He is making, that is to say, a specific truth claim.

Although these levels are in principle distinct, it is not always easy to apply the distinction in practice. Is the "glory" that shone at the birth of Christ physical (level 1) or uncreated (level 4) (Luke 2:9)? Most Orthodox exegetes would choose the second alternative, but the matter is not entirely clear. When it is said, in the prologue of St. John's Gospel, "The light shines in the darkness, and the darkness did not overcome it" (John 1:5), it is reasonable to interpret this in a metaphorical sense (level 2), but in the reference here to the "light" of Christ there may also be a hidden allusion to the light of the Transfiguration (level 4). The light shining from the risen Christ, in the vision of the Apocalypse (Rev. 1:13-16), is more obviously di-

---

6. *Extracts from Theodotus* 5, 3: ed. F. Sagnard, Sources chrétiennes, Série annexe de textes hétérodoxes (Paris: Cerf, 1948), p. 62.

7. *Homily after the Capture of Eutropius outside the Church* 10 (PG 52:404-5).

8. *On Baptism, Oration* 40, 6 (PG 36:365A).

9. *Ambigua* 10 (PG 91:1160C).

10. *The Festal Menaion,* pp. 486, 478, 491, 469.

vine and uncreated (level 4). Orthodox writers also understand in similar terms the "light from heaven, brighter than the sun" that blinded Paul on the road to Damascus (Acts 26:13; cf. Acts 9:3). Yet in all these cases different interpretations are possible.

While the imagery of light bears usually a positive sense, this is not invariably the case. According to St. Paul, "Even Satan disguises himself as an angel of light" (2 Cor. 11:14); and there are frequent warnings in ascetic writers against visions of light that are deceptive and demonic.[11]

Turning now from light to darkness, we find that the term "darkness" can also be understood on at least four levels, although these do not correspond exactly to the four levels in the case of light:

1. The darkness may be part of the created order, that is to say, perceived by the physical senses. This is presumably the case with the primeval darkness of chaos that "covered the face of the deep" (Gen. 1:2), although there was at that stage no created being in existence to behold it. More obviously it is the case with the darkness that is separated from the light on the first day of creation (Gen. 1:4-5). If the entry of Moses into the "thick darkness" of Sinai (Exod. 20:21) is understood as a historical incident — and this is indeed the way in which most Orthodox exegetes understand it — then this darkness belongs equally to the physical order. It is a mass of somber thunderclouds gathered around the summit of the mountain; yet at the same time the darkness of Sinai has, beyond this, distinctive spiritual implications, associated as it is with the experience of mystical union. At the Last Supper, Judas goes out from the light of the upper room into the physical darkness of night (John 13:30); here again, however, the darkness has spiritual connotations. The same is true of the physical darkness "over all the earth" at the time of Christ's Crucifixion (Matt. 27:45; Mark 15:33; Luke 23:44). This first level, that of darkness in the natural world, does not correspond exactly to the first level in the case of light, for there is an asymmetry between light and darkness. Darkness is not a material reality in the way that light is, since darkness is nothing but the absence of light, and there are no particles in darkness.

---

11. See, for example, Evagrius, *On Prayer* 114-15 (*PG* 79:1192D-1193A), and Diadochus, *Chapters* 36, 40, ed. E. des Places, Sources chrétiennes 5 *bis* (Paris: Cerf, 1955), pp. 105, 108; ET *The Philokalia,* trans. G. E. H. Palmer, Philip Sherrard, and Kallistos Ware, vol. 1 (London/Boston: Faber, 1979), pp. 68, 263, 265 (see below, notes 39, 42).

2. The word "darkness," like the word "light," may be understood in a metaphorical or figurative sense, as in the phrases: "The Lord my GOD lights up my darkness" (Ps. 18:28), "The way of the wicked is like deep darkness" (Prov. 4:19), "the unfruitful works of darkness" (Eph. 5:11), or "He who hates his brother is in darkness" (1 John 2:11). In all these and other such instances, the metaphorical use of the term "darkness" bears a pejorative sense; it is associated with sin and ignorance. The darkness of chaos (Gen. 1:2) is likewise negative in character (cf. level 1). But the darkness of Sinai (Exod. 20:21), on the contrary, is highly positive. It is a sign not of the absence but of the presence of God; it denotes not distance from God but union with him.

3. In Western mystical writers, such as John of the Cross (1542-91), darkness is understood in a purgative sense: passing through the "night of the senses" and the "night of the spirit," the soul is progressively detached from dependence on sensory things and prepared for the unitive encounter with God. Here, then, the symbol of darkness is positive, signifying an experience that, though painful, is at the same time creative and grace-given.

4. There is, in both Eastern and Western writers, a higher, mystical darkness, the "thick darkness" into which Moses entered on Sinai, the darkness not of purgation but of union.[12] Here darkness denotes the divine incomprehensibility, but at the same time, as we have just emphasized, it signifies oneness with the living God, not separation from him. Just as there is no exact symmetry between level 1 of light and level 1 of darkness, so here at level 4 there is no complete correspondence between the mystical experience respectively of light and of darkness. The divine light, whether beheld on Tabor or by the saints, is regarded in the Eastern Christian tradition as a specific reality that, while nonmaterial, is also objective and "hypostatic." On the other hand, the mystical darkness, while symbolizing the divine presence, unlike the light of Tabor is not to be identified with the divine energies. The relevant texts do not attribute to divine darkness the objective and "hypostatic" character that is possessed by the vision of divine light. Scripture and tradition affirm that "God is light" (1 John 1:5), but

12. On the relation between levels 3 and 4 of darkness, see Andrew Louth, *The Origins of the Christian Mystical Tradition: From Plato to Denys* (Oxford: Clarendon, 1981), pp. 179-90. I would make a somewhat clearer distinction than he does between the darkness of purgation and the darkness of union.

nowhere is it said in Scripture that "God is darkness"; it is only stated that God is *in* the darkness.

References to light and darkness on level 4 are to be construed as analogical rather than metaphorical. (I follow here the distinction between metaphor and analogy made in the introduction to this volume, and also by John Polkinghorne in his contribution.) That is to say, in applying the terms "light" and "darkness" to the divine/human encounter, we are not simply employing a figure of speech but are making a statement about the reality of that encounter. Whereas in metaphor there is always a degree of arbitrariness, in the case of analogy there is an intrinsic, if necessarily qualified, relationship between the two components in the analogy; and that is true more particularly when we speak of God as light or assert that he dwells in darkness. Yet, although in this context the language of light and darkness is not arbitrary but inherently appropriate, at the same time the terms "light" and "darkness" are being used in a special sense, different from their use when applied to the physical realm (level 1). So, when saying "God is light," we need to add, "yet he is not light as we know it, but in an incomparably higher sense"; and, when saying "He dwells in darkness," we need to add, "yet the darkness is supremely bright" (cf. Ps. 139:12).

Images of light evoke primarily a sense of height and transcendence, whereas images of darkness evoke a sense of depth and immanence. Light is associated in our minds with the clear blue of the sky, with the sun and its rays, with forked or sheet lightning. Darkness, on the other hand, is associated with the bowels of the earth or the bottom of the sea, with caves or thick forests. But of course this contrast must not be exaggerated. Light, as Andrew Steane points out, can permeate the inside of things as well as illuminate their outside. The Quaker George Fox (1624-91) spoke characteristically of the "Inner Light." By the same token, darkness calls to our minds not just subterranean caverns but the night sky; and it is significant that Christ speaks of "the *outer* darkness" (Matt. 8:12; 22:13; 25:50).[13]

Keeping in mind these fourfold distinctions, let us consider how light and darkness are interpreted by the Greek Fathers. But first it will be appropriate to review the evidence in Hellenic philosophy and in Scripture.

13. Light is present even in this "outer darkness," for the "outer darkness" contains the "fire that never shall be quenched" (Mark 9:43). Many Orthodox consider that this fire of hell is nothing other than the uncreated glory of God; what the saints experience as joy, the damned through their own choice experience as torment. See Kallistos Ware, *The Inner Kingdom* (Crestwood, NY: St. Vladimir's Seminary Press, 2000), pp. 207-8.

1. The Hellenic Tradition: "The Self Rendered Radiant"

The use made of the imagery of light and darkness in the mystical theology of the Greek Fathers has two sources: on the one side, Hellenic philosophy, and more particularly Platonism; on the other, the Old and New Testaments. In the Platonic tradition, the divine is regularly expressed in terms of light. In the famous analogy of the cave, developed by Plato (c. 429-347 BCE) in his *Republic,* God is envisaged as the noetic Sun that illumines the transcendent realm, casting shadows on the walls of the cavern where we are imprisoned.[14] The neo-Platonist Plotinus (205-269/70 CE) compares the One, the first and highest Hypostasis, to light, and the second Hypostasis to the sun.[15] He speaks more particularly about a vision of pure intellectual light, in which the visionary does not see any specific object in the light, but "the light itself is the vision."[16] This vision of intellectual light has a transformative effect, such that the one who beholds the light himself becomes the light that he contemplates:

> There one can see both God and oneself as it is right to see them: the self rendered radiant, filled with noetic light, or rather itself turned into light, pure, weightless, floating free, having become — or rather, actually being — god; at that moment set on fire, but the fire seems to go out if one is weighed down again.[17]

Although Plotinus states here that the self becomes pure light, he does not say explicitly that the *body* shines with noetic light. Taking into account his view of materiality in general and of the human body in particular,[18] it seems improbable that this is something he would have wished to assert. In this regard Christian mystical theology advanced much farther than neo-Platonism was able to do.

To the best of my knowledge, the Platonist tradition nowhere describes the divine in terms of darkness. It is "solar," not "nocturnal," in its imagery. The reason for this is presumably that darkness, being formless and indeterminate, is therefore regarded by Platonism in negative terms as imperfect and irrational.

14. *Republic* VII, 514a-517c.
15. *Enneads* V, 6, 4.
16. *Enneads* VI, 7, 36.
17. *Enneads* VI, 9, 9.
18. See Porphyry, *On the Life of Plotinus and the Order of His Books,* 1: "Plotinus, the philosopher of our times, seemed ashamed of being in a body."

2. The Old Testament: "The Thick Darkness Where God Was"

To discover the source of the darkness symbolism exploited by Christian authors, it is necessary to turn to the Old Testament, and more especially to the life of Moses, who came to be regarded by Christian writers as a paradigm of the mystical quest. Sometimes the theophanies of the Old Testament take the form of light, as in the manifestation of God to Moses at the Burning Bush (Exod. 3:2). Elsewhere, however, God reveals himself in mingled light and darkness. This is the case, for example, with the strange ritual in Genesis 15:12-17, discussed by David Brown, and also with the Exodus from Egypt, when God's presence accompanies the people of Israel in a pillar of cloud by day and a pillar of fire by night (Exod. 13:21). This combination of light and darkness is to be found particularly in the "storm of theophanies" (cf. Isa. 19:1), when God shows himself — and at the same time conceals himself — in dark thunderclouds and flashes of lightning. Here, according to the context, it is sometimes the imagery of light that prevails, as in Ezekiel 1:1-28 and Habakkuk 3:3-4, and sometimes that of darkness.

This variation between the luminous and the tenebrous is evident above all in the different accounts to be found of Moses' ascent of Mt. Sinai. At times the symbolism is predominantly that of light, as when it is said that Moses and Aaron, together with the elders of Israel, climbed Sinai and "they saw the place where the God of Israel stood. Under his feet there was something like a pavement of sapphire stone, like the very heaven for clearness" (Exod. 24:10). Here the imagery suggests radiance and transparency rather than gloom and obscurity. Yet there is at the same time a certain apophatic reserve. For, in the Septuagint rendering that I have followed, it is only said that they saw "the place where the God of Israel stood," not that they saw God himself. The Hebrew text is less guarded, stating in direct terms, "They saw the God of Israel."

In sharp contrast, however, to this vision of sapphire stone and celestial clarity, elsewhere in the Sinai narrative it is said, in the passage to which we have already referred, "Moses entered the thick darkness where God was" (Exod. 20:21). Here, in a text of seminal importance for Christian mysticism, the encounter with the divine is spelled out emphatically in terms of darkness. Again, as in Exodus 24:10, there is a certain apophatic reserve: we have already noted how it is not said that God *is* darkness, but only that he is *within* the darkness. Later writers, as we shall see, hesitate to say even as much as this.

In these and other such passages where the imagery of darkness is used, the effect of this symbolism is to inspire a feeling of awe and reverent wonder. Darkness symbolizes the *mysterium tremendum et fascinans* of which Rudolf Otto speaks in *The Idea of the Holy,* the mystery that makes us tremble and yet attracts and enchants us. This sense of fear and mystery is evoked in the Old Testament above all by the darkness of the Holy of Holies. It is deeply significant that the innermost sanctuary, where for Judaism the divine presence was to be found in its most immediate and intense form, was a place not of light and radiance but of dimness and obscurity: "And when the priests came out of the holy place, a cloud filled the house of the LORD, so that the priests could not stand to minister because of the cloud; for the glory of the LORD filled the house of the LORD. Then Solomon said, 'The LORD has said that he would dwell in thick darkness'" (1 Kings 8:10-12). Here, significantly and surprisingly, glory and darkness are associated closely together.

Elsewhere in the Old Testament, in a work that has constantly inspired Christian mystical theology, the Song of Songs, the symbolism of darkness is likewise predominant: the encounter between the Bride and the Bridegroom occurs at night (Song of Songs 3:1; 5:2). Daniel likewise receives his vision of the Son of man and the Ancient of Days in nocturnal dimness: "As I watched in the night visions, I saw one like the Son of man coming in the clouds of heaven" (Dan. 7:13).

In the Psalms there is a striking variation between light and darkness. Sometimes it is said that God is "wrapped in light as with a garment" (Ps. 104:2), elsewhere that he "made darkness his secret place" (Ps. 18:11: cf. Ps. 18:9 and 2 Sam. 22:10, 12). There is thus, within the Old Testament, a rich and varied use of the imagery of both light and darkness, and it cannot be said that either symbol enjoys decisive preponderance.

In later Judaism, the tradition of "light mysticism" is expressed notably in the Rabbinic concept of the Shekinah, the luminous and radiant presence of God with his people. "Darkness mysticism," on the other hand, finds a striking exponent in the person of Philo of Alexandria (c. 20 BCE–c. 50 CE), who makes particularly significant use of the "thick darkness" of Sinai. In his customary fashion he combines Scripture and philosophy, and so in this instance he takes the distinctively Jewish notion of divine darkness — something not to be found in Platonism — and then interprets it in Platonic terms to denote the radical transcendence and incomprehensibility of God. For Philo the darkness symbolizes, not God as he is in himself, but rather the limitations of the human mind, our ignorance and unknowing when confronted by the divine, our inability to comprehend the super-eminent and ineffable Deity:

> See Moses enter into the thick darkness *(gnophos)* where God was, that is, into conceptions regarding the Existent Being that belong to the un-approachable region where there are no material forms. For the Cause of all is not in the thick darkness, nor locally in any place at all, but high above both place and time. For he has placed all creation under his control, and is contained by nothing, but transcends all. Yet though transcending and being beyond what he has made, none the less he has filled the world with himself; for he has caused his powers to extend themselves throughout the universe to its utmost bounds, and in accordance with the laws of harmony has knit each part to each. When therefore the God-loving soul probes the question of the essence of the Existent Being, she enters on a quest of that which is beyond matter and beyond sight. And out of this quest there accrues to her a vast boon, namely to apprehend that God in his essence is apprehensible by no one, and to see precisely this, that he is incapable of being seen.[19]

Here Philo is concerned to uphold the double truth that God is both transcendent and immanent. He is transcendent and unknowable in his essence *(kata to einai),* and it is this unknowability that is signified by the "thick darkness"; but he is immanent and knowable through his "powers" *(dynameis)* that extend throughout creation. This distinction between God's essence and his powers or energies has a long history in Christian thought, and it is used by, among others, the Cappadocians and Gregory Palamas.

It will be noticed that Philo, in his desire to safeguard the divine transcendence, is strongly apophatic in this passage. Not only does he refrain from saying that God *is* darkness, but he also denies that God is *in* the darkness, for the "Existent Being" is "high above place and time" and "beyond what he has made." Apophatic language, in this manner, is not simply a method of negating positive statements, but it is also — as George Hunsinger makes clear — a way of asserting divine supereminence. The negations do not merely counterbalance the affirmations, but they reach out to a higher realm that is totally beyond both affirmation and negation.

---

19. *On the Posterity of Cain* V, 14-15. Cf. *On the Change of Names* II, 7-10.

3. The New Testament: "In Him Is No Darkness at All"

What of the New Testament? Here darkness is never used positively as a symbol of the divine, but it is associated negatively with sin and evil (see, for example, Luke 22:53; Eph. 6:12; Jude 6, 13). So far as God is concerned, his "secret place" is not darkness but light: "He dwells in unapproachable light" (1 Tim. 6:16). In the Synoptic Gospels, as we have already seen, light is associated with God above all at the Transfiguration of Christ on Tabor, when "his face shone like the sun, and his clothes became dazzling white" (Matt. 17:2: cf. Mark 9:3; Luke 9:29). The "bright cloud" that overshadows Jesus (Matt. 17:5) recalls the Jewish Shekinah.

The imagery of light, or more exactly the contrast between light and darkness, is especially evident in the Johannine writings. Although the Fourth Gospel contains no separate account of the Transfiguration, the themes of light and glory are everywhere present in it, from the prologue onwards. Of the preexistent Logos it is said, "He was the true light" (John 1:9), while one of the great "I am" sayings of Jesus refers precisely to light: "I am the light of the world" (John 8:12; cf. 9:5; 12:46). Particularly striking is the affirmation in the Johannine epistles: "God is light, and in him there is no darkness at all" (1 John 1:5).

4. Mystics "Solar" and "Nocturnal": From Irenaeus to Gregory of Nyssa

Drawing on this double tradition, Hellenic and Judaic, the Greek Fathers speak both of divine light and of divine darkness. It is possible to draw up two parallel lists, of "solar" mystics and of "nocturnal" mystics respectively (see Figure 1). The "solar" mystics are the more numerous, but among the "nocturnal" mystics there are writers of particular weight and influence. As time passes, there is an increasing *coincidentia oppositorum*, with many Fathers combining the two symbols together; for, although contrasting, they are in no way contradictory.

In the second century, St. Irenaeus of Lyons (c. 130–c. 200) stands firmly in the tradition of "light mysticism." In his theology he assigns a central place to the vision of God: "The glory of God is a living human being; the life of each human being is the vision of God" *(gloria enim Dei vivens homo, vita autem hominis visio Dei).*[20] When speaking of this "vi-

20. *Against the Heresies* IV, 20, 7.

Figure 1

Light Symbolism	*Darkness Symbolism*
Plato	
Plotinus	Philo
Irenaeus	Clement of Alexandria
Origen	Gregory of Nazianzus
Gregory of Nyssa	
Evagrius	
Macarian Homilies	Dionysius the Areopagite
Symeon the New Theologian	
Gregory Palamas	

sion of God" Irenaeus uses language reminiscent of the Transfiguration of Christ on Mt. Tabor. He is in fact the first Christian writer to make a connection between the Transfiguration of Christ and the believer's experience of mystical union. The "light of the Father" *(paterna lux),* he says, passes into the "flesh" *(caro)* of Christ; and from Christ's flesh it shines forth upon us, so that each of us is "enfolded" *(circumdatus)* in the Father's light, and so we become incorruptible.[21] In and through the transfigured Christ, then, we humans come to participate in the glory of the Father. Pursuing the theme of light, Irenaeus continues:

> Just as those who see the light are within the light and participate in its splendour, so those who see God are within God and participate in his splendour. For the splendour of God is life-giving. Those, then, who see God participate in life. Thus God who cannot be contained, who is incomprehensible and invisible, renders himself visible, comprehensible and accessible to humankind, so as to give life to those who lay hold of him and behold him.[22]

It is evident here that Irenaeus, although limiting himself to the symbolism of light, insists at the same time that God is incomprehensible. He is not only a cataphatic but an apophatic theologian. Thus it should not be assumed that, while "darkness" theologians such as Philo are apophatic, the theologians of light are exclusively cataphatic; for in reality it is per-

21. *Against the Heresies* IV, 20, 2. Cf. John 17:22-23.

22. *Against the Heresies* IV, 20, 5. The Greek text can be found in John of Damascus, *Sacra Parallela,* apud Adelin Rousseau, ed., Sources chrétiennes 100 (Paris: Cerf, 1965), p. 640.

fectly possible for a "solar" mystic to find a place for apophaticism. Irenaeus, concerned as he is to safeguard the transcendent mystery of the divine, insists that the language of light does not in any way constitute an exact description of God: "He is most aptly called 'light,' but he is nothing like the light that we know."[23] The term "light," that is to say, can indeed be appropriately applied to God, yet at the same time God infinitely transcends all that we humans understand by the word. As an apophatic symbol, the light reveals God and yet conceals him.

It may also be noted that, unlike Plotinus, Irenaeus regards the vision of divine light as involving the body as well as the soul. His doctrine of the human person is consistently unified and holistic:

> The flesh is to be interpenetrated by the power of the spirit, in such a way that it is no longer simply carnal but becomes truly spiritual through its communion with the spirit. . . . Just as the flesh is liable to corruption, so it is also capable of attaining incorruptibility.[24]

Whereas Irenaeus adheres to the symbolism of light, his younger contemporary Clement of Alexandria takes over from Philo the concept of divine darkness, reproducing his language almost word for word. For Clement, as for Philo, the darkness signifies divine incomprehensibility:

> Moses, convinced that God will never be known by human wisdom, says: "Show yourself to me" (cf. Exod. 33:13, 18). Thus he is compelled to enter into the "thick darkness" (Exod. 20:21) where the voice of God was, that is, into conceptions regarding the Existent Being that belong to the unapproachable region where there are no material forms. For God is not in the thick darkness, nor locally in any place at all, but high above place and time and the distinctive character of specific objects.[25]

Thus for Clement, as for Philo, God is not actually said to be darkness, nor is he within the darkness in such a way as to be confined within it spatially. By the same token, God is above "the distinctive character of specific objects," in the sense that he is not just one among many different existent objects.

Face to face with this ultimate mystery, plunged into "thick darkness," we recognize the utter inadequacy of all human speech. As Clement puts

23. *Against the Heresies* II, 13, 4.
24. Fragment 6 (Armenian), in *Patrologia Orientalis* 12:738.
25. *Stromateis* II, 2 (6, 1).

it, we cease to use language, and we worship God "in awe and silence, and with holy wonder."[26] This recalls the words of Plato, quoted elsewhere by Clement, "The beginning of philosophy is to feel a sense of wonder."[27] And if philosophy begins in wonder, that equally is where it concludes, as Coleridge affirms: "In Wonder all Philosophy began: in Wonder it ends: and Admiration fills up the interspace."[28] What applies to philosophy applies incomparably more to theology. If it is true that the theologian is the one who prays,[29] then the theologian is also the one who has an unlimited capacity for astonishment. "He shall not cease from seeking until he finds," says Clement, citing the Gospel according to the Hebrews, "and having found he will be amazed."[30]

Closely associated with Clement is his fellow-Alexandrian Origen (c. 185–c. 254). Yet, as regards their use of the symbolism of light and darkness, there is a striking contrast between the two. Origen is almost exclusively a theologian of light, who sees the mystical ascent as an ever-increasing illumination, not as an entry into "thick darkness." In his *Homilies on Exodus* he never once cites Exodus 20:21; what was a central moment in the story of Moses, as interpreted by Philo and Clement, is simply ignored and passed over by Origen.[31] Since he was familiar with their writings, this omission is certainly deliberate. It is true that elsewhere in his writings he does make occasional allusions to Exodus 20:21 and Psalm 18:11, understanding these texts to indicate the inability of the human mind to comprehend God.[32] Even though, as we noted in regard to Irenaeus, a preference for light symbolism does not necessarily exclude an apophatic approach to the divine, it has to be said of Origen that he is consistently less apophatic than Clement.

St. Gregory of Nazianzus follows Origen in speaking of God as light:

26. *Stromateis* VII, 1 (2, 3).

27. *Theaetetus* 155D; cf. Clement of Alexandria, *Stromateis* II, 9 (45, 4).

28. S. T. Coleridge, "Aphorisms on Spiritual Religion" IX, in *Aids to Reflection*, ed. J. Beer, *The Collected Works*, vol. 9 (Princeton: Princeton University Press, 1993), p. 236.

29. Evagrius of Pontus, *On Prayer* 60 (61) (*PG* 79: 1180B); *The Philokalia*, vol. 1, p. 62.

30. *Stromateis* V, 14 (96, 3); cf. M. R. James, ed., *The Apocryphal New Testament* (Oxford: Clarendon, 1924), p. 2.

31. There is a brief reference to the cloud on Sinai (Exod. 19:9) in Origen, *Homilies on Exodus* 11:7, but no particular significance is attached to it. The "light" theophany in Exodus 24:9-18 is nowhere mentioned by Origen, but the light on the face of Moses (Exod. 34:29-35) is discussed at some length in *Homily* 12.

32. See *Commentary on John* II, xxviii (23), 172; *Contra Celsum* VI, 17. Cf. *Contra Celsum* II, 55, which quotes Exodus 20–21 in passing.

echoing Plato, he says, "What the sun is in the realm of the senses, God is in the noetic realm."[33] His disciple Evagrius of Pontus (346-99) stands likewise in the tradition of "light mysticism." He distinguishes between two different levels in the vision of light. First, the ascetic attains a vision of the light of the intellect *(nous)*: "It is a sign of dispassion when the intellect begins to see its own light.[34] . . . In the time of prayer they see the light characteristic of the intellect shining around them.[35] . . . If someone wishes to see the state of the intellect, let him deprive himself of all concepts; then he will see himself as sapphire and the colour of the sky."[36] At this first stage Evagrius is evidently referring to an experience of the created light inherent in the intellect (level 3, *supra*); there are parallels here in Yoga.[37] But then in the second place he alludes to a higher experience in which the intellect beholds, not its own created light, but the divine light (level 4): "it will be totally mingled with the light of the Holy Trinity."[38] At neither of these two levels — whether the vision be of created or of uncreated light — does the visionary see any shape, figure, or face in the light. The experience is one of pure luminosity; as with Plotinus, the light itself is the vision. "Never try to see a form or shape during the time of prayer," warns Evagrius. "Do not try to see angels or Christ in a visible way. . . . I shall say again what I have said elsewhere: blessed is the intellect which at the time of prayer has gained complete freedom from forms *(amorphia)*."[39]

St. Diadochus of Photice (mid-fifth century) reproduces the teaching of Evagrius on the two levels of the vision of light. Alluding to the invocation of the Name of Jesus, Diadochus writes: "Those who meditate unceasingly upon this holy and glorious Name in the depths of their heart can sometimes see the light of their own intellect *(nous)*."[40] Elsewhere he speaks also of a vision of divine light:

33. *Oration* 21, 1 (*PG* 35:1084A).

34. *Praktikos* 64, ed. A. and C. Guillaumont, Sources chrétiennes 171 (Paris: Cerf, 1971), p. 648.

35. *Gnostikos* 45, ed. A. and C. Guillaumont, Sources chrétiennes 356 (Paris: Cerf, 1989), p. 178.

36. *Skemmata* 2, in J. Muyldermans, "Evagriana," *Le Muséon* 44 (1931): 374. Cf. Exodus 24:10.

37. See the note of John Eudes Bamberger in his translation of Evagrius, *The Praktikos: Chapters on Prayer*, Cistercian Studies Series 4 (Spencer, MA: Cistercian Publications, 1970), p. 34, n. 54.

38. *Kephalaia gnostika* II, 29, ed. A. Guillaumont, *Patrologia Orientalis* 28:1 (134), 72-73.

39. *On Prayer*, 114-15, 117 (*PG* 79: 1192D-93A), *The Philokalia*, vol. 1, p. 68.

40. *Chapters* 59: des Places, 119; *The Philokalia*, vol. 1, p. 270.

You should not doubt that the intellect, when it begins to be strongly under the influence of the energy of divine light, becomes so completely translucent that it sees its own light in full abundance. It is said that this takes place when the power of the soul gains control over the passions.[41]

Here Diadochus makes a clear distinction between the light of the intellect and the divine light: the influence of the latter enables us to perceive the former, but the former is evidently no more than a created and natural light.

In common with Evagrius, Diadochus insists that we should not seek to see any shape or form in the light:

Let no one who hears us speak of the perceptive faculty of the intellect imagine that by this we mean that the glory of God appears to people visibly. We do indeed affirm that the soul, when pure, perceives God's grace, tasting it in some ineffable manner; but no invisible reality appears to it in a visible form, since now "we walk by faith, not by sight," as St. Paul says (2 Cor. 5:7). . . . Everything that appears to the intellect, whether as light or as fire, if it has a shape, is the product of the evil artifice of the enemy.[42]

The unknown author of the *Homilies of Macarius,* who was probably contemporary with Evagrius, although the two are entirely independent of one another, likewise envisages two levels of visionary light, although in the *Homilies* the distinction between them is less clear-cut than in Evagrius. Sometimes the *Homilies* mention an experience in which the soul sees itself as light;[43] on this level the light is created. At other times the *Homilies* refer to a vision of "the light of God" or of "divine light";[44] evidently the light here is uncreated. Elsewhere the *Homilies* speak of a union with "non-material and divine fire."[45]

The *Homilies* draw attention to various decisive moments when divine light and glory are manifested in Scripture and in the history of salvation:

41. *Chapters* 40: des Places, 108; *The Philokalia,* vol. 1, p. 265.

42. *Chapters* 36, 40: des Places, 105, 108; *The Philokalia,* vol. 1, pp. 263, 265.

43. Collection II (H), ed. Hermann Dörries, Erich Klostermann, and Matthias Kroeger, Patristische Texte und Studien 4 (Berlin: Walter de Gruyter, 1964), 7:5-6 (there is also a reference to "divine light" in this passage).

44. II, 1:8, 10.

45. II, 25:9.

1. Prior to the Fall, Adam and Eve in Paradise were physically clothed in the glory of God, which covered their nakedness. After they had transgressed God's commandment, this glory was taken away from them, so that they saw that they were naked (see Gen. 3:7).[46]
2. The glory that clothed Adam before the Fall shone also from the face of Moses when he descended from Mt. Sinai. So bright was the light that he had to cover his face with a veil (see Exod. 34:29-35).[47]
3. The same bodily glory radiated from the Savior at the Transfiguration: "The body of the Lord was glorified, when he went up into the mountain, and was transfigured into divine glory and into infinite light."[48]
4. This bodily glory of the Transfiguration has an eschatological character. What happened to Christ's body on Tabor will happen to the bodies of the saints at the Resurrection on the Last Day:

> As the body of the Lord was glorified . . . so are the bodies of the saints glorified and shine like lightning.[49]
>
> What the soul now has treasured up within her, will be revealed then [on the Last Day] and displayed outwardly in the body. . . . At the day of Resurrection the glory of the Holy Spirit comes out from within, decking and covering the bodies of the saints. This glory they had before, but it was hidden within their souls. What someone has now, the same will come forth then externally in the body.[50]

In all four of these instances, the divine glory of which the *Homilies* speak is directly associated with the body. Here the *Homilies* are in full agreement with the holistic anthropology of Irenaeus.

In the Macarian *Homilies* the transfiguration of the body by divine light is said to occur only at the Resurrection of the dead on the Last Day. But in an early text from Egypt, the *Apophthegmata* or *Sayings of the Desert Fathers*, referring to monks of the fourth or fifth century, examples are given in which the bodily transfiguration occurs during the present life. It is recorded of Abba Pambo, "God so glorified him that no one could look at his face, be-

---

46. II, 12:7-8.

47. Collection III (C), ed. Vincent Desprez, Sources chrétiennes 275 (Paris: Cerf, 1980), 20:3.

48. Collection I (B), ed. Heinz Berthold, Griechischen Christlichen Schriftsteller (Berlin: Akademie Verlag, 1973), 45:2; II, 15:38. Cf. I, 18:7:3.

49. I, 45:2; II, 15:38.

50. II, 5:8-9.

cause of the glory that his face had. . . . Just as Moses received the image of the glory of Adam, when his face was glorified, so the face of Abba Pambo shone like lightning, and he was as a king seated on his throne."[51] When Abba Sisoes lay on his deathbed, "his face shone like the sun," and the brightness increased ever more and more until the actual moment of his death, when "he became like lightning, and the whole dwelling was filled with a sweet fragrance."[52] Elsewhere the *Apophthegmata* speak of fire rather than light, as in the case of Abba Arsenius: when he was praying, one of his disciples, coming upon him unawares, "saw the old man entirely as fire."[53] These examples call to mind the occasion when, at a much later date, Nicolas Motovilov saw St. Seraphim of Sarov (1754-1833) transfigured by divine light.[54]

Another notable occasion in the fourth century on which light symbolism occurs is in the Nicene Creed (325), as likewise in the Nicene-Constantinopolitan Creed (381), where it is said that Jesus Christ is "light from light" (cf. Heb. 1:3). In this way, the imagery of light plays a decisive role in the formulation of Christology and the doctrine of the Trinity. Nowhere in the Creed is there any use of darkness symbolism; apophatic language is also entirely absent from the Creed.

Whereas both Evagrius and the *Homilies of Macarius* stand definitely within the tradition of "light mysticism," and neither of them employs the symbolism of divine darkness, at almost exactly the same time the theme of mystical darkness was being revived by another Greek writer, St. Gregory of Nyssa (c. 330–c. 395). While it is natural to classify Gregory of Nyssa as one of the three Cappadocian Fathers, and so to associate with him St. Gregory of Nazianzus, the close friend of Nyssa's elder brother St. Basil of Caesarea, yet as regards the symbolism of light and darkness the two Gregories differ markedly from one another. Where Gregory of Nazianzus follows Origen in interpreting the Christian life as an ever-increasing illumination, Gregory of Nyssa in his *Life of Moses* reverses the sequence, seeing the mystical journey paradoxically as a progress not from darkness to light but from light to darkness. Thus, initially, Moses beholds God in light at the vision of

51. *Apophthegmata,* alphabetical collection, Pambo 1 and 12. Cf. Silvanus 12.
52. Sisoes 14.
53. Arsenius 27.
54. See Kallistos [Timothy] Ware, "The Transfiguration of the Body," in *Sacrament and Image: Essays in the Christian Understanding of Man* ed. A. M. Allchin (London: Fellowship of St. Alban and St. Sergius, 1967), pp. 17-32, esp. 17-19. Compare also, in the same volume, pp. 40-41, the remarkable comments by Metropolitan Antony (Bloom) of Sourozh on the light of the Transfiguration as depicted in two icons in the Tretyakov Gallery, Moscow.

the Burning Bush (Exod. 3:2), but this is no more than a preliminary stage; the decisive moment of encounter comes subsequently, when he enters the "thick darkness" of Sinai (Exod. 20:21). There is also a further "theophany" in the *Life of Moses*, when Gregory interprets Exodus 33:21-23 as signifying perpetual progress *(epektasis)* throughout all eternity. This last is seen as a revelation of God's glory, but there is here no reference to darkness.

In his exegesis of Exodus 20:21, Gregory adheres closely to Philo and Clement of Alexandria:

> What does it mean that Moses entered the thick darkness *(gnophos)* and then saw God in it? What is now recounted seems somehow contradictory to the first theophany [the Burning Bush], for then the divine was beheld in light but now it is seen in darkness. . . . Scripture teaches by this that religious knowledge comes at first to those who receive it as light. . . . But as the intellect progresses and, through an ever greater and more perfect attentiveness, comes to apprehend reality, the closer it approaches to contemplation, the more clearly it sees that the divine nature cannot be contemplated.
>
> For, leaving behind everything that is observed, not only what sense comprehends but also what the intelligence thinks it sees, the intellect keeps penetrating deeper until through the intelligence's yearning for understanding it gains access to the invisible and incomprehensible, and there it sees God. This is the true knowledge of what is sought; this is the seeing that consists in not seeing, because that which is sought transcends all knowledge, being separated on all sides by incomprehensibility as by a kind of darkness. Therefore John the sublime, who penetrated into the luminous darkness, says, "No one has ever seen God" (John 1:18), thus asserting that knowledge of the divine essence is unattainable not only by human beings but also by every intellectual nature.[55]

Thus the entry of Moses into the "thick darkness," Gregory concludes, signifies that "the divine is by nature beyond all knowledge and comprehension."[56]

Here, then, Gregory of Nyssa follows Philo and Clement in interpreting the darkness of Sinai to mean the divine incomprehensibility. He is careful to specify that it is knowledge of God's essence that is unattainable

---

55. *Life of Moses* II, 162-63, ed. Jean Daniélou, Sources chrétiennes 1 *bis* (Paris: Cerf, 1955), pp. 80-82.

56. *Life of Moses* II, 164: Daniélou, p. 82.

by the human mind; for, agreeing with Philo, Gregory considered that humans can indeed know God through his energies or "powers," although never exhaustively so.

A further point to note is Gregory's use of the oxymoron "luminous darkness" *(lampros gnophos)*. Gregory's language recalls the teaching of Nicolas of Cusa (1401-64), concerning the *coincidentia oppositorum*. It recalls equally the "dazzling darkness" of which Henry Vaughan (1621/2-1693) speaks in his poem "The Night":

> There is in God (some say)
> A deep, but dazzling darkness. . . .
> O for that night! where I in him
> Might live invisible and dim.

The fact that the darkness is described in positive terms as "luminous" or "dazzling" indicates that it is not a void but a superabundant fullness; if this fullness appears to us as darkness, that is because our minds are incapable of apprehending its superabundance.

5. The Areopagitic Writings: The Two Ways

The same "coincidence of opposites" is to be found in the writings attributed to Dionysius the Areopagite (c. 500). He is usually classified as a "darkness mystic," but it would be more exact to say that he makes use equally of the symbols of both darkness and light. Fundamental to the mystical theology of the Areopagitic writings is the distinction between the two ways, cataphatic and apophatic. First, there is the Way of Affirmation or the Way of Descent, that is to say, God's self-revelation through descending "processions" *(proodoi)* and divine names, and through the two hierarchies, angelic and ecclesiastical; and the characteristic symbol of the Way of Affirmation is light. Second, there is the Way of Negation or the Way of Ascent, that is to say, the mystical ascent of the human person to the divine; and the characteristic symbol of this second way is darkness. The two ways, while distinct, are inseparable; in the words of Heraclitus (c. 500 BCE), "The way up and the way down are one and the same."[57]

In his work *The Mystical Theology*, Dionysius takes Moses' ascent of

---

57. Fragment 60 (Diels), in C. J. de Vogel, ed., *Greek Philosophy: A Collection of Texts*, vol. 1, 4th ed. (Leiden: Brill, 1969), p. 26; used by T. S. Eliot as an epigraph in *The Four Quartets*.

Sinai as exemplifying the Way of Negation. Moses passes through three stages: purification (Exod. 19:10-15), illumination (Exod. 19:16-19), and finally union, symbolized by his entry into the "thick darkness" (Exod. 20:21). Of this third stage, Dionysius writes:

> [Moses] breaks free from all that is seen and from all that sees, and plunges into the truly mystical darkness *(gnophos)* of unknowing. Here, renouncing all intelligible concepts, and taken up entirely into the intangible and the invisible, he is united completely to him who is beyond everything. Belonging neither to himself nor to anything else, through a suspension of all knowledge he is supremely made one with him who is altogether unknowable and, by knowing nothing, he knows in a manner that transcends the intellect.[58]

Here, exactly as in Philo, Clement, and Gregory of Nyssa, the "thick darkness" represents the transcendence and unknowability of God. Moses is "taken up entirely into the intangible and invisible," experiencing a total "unknowing." But the darkness in Dionysius, although symbolizing God's unknowability, expresses not separation but union: Moses is made one with God in the darkness.

In this connection, emphasizing the positive character of the darkness, Dionysius takes up Gregory's oxymoron "luminous darkness." In particular he uses the striking phrase *hyperphotos gnophos*, "darkness brighter than light," darkness that is dazzling and surpassingly radiant, and he refers to the "ray of divine darkness."[59] He insists explicitly on the "coincidence of opposites": "The divine darkness *is* the unapproachable light in which God is said to dwell."[60] Developing the point, he maintains that negations, when applied to God, do not signify any imperfection or "defect" *(elleipsis)* but rather a "superabundance" *(hyperochē)*: "We ascribe an intangible and invisible darkness to that Light which is unapproachable, because it superabundantly surpasses the visible light."[61] The very splendor of God's light hides him from us. The darkness, in other words, is not so much in God as in us; it indicates our inability to comprehend God as he is in himself. The divine itself is supremely positive, a light so radiant that we are overwhelmed by its brightness and can only experience and express it in terms

58. *The Mystical Theology* I, 3.
59. *The Mystical Theology* I, 1.
60. *Letter* 5. Cf. 1 Timothy 6:16.
61. *The Divine Names* VII, 2.

of darkness. In the words of Jakob Boehme (1575-1624), "Darkness is not the absence of light but the terror that comes from the blinding light."[62]

6. "Your Light, My God, Is You Yourself": Symeon and Palamas

In the later period of Greek patristic theology, there are two outstanding "mystics of light," St. Symeon the New Theologian (959-1022) and St. Gregory Palamas (1296-1359).[63] Neither of them made any significant use of the symbol of darkness. Symeon for his part has left vivid descriptions of the series of visions of divine light that he was granted in the course of his life. Here, for example, is his account of his first such vision, which he received while still a layman, aged about twenty. He speaks of himself in the third person:

> One day, as he stood repeating more in his intellect than with his mouth the words "God, have mercy upon me, a sinner" (Luke 18:13), suddenly a profuse flood of divine light appeared above him and filled the whole room. As this happened the young man lost his bearings, forgetting whether he was in a house or under a roof; for he saw nothing but light around him and did not even know that he stood upon the earth. . . . He was wholly united to non-material light, so much so that it seemed to him that he himself had been transformed into light.[64]

There are several points of importance to be noted here. First, the light is explicitly termed "divine." Second, Symeon apparently sees the light through his bodily eyes, and yet the light is not an ordinary physical light but is "non-material" *(aülos)*. Third, the light — as in the case of Plotinus — has a transfiguring effect: Symeon feels himself to have been "transformed into light." Fourth, in this and in his later visions it is not suggested that Symeon per-

---

62. Quoted in M.-M. Davy, *Nicolas Berdyaev: Man of the Eighth Day* (London: Geoffrey Bles, 1967), p. 124.

63. Light also plays an important part in the theology of St. Maximus the Confessor, who follows Evagrius in distinguishing between the light of the intellect and the light of the Holy Trinity; but, unlike Evagrius, he also refers to the entry of Moses into the divine darkness. See *Centuries on Love* I, 10, 33, 97; II, 6 (divine light); IV, 79-80 (light of the intellect); *Centuries on Theology* I, 84-85 (divine darkness); ET *The Philokalia*, vol. 2 (London/Boston: Faber, 1981), pp. 54, 56, 64, 66, 110, 133.

64. *Catechesis* XXII, 88-98, ed. Basile Krivochéine, Sources chrétiennes 104 (Paris: Cerf, 1964), p. 372; ET, *The Philokalia*, vol. 4 (London: Faber, 1995), p. 18.

ceived any shape, form, or face within the light: as with Plotinus, Evagrius, and Diadochus, the light itself is the vision.[65] It is true that in a later vision, although not on this first occasion, Christ speaks to Symeon from out of the light;[66] but he does not see the one whose voice he hears.

Symeon is quite clear about the divine and uncreated character of the light that was revealed to him: "Your light, my God, is you yourself."[67] Sometimes he links the light with the Trinity as a whole, and sometimes more specifically with the Holy Spirit, but most often he interprets it as the light of Christ. As John Behr observes, what matters ultimately to Symeon is not the light as light, but who the light is; he is not photocentric but Christocentric. Symeon is not consistent in making a distinction between the divine energies and the divine essence; at times he treats the manifestation of the light as identical with God's energies, but occasionally, unlike Gregory of Nyssa, he implies that human beings can be united with God's essence.[68]

Gregory Palamas was writing at a time of controversy, and so he was obliged to be more precise than Symeon had been. Around 1337 he became involved in a dispute with a learned Greek from South Italy, Barlaam the Calabrian, who maintained that the light the hesychast monks of Mt. Athos beheld in prayer was not the uncreated light of the Godhead but no more than a created light, the result of their own imagination. In response Gregory argued, in conformity with earlier tradition — and especially with the Macarian *Homilies* — that what the hesychast monks beheld in prayer was nothing other than the divine light of Tabor, the same light that will also be manifested at the Second Coming of Christ:

> Is it not evident that there is but one and the same divine light, that which the apostles saw on Tabor, which purified souls behold even now, and which is the reality of the eternal blessings that are to come?[69]

65. In his initial vision, Symeon beholds also a second light, "more lucid than the first," and he then perceives his spiritual father, Symeon the Studite, standing close to this second light (*Catechesis* XXII, 100-104). This is unusual; in his later visions, the figure of a person never appears to him. But even in this instance, the Studite is only standing close to the light and not actually in it.

66. *Catechesis* XXXVI, 223-33: ed. Krivochéine, Sources chrétiennes 113 (Paris: Cerf, 1965), p. 348.

67. *Hymn* XLV, 6, ed. Johannes Koder, Sources chrétiennes 196 (Paris: Cerf, 1973), p. 102.

68. See Basile Krivochéine, "'Essence créée' et 'Essence Divine' dans la théologie spirituelle de S. Syméon le Nouveau Théologien," *Messager de l'Exarchat du Patriarche russe en Europe occidentale* 75-76 (1971): 151-70.

69. *Triads* I, 3, 43; Meyendorff, p. 205.

Here Palamas's teaching was confirmed by three Councils of Constantinople (1341, 1347, 1351). Summing up and clarifying the views of earlier writers, he affirmed seven things about the divine light:

1. It is a "non-material" light — here Palamas uses the same adjective as Symeon, *aülon*[70] — "a light that is noetic and intelligible, or rather spiritual,"[71] not a physical light of the senses.

2. Although nonmaterial, the light is not merely imaginary or figurative; it is not just a metaphorical "light of knowledge" but is "hypostatic," an existent reality.[72]

3. While not a physical light of the senses, the divine light can nonetheless be perceived through the senses, provided that the latter are transformed by the grace of the Holy Spirit. Here, adhering to the holistic anthropology characteristic of Irenaeus and the Macarian *Homilies,* Palamas affirms that the body shares with the soul in the vision of God. Thus the three disciples on Tabor beheld the glory of the Transfiguration through their bodily eyes; and the righteous at the resurrection of the body on the Last Day will likewise look at the light of the glorified Christ through their physical senses. Yet what enables human beings to see the divine light is not the organs of sense-perception by virtue of their own intrinsic power, but rather the grace of the Holy Spirit that is active within them. None can behold the light except those who are spiritually prepared so to do; that is why Christ was transfigured only before the three chosen disciples, and not before the multitude. In this way the light is to be termed both "invisible" and yet "visible."[73]

4. The light manifested to the hesychasts is not created but uncreated and eternal. It is the light of the Holy Trinity — Father, Son, and Holy Spirit. Because it is divine and is God himself, it divinizes the beholder, conferring upon him the gift of *theōsis.* Yet, while the light is God, it is God in his energies, not in his essence. It manifests God's glory, not his inner nature. At this point Palamas's standpoint is more carefully nuanced than that of Symeon.[74]

---

70. *Triads* III, 1, 22; Meyendorff, p. 599.
71. *Triads* I, 3, 10; Meyendorff, p. 131.
72. *Triads* I, 3, 7; Meyendorff, p. 123.
73. *Triads* I, 3, 16; Meyendorff, p. 143.
74. Critics of Palamas, both Eastern and Western, since the fourteenth century have argued that his distinction between the essence and the energies of God impairs the divine simplicity (on God's simplicity, see the chapter by George Hunsinger). For a brief response to this

5. The divine light is infinite, "like an ocean without limits";[75] and so human beings will never comprehend the whole of it, either in this life or in the age to come. God is truly revealed in his divine energies, but never exhaustively revealed. Like Gregory of Nyssa, Palamas envisages perfection in terms of never-ending progress.

6. The divine light may rightly be termed both radiance and darkness. Here Palamas takes up the *coincidentia oppositorum* propounded by Gregory of Nyssa and the Areopagitic writings. "In the strict sense it is light," says Palamas, for it is a supremely positive reality; but, "by virtue of its transcendence" it is experienced by us as "darkness."[76] "Even though it is darkness, yet it is surpassingly bright; and in that dazzling darkness, as the great Dionysius says, things divine are granted to the saints."[77]

7. Palamas, like Symeon, considers that the light has a transforming effect upon the visionary beholders. Taken up into the uncreated splendor, they themselves shine outwardly with the divine radiance that they contemplate, "transfigured from glory into glory" (2 Cor. 3:18): "Participating in that which surpasses them, they are themselves transformed into it . . . the light alone shines through them, and it alone is what they see . . . and in this way God is all in all."[78] A little later, Palamas adds: "It is in the light that the light is beheld (cf. Ps. 36:9). . . . Our visual faculty in its entirety becomes itself light and is assimilated to that which it beholds; or rather, it is united to it without confusion, being light and beholding light through light. If it looks at itself, it sees light; if it looks at the object of its vision, it sees light once more; and if it looks at the means whereby it sees, this too is light."[79] This glorification of the body, while reserved in its plenitude to the Last Day, is partially anticipated even in this present life.

In this present survey of light and darkness imagery, we have been considering it primarily in the context of mystical prayer; and so we have spoken of inner, personal experience rather than the corporate life of the

---

criticism, see Kallistos Ware, "God Hidden and Revealed: The Apophatic Way and the Essence-Energies Distinction," *Eastern Churches Review* 7 (1975): 125-36, especially 134-36.

75. *Triads* III, 1, 33; Meyendorff, p. 621.

76. *Triads* II, 3, 51; Meyendorff, p. 491.

77. *Triads* I, 3, 18; Meyendorff, p. 149.

78. *Triads* II, 3, 31; Meyendorff, p. 451. Cf. 1 Corinthians 15:28.

79. *Triads* II, 3, 36; Meyendorff, p. 459.

church. It should be remembered, however, that many of those whom we have quoted, from Irenaeus to Palamas, were bishops, directly responsible for pastoral and social work; and all of them, whether bishops or not, assumed that anyone practicing inner prayer would be at the same time fully a member of the ecclesial community, regularly receiving the sacrament of Holy Communion. If this is not explicitly mentioned in the texts we have examined, that is because it is taken for granted.

Indeed, the imagery of light is applied not only to mystical union but to the sacraments of Baptism and the Eucharist. In one of the "Agrapha" — sayings and traditions about Jesus, not recorded in the Gospels — it is said that light shone forth at the moment of Christ's Baptism in the Jordan: "When he was being baptized, a very great light shone round about from the water, so that all that had come thither feared."[80] This establishes a close link between Christ's Baptism and his Transfiguration. Significantly, in modern Greek usage the Feast of Christ's Baptism (Epiphany, January 6) is known as "The Lights" *(Ta Phota)*. This language of light is applied not only to the Baptism of Jesus but to our own Baptism. In early sources Baptism is regularly described as "illumination" *(photisma* or *photismos)*. After immersion in the font, the newly baptized is clothed in a white robe, as the words are sung, "Grant to me a garment of light, O most merciful Christ our God, who wrap yourself in light as with a garment" (cf. Ps. 104:2); and he or she is then given a lighted candle to hold.

Similar language is applied to the Eucharist. The Holy Gifts received in Communion are regularly described as "light" and "fire." Before the reading of the Gospel, the celebrant prays, "Shine in our hearts with the pure light of your divine knowledge." Immediately after Communion the people sing, "We have seen the true light." In the concluding "Prayer behind the Ambo," God is invoked as "Father of lights" (cf. James 1:17); and during the prayers of thanksgiving the Blessed Virgin Mary is addressed as "the light of my darkened soul." These are but a few examples out of many.

The imagery of divine light, whether applied in an ecclesial or in a personal context, is by no means limited to the Christian East. It is true that the Feast of the Transfiguration (August 6) enjoys a greater prominence in the East than in the West: in the Orthodox calendar it is one of the twelve Great Feasts of the church year, whereas in the Roman rite (pre–

---

80. M. R. James, *The Apocryphal New Testament* (Oxford: Oxford University Press, 1924), p. 33. James notes parallels in Justin Martyr, Ephraim the Syrian (p. 33), and the Gospel of the Ebionites (p. 9).

Vatican II) it is merely a "Double of the Second Class," and in the Anglican 1662 Book of Common Prayer there are no collect and no Scripture readings whatsoever for August 6 (this was changed in twentieth-century reforms). At the same time it should not be forgotten that one of the finest books on the Transfiguration in the last hundred years is from the pen of an Archbishop of Canterbury.[81]

Even though the theme of divine light is more prominent in the Greek East than in the Latin West, and even though the Palamite interpretation of the divine light has sometimes been attacked by Western writers, yet in reality there is no serious conflict between East and West over the application of light imagery to the divine realm. As Robert Dodaro's contribution to this volume makes clear, St. Augustine of Hippo (354-430) refers to the divine light in much the same terms as Palamas, calling it "unchanging," "incorporeal," and "uncreated." Admittedly, Augustine's approach is mainly epistemological, while that of Palamas is experiential: Augustine is concerned more with the knowledge of God, Palamas with mystical union. But this is a difference of context, not of substance.

Christian East and West are agreed that the mystical union may be manifested outwardly in the body. In the West, this outward manifestation has frequently taken the form of the reception of the *stigmata* — an entry into the mystery of the Crucifixion rather than that of the Transfiguration — with Francis of Assisi (1181/2-1226) as the best-known example; and this marking with the wounds of Christ is something unknown in the Orthodox East. There are also, however, many Western saints who have been transfigured bodily by the divine light in the same way as the Desert Fathers and Seraphim of Sarov. What is at issue here is at most a difference of emphasis, not a stark contrast or (still less) a spiritual contradiction. So far as the theology of the divine light is concerned, this is fundamentally part of the shared heritage of Christendom, both Eastern and Western.

Epilogue: Why Light? Why Darkness?

While the images of light and darkness are more complex than might appear at first sight, our exploration of their use in Scripture and in the Greek patristic tradition has also revealed some clear threads of continuity. In

81. Arthur Michael Ramsey, *The Glory of God and the Transfiguration of Christ* (London/New York/Toronto: Longmans, Green, 1949) (written while professor at the University of Durham).

particular, it has become evident that references to the divine light are not to be understood solely in a metaphorical sense, but — at least in the intention of those who make such references — they often denote a specific spiritual experience, undergone not only inwardly but sometimes also outwardly in the body. In the writings of the Greek Fathers, the divine light is not a figure of speech but an objective reality revealed through grace to the saints. Yet, when this reality is termed "light," this is not and cannot be an exact description; for what the saints experience far transcends the physical light present in the material world, and for this reason it may equally be termed "darkness."

It remains to ask, in conclusion, why the symbols of light and darkness have been chosen in this way to express the divine. An obvious response is to point out that both symbols possess a firm scriptural basis, in the Old Testament account of Sinai and in the New Testament account of Christ's Transfiguration. Yet this merely pushes the question one stage further back. Why, we ask, should these two symbols have been assigned a privileged place in salvation history and in the Bible? Light, it may be answered, is an apt description of the divine because, among all the constituents of the physical world, it is the least material. It illumines the objects upon which it falls without suffering loss or change in itself. It spreads throughout space yet remains undivided, conveying the impression of being present everywhere at once. It holds the universe together. It is pure and clear, simple and incorrupt, immediately accessible to us and yet at the same time eluding our grasp. More important, it is dynamic and life-giving, bestowing on us a sense of warmth, hope, and beauty.

As for darkness, it expresses the awe and numinous wonder instilled by the divine, the sense of living mystery. Here let us remind ourselves that in the religious context a mystery signifies, not an unsolved problem or a baffling enigma, but something that is revealed to our understanding; yet something, at the same time, that is never totally revealed, for it reaches out into the infinite depths of God. Such precisely is the meaning of darkness when used to symbolize the mystical union. God's presence is indeed directly experienced in the darkness, yet he remains concealed. In the words of Novalis, "The great mystery is revealed to all, and remains for ever unfathomable."[82]

---

82. Cited in Catherine Evtuhov, *The Cross and the Sickle: Sergei Bulgakov and the Fate of Russian Religious Philosophy* (Ithaca/London: Cornell University Press, 1997), p. 180.

"The Darkness and the Light Are Both Alike to Thee": Light as Symbol and Its Transformations

David Brown

In the scientific contributions to this volume inevitably much attention has been given to light behaving as both particle and wave. Against such a backdrop it would be tempting to deny any comparable complexity in Christian use of light imagery. Certainly, within the biblical tradition "light" is almost always used to symbolize divine integrity, truth, and goodness, with "darkness" then applied to all that is evil and opposed to God.[1] Nor do I want to deny the richness in such symbolism as it is deployed subsequently in Christian art, architecture, and poetry. Occasionally, however, some different patterns emerge, and it is these that I want to explore in this essay. Symbols naturally encourage exploration more readily than literal language through opening up unexpected possibilities, as when apparently contradictory images are permitted, with God described, for example, as both rock and water, or as both shepherd and lamb. Similarly then here, as we shall see, God has been associated not just with brilliant or clear light but also with dim light, a cloudy sky, shadow, and even pitch darkness. Nor is it the case that, even where light alone is employed, the meaning is always the same. For example, light is not always used to suggest clarity, but sometimes its dazzle is portrayed as having similar effects to darkness itself.

In exploring some of these transformations I shall begin with two examples from the biblical world. Thereafter, I shall take a rather different pair from the world of art and architecture, before concluding with consideration of three contrasting approaches to light in the modern, scientific world.

---

1. For itemization of the more conventional range, see Gerald O'Collins's chapter, esp. pp. 105-14.

1. The Biblical World

Here I want to offer two case studies: first, at greater length, the identification of God with darkness, and then much more briefly, a similar identification with cloud and shadow. In both cases subsequent exegesis modified the original meaning in illuminating ways, but not so as to exclude altogether continuing relevance for the original meaning. Admittedly, in respect of the first, it would be possible to argue on the basis of the psalm from which my chapter's title is drawn (Ps. 139:12) that no more is meant in the Old Testament passages that equate God with darkness than that God's presence is to be found everywhere, even in the darkness; so darkness then becomes as day.

But rather more than this seems indicated, for it looks as though darkness may even have been the primal image for God, with divine mystery thus the primary connotation. Even in the creation story God's presence in the world antedates creation of light: "darkness was on the face of the deep; and the spirit of God moved upon the face of the waters" (Gen. 1:4). Although in its present context the verse is relatively late (according to source criticism, part of P's creation narrative), its assumption of an antecedent chaos rather than *creatio ex nihilo* argues for adaptation from earlier material. Certainly, in an indisputably early passage (Gen. 15) that describes God's inaugural covenant with his chosen people, the strange ritual of the "cutting" of the covenant only takes place when the sun had gone down (v. 17).[2] Although the smoking fire pot and flaming torch that are described as passing between the various animal sacrifices are no doubt intended to indicate divine endorsement of the covenant, even so they do so in a context of darkness and mystery rather than unqualified light.

Turn now to a better-known appearance, on Mt. Sinai, and a similar complexity is to be observed. Because of Paul's various allusions to the incident (2 Cor. 3:7; 4:6), Christians are likely to think first of how the skin of Moses' face shone when he came down from the holy mountain (Exod. 34:30), and the greater glory that now shines on the face of Christ. But in its immediate context we are told how, in order to encounter God, Moses had to enter a descending cloud (Exod. 34:5) that at the earlier giving of the Decalogue had been described as "thick darkness" (20:21), accompanied

---

2. "Probably one of the oldest narratives in the tradition about the patriarchs": Gerhard von Rad, *Genesis* (London: SCM, 1972), p. 189.

by "thunderings and lightnings" (20:18).[3] Nor are we left in any doubt as to the point in this context: "when the people saw it, they trembled, and stood afar off." Darkness is thus once again being used to evoke the divine, and with it an accompanying sense of awe and mystery.

Equally, the application of light and darkness to the Temple is not quite as straightforward as may initially appear. Certainly there are plenty of passages, especially in the Psalms, that speak of the presence of a divine glory in ways that make it natural to interpret such glory in terms of the splendor of light (e.g., Pss. 26:8; 63:2), while others allow of no other alternative. Ezekiel, for example, tells us that the earth "shines" with such glory (43:2). Yet in the two key passages describing the dedication of the Temple under Solomon, that same "glory" is interpreted as "deep darkness": "When the priests came out of the holy place, a cloud filled the house of the LORD, so that the priests could not stand to minister because of the cloud; for the glory of the LORD filled the house of the LORD. Then Solomon said, 'The LORD has set the sun in the heavens, and has said that he would dwell in thick darkness'" (1 Kings 8:10-12).[4] One way of reconciling these two views is to look to the more literal meaning of the Hebrew word for "glory" *(kabod),* with its notion of a "weight" or what overwhelms, for light or darkness might thus have very similar effects. Both brilliant light and impenetrable darkness might "weigh" or "press down" on the human observer in similar ways, creating awe and fear.

But, that said, it is still worth pursuing further the question of why darkness might nonetheless have once been the preferred image for representing the divine. It may have had something to do with the features that differentiated the Temple from other such structures in the ancient world. Admittedly, in most respects it was remarkably similar. As with temples in the ancient world more generally, animal sacrifice and other forms of worship took place out of doors, while the building itself remained reserved as a dwelling place for the deity. So the Temple at Jerusalem was by no means unique in this respect. Where the difference lay was in the absence of any symbolic representation of the deity, with no statue of YHWH to compare with that of Athena on the Acropolis, or of Zeus at Olympia. Instead, in the Holy of Holies the place between the sculpted Cherubim and above the Ark of the Covenant remained vacant. Not that these were the only forms of decoration, but it was all shrouded in darkness. The building as a whole

---

3. Parallel imagery is used in Deuteronomy 4:11 and 5:23.
4. Paralleled in 2 Chronicles 5:13–6:1, apart from the omission of any reference to the Sun.

lacked any proper windows, while this, the smaller and more sacred part, was separated by a curtain from the main source of light in the building, the seven-branched candlestick known as the menorah. Even here, the seven lights seem scarcely adequate for so large a building, and so suggest a marked contrast from, for example, Olympia, where various means were employed to augment visibility and luminosity.[5]

The nineteenth-century New Testament scholar and Bishop of Durham B. F. Westcott, in an appendix to one of his commentaries, wrestles with the question of why such differences should have existed. In what is a fascinating essay he argues that the darkness in the Holy of Holies must play a key role in any adequate Christian approach to art. Commenting on the apparent violation of the second commandment in the Temple's contents, he observes that the ancient Israelite "learnt from the records of the Old Testament that it was the Divine will that in the unapproachable darkness of the Holy of Holies the costliest works of Art should render service before the revealed presence of the Lord. No human eye could rightfully ever again trace the lineaments of those cherubim and palm trees and open flowers when they were once placed in the oracle, but it was enough to know that they were there. In no other way could the Truth be more eloquently or solemnly enforced that the end of Art is to witness to the inner life of Nature and to minister to God. . . . Philosophers and poets have dwelt upon the veiled statue at Sais; there is an open secret in the sacred gloom of the Holy of Holies more sublime and inspiring."[6] In short, for Westcott the Temple strikes a body blow to the notion of art as imitation. It is not there to copy, but to point beyond itself to the underlying spiritual character of the visible world and its eventual transfiguration under God. The merely partial veiling of a deity like Neit at the Egyptian temple of Sais was thus a poor hint of what the Temple expressed more profoundly in its far deeper veil of darkness.[7]

As a matter of fact, it is doubtful whether Westcott's analysis can be sus-

---

5. An image of Zeus (thirteen meters high) was reflected in a pool of oil at its base, which also prevented the ivory covering from drying out. Pausanias informs us that there was a spiral staircase to an upper gallery for closer viewing of the face. For an imaginative reconstruction, see J. Swaddling, *The Ancient Olympic Games,* 2nd ed. (London: British Museum, 1999), p. 18.

6. B. F. Westcott, "The Relation of Christianity to Art," in *The Epistles of St John* (London: Macmillan, 1883), pp. 319-60, esp. 323.

7. Neit came to be identified with Athena/Minerva, and so was used as a model for divine "Wisdom."

tained. Artistic representation was after all found elsewhere in the Temple, and not just in this dark place. Taking their clue from later Jewish writers, many commentators now find in the art of the Temple deliberate cosmological allusions, with the menorah, for example, intended to represent the then seven known planets and the laver or basin of water outside the Temple the waters held back at creation.[8] If so, the emphasis might be more on the mystery already inherent in creation rather than a mysterious transcendence or future transfiguration. However, either way the art, like the darkness, was not intended to explain but rather to enhance a sense of mystery. Just as the laver and menorah point beyond themselves, so does the darkness: a God present in the Holy of Holies yet not grasped or contained.

The image is thus the very opposite of the Prologue to St. John's Gospel, where the positions of light and darkness are reversed, with darkness unable to penetrate or contain the Light (1:5). Later in his Prologue (at v. 14) John uses temple imagery to describe Christ "tabernacling" among us. So it could be that he is deliberately inverting Old Testament imagery here, in order to suggest the different character of the divine presence that is now in our midst. The Logos is here to bring clarity and intelligibility to our lives rather than mystery. Certainly, that is how Light functions throughout the rest of John's Gospel.

But divine mystery of course continued to be a key element within Christian theological understanding of the divine. So it is not surprising that mystical theology wrestled with the exegesis of such passages, and in particular with the question of whether the heart of the divine presence could best be described as light or darkness. As the history is discussed at some length in two other contributions to this book, I will only mention the issue in passing as it pertains to how such imagery should be read.[9] One patristic tradition deriving from Origen and followed by Gregory of Nazianzus, had it triumphed, might well have resulted in exclusive use of light imagery and unqualified optimism about the possibilities of transcending human limitations in a joyful union. But in the end it was Gregory of Nyssa's account of Moses' two experiences on Mt. Sinai that was the more influential.[10] Light, he maintains, is succeeded by darkness because

8. For the menorah representing the sun, moon, and five planets, see Philo, *Quis Heres*, 221-24. For later understandings of the Temple more generally, see R. C. T. Hayward, ed., *The Jewish Temple* (London: Routledge, 1996).

9. For the history, see especially the essays by John Behr and Kallistos Ware.

10. A contrast was drawn between the darkness of Exodus 20:21 and God's earlier appearance to Moses as fire (19:18).

darkness reveals the more fundamental reality. "When, therefore, Moses grew in knowledge, he declared that he had seen God in the darkness, that is, that he had then come to know that what is divine is beyond all knowledge and comprehension, for the text says, *Moses approached the dark cloud where God was.* What God? He who *made darkness his hiding place,* as David says, who also was initiated into the mysteries in the same inner sanctuary."[11] In other words, what is sought is envisaged as an experience that "transcends all knowledge, being separated on all sides by incomprehensibility, as by a kind of darkness."[12]

The result was a tension transmitted to all subsequent writers, with some attempting reconciliation between the images of light and darkness, and others not. Denys the Areopagite is the most noted reconciler. Although he follows Gregory of Nyssa in accepting that all ends in a "truly mysterious darkness of unknowing," he gives the expression a much more positive and intimate aspect than Gregory had seemed prepared to allow.[13] So the final result is one in which the individual concerned "belongs completely to him who is beyond everything . . . united by a completely unknowing inactivity of all knowledge, and knows beyond the mind by knowing nothing." While such language verges on the incoherent, what Dionysius seems to want to affirm is that the union is an affective and ecstatic one, but inexplicable in words. As he promises elsewhere, "shedding all and freed from all, you will be uplifted to the ray of the divine shadow which is above everything that is."[14] Indeed, that talk of "a ray from a shadow" is even more prominent in the words with which his *Mystical Theology* begins, where darkness is almost in effect equated with light: "the mysteries of God's Word lie . . . in the brilliant darkness of a hidden silence. Amid the deepest shadow they pour overwhelming light on what is most manifest." Dazzling light can of course have the same effect as deep darkness in preventing vision. Paul's experience on the Damascus Road is a case in point.[15] But I think that probably rather more is implied here. Ver-

11. The passages in italics are quotations from Exodus 20:21 and Psalm 17:12 (Septuagint).

12. Gregory's *Life of Moses,* book II, 164, 163; translated in The Classics of Western Spirituality series (New York: Paulist, 1978), p. 95.

13. This and the next quotation are drawn from *Mystical Theology* 1.3, 1001A, in *Pseudo-Dionysius: The Complete Works,* Classics of Western Spirituality (London: SPCK, 1987), p. 137. For a similar positive interpretation, see A. Louth, *The Origins of the Christian Mystical Tradition* (Oxford: Clarendon, 1981), pp. 159-78, esp. 174-76.

14. For this and the subsequent quotations, see *Mystical Theology,* 1.1, 997A-1000A (p. 135).

15. Acts 9:3-4; 22:6; 26:13-14. Not dissimilar effects are suggested by the evangelists' ac-

balized, intellectual knowledge has been denied, but not the warmth of personal intuitive insight that cannot be so expressed. So the brilliant ray lifts up the believer into the divine presence, but not in a way communicable to others.

By no means all, however, followed Denys. A more negative strain (that was probably also the position of Gregory of Nyssa) continued into the Western medieval tradition, and can be found in the German Meister Eckhart and the English mystical treatise *The Cloud of Unknowing*.[16] Some modern exegetes see in such writers a denial of even the possibility of any human experience of God.[17] In my view that is to go too far. Nonetheless, the experience is clearly quite different from later talk of "the dark night of the soul," as in St. John of the Cross. This alludes to the penultimate stage of encounter before the deepest affective relationship is formed. The term is intended to describe how, as the soul draws closer to God, it becomes ever more aware of its own unworthiness, and so of the yawning gap that exists between divinity and humanity, unable to be crossed without divine aid. Nonetheless, divine love can draw our wills and emotions across that great abyss.[18]

The second biblical image that I want to consider here (but more briefly) is that of "cloud" and "shadow," and again with respect to both possible original meanings and subsequent applications in later exegesis. The people of Israel were accompanied in their wanderings through the wilderness by a pillar of fire at night and by cloud during the day. While some passages suggest that the cloud also partakes of light and so reflects the glory of the Lord (e.g., Exod. 16:10), others assume the more mundane purpose of simply guiding the people on their way (e.g., Exod. 13:21). Given the usually cloudless desert sky, the latter is perhaps the earlier explanation, though eventually it was the theme of divine glory that came to predominate, and it is in this sense that the cloud of divine glory is said to fill the Temple (e.g., 1 Kings 8:10-11; 2 Chron. 5:13-14). Even so, other passages do seem to pull in a rather different direction.

---

counts of the Transfiguration. Although only Matthew has the disciples fall on their faces (Matt. 17:6), both he and Luke describe a dazzling effect: Matthew 17:2; Luke 9:29.

16. Philo was probably a key influence on Gregory. See Philo's discussion in *De Posteritate Caini*, 4.12–5.16.

17. E.g., D. Turner, *The Darkness of God* (Cambridge: Cambridge University Press, 1995).

18. For a helpful exposition, see R. Williams, *The Wound of Knowledge* (London: Darton, Longman & Todd, 1979), pp. 173-75.

In Canaanite mythology Baal is frequently described as "rider on the clouds," and it may well be a borrowing of such imagery that leads to clouds being treated in the Bible as God's chariot for war and judgment: "Behold, the LORD is riding on a swift cloud . . . and the idols of Egypt will tremble at his presence, and the heart of the Egyptians will melt within them" (Isa. 19:1). In similar vein Nahum tells us that "the clouds are the dust of his feet" (1:3), while a variant reading in one of the psalms (adopted by the AV) equates such conduct with the desert itself: "cast up a highway for him that rideth through the deserts" (68:4). Ultimately of course that same imagery enters Christianity through Daniel's "night" vision of the "one like unto a son of man" coming "on the clouds of heaven" (Dan. 6:13). While all such images are externally directed (it is others whom the cloud separates from God), in Lamentations a similar fate befalls Israel itself: "How the LORD in his anger has set the daughter of Zion under a cloud! He has cast down from heaven to earth the splendor of Israel" (2:1). So clouds in this sense are clearly indicative of divine judgment, and have little, if anything, to do with the imagery of light with which they have been elsewhere associated. Instead, they represent the dark and threatening side of God.

In most subsequent Christian exegesis it was the positive side of cloud imagery that was to take precedence, with cloud simply directly equated with light. But there are some exceptions. One of the most intriguing, not least because it is pursued right through his writings, is in the work of the Scottish nineteenth-century blind preacher and poet, George Matheson. Commenting, for example, on Isaiah 32:3 (God described as "the shadow of a great rock in a weary land"), Matheson observes: "There are times in which man needs nothing so much as a withdrawal of light. There are times in which the only chance for a human soul is in the pulling down of the window blinds. We pray 'Enlighten our eyes!' but often we can only get our inner eye enlightened by having the outer eye shaded. . . . God puts the multitude all out, and locks the door. He closes the shutters of the casement. He interrupts the music in the street; he forbids the dancing in the hall. He says, 'Your nerves are weary with excitement; in this desert place you shall rest awhile.'"[19] In other words, instead of reading the nonlight and negative references to cloud in purely negative terms, Matheson insists on positive results emerging from such negativity.

19. For this and other examples in Matheson, see I. C. Bradley, ed., *O Love that wilt not let me go: Meditations, Prayers and Poems by George Matheson* (London: Collins, 1990), pp. 49-59, esp. 54-55 and 50.

There is not the space here to explore what may be termed Matheson's shadow theology. Undoubtedly, through such reflections he was enabled to perceive his own blindness in a more positive light as conferring advantages not necessarily so easily secured by the sighted. Indeed, Job 12:22 with its talk of light emerging from the shadows is taken as indicative for a general stance on life: "How couldst thou learn, if the natural life never failed thee? How could faith begin, if sight were perfect? How could trust exist if there were no darkness? . . . Out of thy deepest darkness God says, 'Let there be light.'" Although he never expresses matters quite so explicitly in his writings, clearly for Matheson cloud and shade have become more than just surrogates for light, but in themselves the very best mediators of the divine presence.

2. In the World of Art and Architecture

Here once again I want to consider two examples, this time both indicative of the acceptance of paradox in Christian understandings of light. One concerns how Gothic architecture's rationale in light is found not to be quite so straightforward as is commonly supposed; the other, the way in which Christ at his weakest comes to be regarded as the greatest focus of light.

Conventionally, the beginnings of Gothic architecture are traced to the work of Abbot Suger in his building of his new abbey church of St. Denis just outside Paris. Arguments continue about the extent of the influence of the writings of Pseudo-Denys on him.[20] In part Suger may have been influenced by the confused identification that was sometimes made with the French missionary saint of the same name to whom the monastery was dedicated. Certainly, Denys had written a great encomium on light as an image of the archetypal Good that is God.[21] In true Platonic fashion, material things, including lights, are seen to mirror their intellectual counterparts, and so to point ultimately to God himself: "So, then, forms, even those drawn from the lowliest matter, can be used not unfittingly, with regard to heavenly beings. Matter, after all, owes its subsistence to absolute beauty and keeps, throughout its earthly ranks, some echo of

20. For a strong statement of the case in favor of such influence, see O. von Simpson, *The Gothic Cathedral,* 3rd ed. (Princeton: Princeton University Press, 1988), pp. 103-41.

21. *Divine Names* 4, 697C-701B (pp. 74-76).

intelligible beauty. Using matter, one may be lifted up to the immaterial archetypes."[22] Suger in similar vein talks of how the loveliness of many-colored stones in the church's altar can lead us from the material to the immaterial, and of how the shining gilded bronze reliefs on its doors are such that they "should brighten the minds (of those who enter) so that they may travel, through the true lights, to the true Light where Christ is the true Door."[23]

So far, such comments might suggest Gothic formulated on quite a simple notion of lightness in contrast to the earlier Romanesque: lightness in materials and light streaming into the church, all intended to draw our contemplation heavenwards. But anyone who has been to that most famous of Gothic cathedrals, Chartres, knows that its magnificent stained glass often renders it quite a dark building, and day and hour need to be quite carefully chosen, if their rich glow is to be fully experienced, far less their details read. Denys had already warned that dissimilarity in the material might be potentially less misleading than similarity, with God as "cornerstone" or even "worm" as more suitable than "sun" or "golden or gleaming men."[24] So perhaps the splendor of the glass appearing only occasionally and even then coming multi-hued and with multiple images could be seen as guarding precisely against any such simple and misleading identifications.

But there is a deeper paradox to be observed. In the nineteenth century Ruskin, like Pugin, believed Gothic to be the quintessential Christian style and again, like Pugin, defended it in terms of the care with which it promoted lightness of overall impression in stone and glass alike. Nonetheless, he rejected any view that supposed such principles simply equivalent to the maximizing of light. Thus no one's outrage could have been greater than his when he learned that it had been the decision of the canons of Amiens Cathedral in the eighteenth century that had led to the removal of much of the cathedral's medieval stained glass, apparently all justified in terms of the production of a stronger, clearer light. Lightness of form and of perception, he insisted, were by no means the same thing as brilliant daylight. If the latter is permitted, then it will deliver its own message rather than allowing the building to speak in its own right.

22. *The Celestial Hierarchy,* 2, 144B-C (pp. 151-52).

23. *De Administratione,* xxiii (pp. 63-64) and xxvii (pp. 47-48), in E. Panofsky, ed., *Abbot Suger and the Abbey Church of St-Denis and Its Art Treasures,* 2nd ed. (Princeton: Princeton University Press, 1979).

24. *Celestial Hierarchy,* 2 (esp. pp. 148, 152). God is referred to as a worm in Psalm 22:6, if it is read Christologically.

David Brown

Somewhat surprisingly, Ruskin finds a twentieth-century ally in Paul Tillich. In an intriguing passage Tillich initially expresses himself in favor of clear glass, partly because "the rational element in religion" is thereby stressed and partly because "the idea is, or should be, to draw nature into the sphere of the Holy Presence." However, he goes on to admit that the opposite in fact often happens: "the members of the congregation are drawn away from concentration on the Holy Presence to the outside world." His solution, therefore, is to accept stained glass. Although he draws attention to the way in which it "effectively shields the congregation from the outside distractions" and can be seen to conform to the principles of Protestant art "because it is an architectural element, even though technically not a necessary one," his real reason for endorsement seems to have been because it sheds "a deeper and more mystical illumination upon the interior of the church."[25]

Given Tillich's somewhat reluctant Protestant concessions to stained glass, it is therefore salutary to note who first coined the phrase "a dim religious light." It was in fact another convinced Protestant, John Milton in his ode to Melancholy, *Il Penseroso*. There he talks of "the high embowed Roof"

And storied Windows richly dight,
Casting a dimm religious light

which, when combined with music,

Dissolve me into extasies,
And bring all Heav'n before mine eyes.[26]

The poem was probably written during Milton's undergraduate days at Cambridge or, if not then, shortly thereafter. So, almost certainly, his sentiments here reflect that great Gothic building at the heart of Cambridge, King's College Chapel.[27] As such, they contrast markedly with his later extensive use of light, as in its invocation at the beginning of book 3 of *Paradise Lost*.[28] Indeed, Milton's use of light imagery is so extensive that he has

25. "Contemporary Protestant Architecture," in P. Tillich, *On Art and Architecture* (New York: Crossroad, 1989), pp. 214-20, esp. 218-19.
26. *Il Penseroso*, lines 155-66, esp. 159-60 and 165-66. Quoted from H. Darbishire, ed., *Poetical Works of John Milton* (London: Oxford University Press, 1958), p. 428.
27. Though his old college of Christ's may also have played its part.
28. *Paradise Lost*, 3, 1-6; Darbishire, p. 53.

been credited with being decisive in moving English poetic use away from "good" and "true" and towards "bright" and "light" as the dominant terms for moral goodness.[29]

Yet already in that same century the phrase "the light of reason" was beginning to be used independently of reference to God, and by the following century such usage had become the norm. Even a Christian poet such as Alexander Pope could speak of reason as "the God within the mind."[30] Significantly, William Cowper finds it necessary to remind his readers of the source of unbelievers' wisdom:

> Their fortitude and wisdom were a flame
> Celestial, though they knew not whence it came.
> Deriv'd from the same source of light and grace
> That guides the Christian in his swifter race.[31]

It is such developments that help explain modern contrasts between "the light of reason" and "the darkness of superstition." But even so the numinous character of "a dim religious light" continues to have appeal. Turn on almost any television program that has a religious context, and churches will be lit, not with just with one or two but many candles, intended to be suggestive, I suspect, of just such an evocative atmosphere. So, while the paradox in Gothic appeal to light now passes most people by, the notion of God found not in brilliant light but in a Gothic suggestive haze continues to resonate in modern secular culture.

The second paradoxical application of light I want to consider here is the placing of the greatest light where it would have been perhaps least expected, at Christ's birth in a stable. Considering Christian art in the abstract and without reference to its history, there are many places where the use of light by artists might have been anticipated, most obviously perhaps in depictions of the creation but also surely in momentous happenings such as the resurrection. As it was, the halo became ubiquitous. Yet the most remarkable use of light finally occurs where it might have been least expected, in the fourteenth century when for the first time in painting we

29. Josephine Miles, "From Good to Bright: A Note in Poetic History," in *Publications of the Modern Language Association of America* 60 (1945): 766-74; cf. also M. Y. Hughes, "Milton and the Symbol of Light," in *Ten Perspectives on Milton* (1965), pp. 63-103.

30. *Essay on Man*, Epistle II, 204; quoted from H. Davis, ed., *Pope: Poetical Works* (London: Oxford University Press, 1966), p. 256.

31. From his long poem on *Truth*, lines 531-54.

find the infant Christ emanating rays of light from his own person: divinity at its apparently most vulnerable now seen as at its most radiant. The person responsible for this new development was not in fact an artist but a saint, St. Bridget or, more accurately, Birgitta of Sweden, who had a vision of the Nativity in 1372 while in the Holy Land. Joseph was seen as an old man, solicitous for his wife but deferential. So he places a lighted candle on the wall of the cave, and then goes outside. Mary then gives birth, painlessly and instantly while kneeling in prayer. Here is how Birgitta describes the scene: "While she was thus in prayer, I saw the one lying in her womb then move; and then and there, in a moment and the twinkling of an eye, she gave birth to a Son, from whom there went out such great and ineffable light and splendour that the sun could not be compared to it. Nor did that candle that the old man had put in place give light at all, because that divine splendour totally annihilated the material splendour of the candle."[32] The Child, trembling from the cold, is then taken up into his mother's arms, but not before she had saluted the infant God: "Welcome my God, my Lord and my Son."

Thereafter, the theme was quickly taken up and disseminated by artists. Perhaps the finest and most familiar painting of this kind in Britain, hanging as it does in the National Gallery in London, is by the fifteenth-century Dutch artist, Geerten Tot Sint Jans.[33] But examples are so numerous for the next few hundred years subsequent to Birgitta's death (in 1373) that regular visitors to galleries have almost come to anticipate and expect just such a depiction, whoever the artist happens to be. There are no haloes in Geerten's painting. It thus anticipates trends in later painting more generally, where internal light is used to identify divinity, eventually, as in Caravaggio, presented in such naturalistic terms that the source of the light is not always immediately obvious to the viewer. A reversal then occurs in Caravaggio's disciple, Rembrandt. Instead of light, it is now darkness that is used to suggest divinity. Ruskin saw such darkness as artificial and dishonest, but, more likely, it was Rembrandt's own distinctive way of opening up the viewer to a larger dimension of the divine: the vulnerability of darkness now disclosing the majesty of divinity.

Rembrandt's approach is altogether too large an issue to pursue fur-

---

32. *Book of Revelations*, VII, 20, 6; quoted from M. T. Harris, ed., *Birgitta of Sweden: Life and Selected Revelations* (New York: Paulist, 1990), p. 203.

33. The unusual name indicates that he lived with the Knights of St. John at Haarlem. He is thought to have died, aged twenty-eight, sometime between 1485 and 1495.

ther here. Suffice it to say that both my examples illustrate how Christian artistic tradition has refused to place God and light in any simplistic relationship with each other. Just as God had been found in dim religious light set against apparently weightless, soaring Gothic architecture, so now here the luminous brilliance of divinity is discovered in the fragility of childhood or in meditative and often elderly figures emerging from deep darkness, as in Rembrandt.

3. In Relation to Modern Science

Attempts to relate religion and theories of light are by no means new. In prescientific Europe at least two forms of connection were postulated. First, the possibility of perception was presumed to presuppose an underlying "sympathy" or connection between the viewer and the object perceived.[34] As early as Empedocles it had been suggested that each object gives off effluences from its spores which, when they come in contact with similar content in the percipient, produce the relevant sensation.[35] Although Plato and Aristotle developed more subtle versions, the basic nature of the relationship between subject and object remained unchanged, and it is such ideas that passed into Christianity, with the Creator now guaranteeing those underlying connections.[36] The way the subject is envisaged as transformed by the object meant of course that vision was seen as having a moral dimension, and so this is sometimes postulated as an element in disputes about images in church.[37]

Then a second factor was the new role Augustine gave to divine aid.[38] Plato had described how "truth flashes upon the soul, like a flame kindled by a leaping spark."[39] For him it had been a metaphor to explicate the rela-

---

34. Such sympathy or influence was part of course of a much larger pattern that included the influence of the stars. For a sympathetic treatment of its use within Christianity, see C. S. Lewis, *The Discarded Image* (Cambridge: Cambridge University Press, 1964), pp. 92-121.

35. Empedocles, fragment 3, 9-13 and 89.

36. For Plato's version, see *Philebus* 33D-34A; *Timaeus* 64A-D; for Aristotle's, see *De anima* II, 412, 417A-418A, 423B-424A.

37. E.g., C. Joby, "The extent to which the rise in the worship of images in the late middle ages was influenced by contemporary theories of vision," *Scottish Journal of Theology* 60 (2007): 36-44.

38. For more detail on Augustine's views, see Robert Dodaro's essay in this volume.

39. *Seventh Letter*, 341C: cf. 344B.

tion of his theory of forms to the sensible world. Augustine, by placing those same forms in the mind of God himself, now ensured that all intellectual understanding required divine aid. That is to say, just as sensible awareness was believed to require the light of sun, so now all intellectual understanding was taken to need divine illumination through participation in awareness of the seminal forms out of which God had created the world. Although Aquinas's revived Aristotelianism weakened this approach, it was really only with Descartes that such ideas were wholly abandoned, with his claim that in effect the capacity to illuminate lay in the objects themselves, in the ability they gave us to form clear and distinct ideas of their nature.[40]

So, as we examine three instances of religion and modern theories of light and their artificial products interacting, we must not think of such interaction as something wholly new. What is new is the range of positions taken. To reflect that range, my examples will include hostility, reconciliation, and something in-between. The accuracy of the science is in some ways less interesting than what is done with it.

My first case study is the use of light to express hostility to religion. A group of Italian artists that includes Giacomo Balla, Umberto Boccioni, Carlo Carrà, and Gino Severini signed in 1910 what they labeled their Futurist Manifesto. It had as its aim the liberation of Italy from the oppressive weight of its past, and the endorsement of everything scientific and modern, in particular machinery, speed, and violence. While their language lacked caution, it helps to remember that such ideas were being expressed without awareness of the horrors to come in the First World War, and to many of their contemporaries they appeared new and exciting. Instead of the Impressionist instant or the rather dull colors of Italian Divisionism, one found, for example, the simultaneous representation of the successive movements of a horse in a race, all within a single frame. Everything from dogs to dancers is subjected to similar treatment, usually in strong and rich colors.

Although Boccioni admired the religious paintings of the Divisionist Gaetano Previati, all the group were united in an antireligious stance, with Christianity, perhaps inevitably, seen as part of the past that had to be rejected.[41] It is perhaps in Giacomo Balla's *Street Lamp* (1909) that this inher-

40. For Aquinas, although the *lumen intellectuale* was no longer thought of as requiring divine aid, it did still participate in the *lumen divinum* that was ubiquitous.

41. For religious themes in Divisionism, see V. Greene, "Divisionism's Symbolic Ascent," in S. Fraquelli et al., *Radical Light: Italy's Divisionist Painters 1891-1910* (London: National Gallery, 2008), pp. 47-59. Mystic gentle colors were preferred.

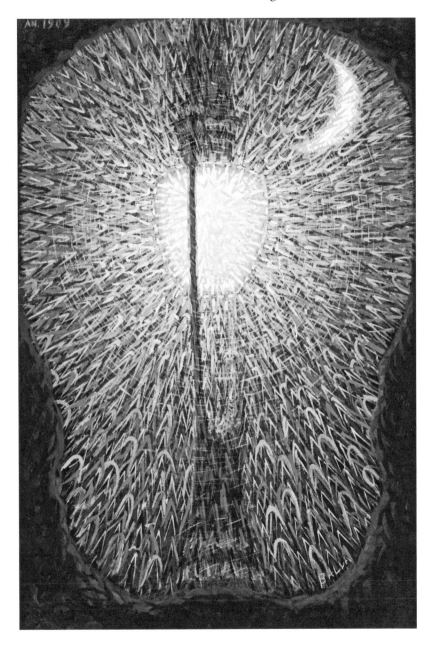

Giacomo Balla, *Street Lamp*

ently antireligious thrust of the movement is made most obvious.[42] The painting is a celebration of the technical achievements of artificial light, in which its diffraction into colored rays is treated as an explosion of light from its own sun. Meanwhile, the moon as part of the created order is set in the top right of the painting in such a way as to suggest by way of contrast its purely passive and insignificant character.

It is intriguing to see that such a stance continues in the world's only museum dedicated exclusively to the use of light in works of art, situated as it is in Italy. Founded by Targetti of Milan, one of the world's major manufacturers of lights (lamps, architectural lighting, and so on), towards the end of last century, it is housed in the Villa Sfacciata, a fifteenth-century villa near the Certosa monastery in Florence. Although the director, Ammon Barzel, is well aware of religious symbolism involving light, he is adamant that light can no longer function in this way. As he observes in the Introduction to the official Guide, "light as the expression and symbol of the divine . . . could now be substituted by real electrical light elements based on technical, scientific and manufacturing achievements."[43] That is then how he reads all the various exhibits he introduces, with even the American artist, James Turrell, well known for his more spiritual use of light, represented by a strictly secular work.[44] W. T. Sullivan's title for his 1968 photograph of the world as viewed from a space satellite is therefore seen as the natural and appropriate culmination of such ideas. "The Light of the World" is no longer Christ but what we ourselves produce with the concentrations of yellow glow in the United States and Western Europe.[45]

At the other end of the spectrum, it is interesting to find Christians drawing apparently diametrically opposed conclusions from the same scientific research. For the painter Salvador Dalì the work of scientists was seen to bring the physical world closer to a religious perspective because the physical was coming to be viewed as less material and more ethereal, like the spiritual world. That at any rate was the intended message of a

---

42. Illustrated in A. Barzel, *Light Art: Targetti Light Art Collection* (Milan: Skira, 2005), p. 8.

43. Barzel, *Light Art*, p. 17.

44. Barzel, *Light Art*, pp. 38-43.

45. Illustrated in Barzel, *Light Art*, p. 25. The title is almost certainly intended as a deliberate contrast to William Holman Hunt's famous nineteenth-century painting of the same name, versions of which are to be found both in Keble College Chapel, Oxford and in St. Paul's Cathedral, London.

number of his paintings such as *Celestial Coronation, Madonna in Particles,* and *Nuclear Head of an Angel.*[46]

The American novelist and poet, John Updike, read matters rather differently. In "Seven Stanzas at Easter," a poem that pleads for a traditional account of the Empty Tomb, Planck's quanta are deployed to give even the observing angel a distinctive kind of materiality:

> Let us not mock God with metaphor,
> analogy, sidestepping transcendence;
> making of the event a parable, a sign painted in the faded
>   credulity of earlier ages:
> let us walk through the door.
>
> The stone is rolled back, not papier-mâché,
> not a stone in a story,
> but the vast rock of materiality that in the slow-grinding
>   of time will eclipse for each of us
> the wide light of day.
>
> And if we will have an angel at the tomb,
> make it a real angel,
> weighty with Max Planck's quanta, vivid with hair, opaque
>   in the dawn light, robed in real linen
> spun in a definite loom.[47]

Presumably, this is Updike's own distinctive way of insisting that the angel has become part of our own material world since "Planck's quanta" are photons, measurable units of real light and not just a spiritual vision. Yet there remains a paradoxical element to the description since photons as pure energy are, strictly speaking, without mass, unless perhaps Updike wants us to think of their gravitational pull. However intended, what is obvious is that Updike's use of physics lies at the opposite pole to Dalí's expectation of the dissolution of matter.

Yet in some ways it is more tentative uses of light imagery that are more appealing, simply because they allow readers or viewers to explore the questions for themselves. That is perhaps why I am particularly fasci-

46. Illustrated in R. Descharmes and G. Néret, eds., *Dalí* (Köln: Taschen, 1997), pp. 444-45, 458-59.

47. "Seven Stanzas at Easter," from *Telephone Poles and Other Poems,* by John Updike, copyright © 1959 by John Updike. Used by permission of Alfred A. Knopf, a division of Random House, Inc.

nated by the work of the American artist Dan Flavin (1933-96). What makes his light installations of particular interest here is the way in which art critics and the general public have often found in his work a strong spiritual dimension, despite his own insistence that none existed. Brought up in a devout Roman Catholic home where he was encouraged to serve daily at mass and to enter a seminary to train for the priesthood to which his father had aspired, Flavin rebelled in early adulthood, and his first art works were pastiches of Catholicism.[48] He then went on to develop the Minimalist art with which his name is associated. When asked, he always insisted that his works bore no more meaning than what appeared on the surface, the standard established at the time by the then dominant art critic of the day, Clement Greenberg. But there are a number of reasons for supposing that at least some of his installations mean rather more.

First, his mentor was Barnet Newman, who had likewise used abstract art to explore religious themes. Newman himself said of Flavin and his work that he was "a man with a personal vision, and that personal vision . . . stretches the imagination. He is not . . . a man intoxicated with a love of science, or the light itself, as are some of the light sculptors, who are bringing together science and art. . . . He has taken the light bulb which is a thing and turned it into an innate material, as if it were paint, or canvas . . . and he has turned this thing, this material, into something personal, in order to make a statement that goes beyond the material as formal material."[49] Second, there is the material he used and the way he used it. His favorite medium was fluorescent light, which, unlike tungsten lamps, produces light not in the wire itself but in a reflective glow from phosphorus or similar materials placed along the inner tube, the color depending on the type of phosphorus used.[50] These colors inevitably opened up possibilities of further meaning, as did the unconventional angles at which the tubes were hung. A third factor is his Catholic background. James Joyce, another lapsed Catholic, developed Aquinas's theory of beauty to speak of "epiphanies" out of ordinary things, and I do not think it too far fetched to envisage Flavin doing the same thing.[51] When prepared to give titles to

48. For Flavin himself on his Catholic upbringing, see M. Govan and T. Bell, *Dan Flavin: A Retrospective* (New Haven: Yale University Press, 2004), pp. 189-90; for an example of pastiche, see Flavin's *East New York Shrine*, on p. 28 of the same book.

49. From the transcript of a talk given by him at the opening of a Flavin exhibition on September 12, 1969: NGC archives, Flavin Exhibition files.

50. Also from the transcript of Newman's talk.

51. James Joyce, *Stephen Hero* (New York: New Directions, 1955), p. 213.

Dan Flavin, *Diagonal of May 25, 1963 (to Constantin Brancusi)*, 1963
Yellow fluorescent light, 8 ft. (244 cm.) long on the diagonal, CL no. 13. Photo by Billy Jim, New York. © 2010 Stephen Flavin / Artists Rights Society (ARS), New York. Courtesy of David Zwirner, New York

Dan Flavin, untitled, 1996
Green, ultraviolet, blue, pink, and yellow fluorescent light. Nave: two sections, each 92 ft.
(28 m.) wide; transept: two sections, each 32 ft. (975 cm.) wide; apse: two sections, each 32 ft.
(975 cm.) high. CL no. 693. Photo by Paola Bobba; courtesy of Fondazione Prada, Milan. © 2011
Stephen Flavin / Artists Rights Society (ARS), New York; courtesy of David Zwirner, New York

specific installations, Flavin honors significant figures in his own life; so why not sometimes something that would transcend his materials in an even more fundamental way, namely God himself? One of his last installations was specifically designed for a church, while several others allude to artists who did avow a spiritual purpose, among them Brancusi, Mondrian, and Newman himself.[52] If I am right, then once again there is an element of subversion with which to end my survey: a manufactured light whose meaning cannot be contained despite its author's best intentions. If so, intriguingly, the relevant examples work in exactly the opposite way from how the Divisionists envisaged their task in their religious paintings: through strong and powerful light, not in gentle translucence; in other words, more like the Futurists who had intended exactly the opposite meaning.

4. Conclusion

What I hope my survey illustrates is the danger of latching onto one single meaning for key Christian metaphors or analogies for God. As I have shown, God's presence has been associated at various times with brilliant light, clear light, dim light, a cloudy sky, and pitch darkness. None of this is to deny that the predominant use is to be found in applications I have chosen not to discuss, where light is in uncomplicated ways identified with goodness and truth and darkness with all that is evil and opposed to God. These other instances do, however, subvert any claim to absolutes in the more common usage. There are at least four reasons why it is important that such a conclusion should be acknowledged. The first is linguistic. Only close attention to context will determine what sort of meaning is appropriate. It is not something that can be imposed in advance. Second, the avoidance of such impositions is essential if Christian experience of the divine is not to be unnecessarily limited. Suppose, for instance, that Tillich's equation of a Protestant perspective with clear light were accepted. Anything like the encounter of the High Priest with God in the darkness of the Holy of Holies would then come to be seen as a matter of pagan influence rather than something that could offer real insight into another facet of God. Third, there is the doctrinal point. Again and again Christianity has

52. For the church example executed in the last year of his life, see *Dan Flavin: A Retrospective*, pp. 104-5. For allusions to the artists mentioned, see pp. 35, 69, 84.

been plagued by single theories imposed on multiple metaphors. To give but one example, Augustine directed the Western church into an absolute equation of water with cleansing, and so baptism became essentially about the remission and washing away of original sin. But water has in fact quite a number of other resonances in Scripture, not least, especially in John, that of being refreshing and life-giving, attention to which might have moved the church in quite a different direction. So similarly here, dazzling light and deep darkness balance the clarity of truth and goodness suggested by clear light. In other words, they subvert any absolute claims by imposing an element of mystery and wonderment. Again, strong light could so easily make us identify divine presence with power, but "dim religious light" hints that this is not always so, as does Birgitta's vision of the Savior at his most glowing when he is also at his weakest and most vulnerable. Finally, the church has nothing to fear from human inventiveness. It is not always essential to look back to analogies with the sun. Even the ordinary fluorescent lamp can evoke a sense of the transcendent, and the agnostic can help us in such perceptions of the divine.

Originally, I had thought of ending this essay by quoting two of Dante's uses of the theme of light. His *Divine Comedy* ends with a clear perception of the Light Eternal as Trinity and limned with our own image, even though a few cantos earlier he had already subverted that image with his vision of the divine unity as a light so intense that it sears his eyes and forces him to close them in wonder.[53] But more appropriate in a volume about relations between science and religion are these lines from a 2009 pop song: "Science broke the news: the only absolute is light. . . . Wasn't that the message of the star on Christmas night?"[54]

The light of science and the Christmas light have after all their common source in God as both Creator and Redeemer.

53. *Paradiso*, XXXIII, 124-85; XXVIII, 16-19.
54. "Earth: The Story So Far" on the Prefab Sprout album *Let's Change the World with Music* (Sony, 2009).

"Let There Be Light!":
A Byzantine Theology of Light

John Behr

"Let there be Light!" So speaks God at the beginning of the narration of our creation. After further decrees, establishing the heavens and the earth, the waters and the dry lands, the plants and the animals, God announces his project, revealing his intent and goal: "Let us make the human being *(anthropos)* in our image, after our likeness." After making males and females, God then rests from his work.

"Let there be light!" Recapitulating the beginning in the prologue to his Gospel, the evangelist John is more specific: it is Christ, the Word of God, who is "the true light, coming into the world, illumining every human being" *(anthropos,* John 1:9). While "God is Light and in Him is no darkness at all" (1 John 1:5), the Son of God is the "Light that shines in the darkness, and the darkness has not overcome it" (John 1:4), and is therefore "true Light of true Light" (Nicaea). The luminosity of God is a common proclamation of the New Testament. Although God "dwells in light unapproachable" (1 Tim. 6:16), nevertheless this light has now become manifest in Christ, or more specifically, through the gospel: "the god of this world has blinded the minds of the unbelievers, to keep them from seeing the light of the gospel of the glory of Christ, who is the likeness of God. . . . It is the God who said, 'Let light shine out of darkness,' who has shone in our hearts to give the light of the knowledge of the glory of God in the face of Christ" (2 Cor. 4:4-6).

It would be easy, but facile, to contrast this emphasis on light in the New Testament with the "thick darkness" penetrated by Moses as he ascended to the place "where God was" (Exod. 20:21). The Old Testament also uses the imagery of light (e.g., Exod. 24:9-14, a passage used by Evagrius to describe the radiance of God; Num. 12:8; Isa. 58:8); and recent studies on Second Temple Judaism, inter-Testamental writings, and later Jewish writings have made us more aware of the importance of the "glory," the "presence," the "throne," and the "chariot" of God for certain strands of Jewish spirituality. Moreover, even within the Old Testament, the import of these terms is significantly qualified: "Even the darkness is not dark to Thee, the night is bright as the day, for darkness is light with Thee" (Ps. 139:12).

1. The Byzantine Vision of the Light of Tabor

The use of the language of light, divine light, to describe the encounter with, and vision of, God is, as is well known, pervasive throughout the Eastern Christian spiritual tradition, culminating in the councils of Constantinople in the fourteenth century, the defining moment of Byzantine hesychasm. The light beheld by the hesychasts, it was affirmed, is the very light that shone from Christ in his transfiguration on Mt. Tabor, and this is nothing other than the eschatological light of the Kingdom to come, a light that transfigures the visionary and all creation. According to St. Gregory Palamas, the leading apologist for the hesychasts, once the intellect has stripped itself of all props and supports, through mental and physical asceticism, it has nothing else on which to rest its activity apart from God, and is thus graced by the illumination of God, seeing the divine light and becoming light in that vision:

> For it is in light that the light is seen, and that which sees operates in a similar light, since this faculty has no other way in which to work. Having separated itself from all other beings, it becomes itself all light, and is assimilated to what it sees, or rather, it is united to it without mingling, being itself light and seeing light through light. If it sees itself, it sees light; if it beholds the object of its vision, that too is light; and if it looks at the means by which it sees, again it is light. For such is the character of the union, that all is one, so that he who sees can distinguish neither the means nor the object nor its nature, but simply has the awareness of being light and of seeing a light distinct from every creature.[1]

---

1. Gregory Palamas, *The Triads* 2.3.36 (trans. pp. 65-66), J. Meyendorff, ed., in *Gregoriou tou Palama Syggrammata*, ed. P. Christou, vol. 1 (Thessalonika, 1962); partial trans. N. Gendle, Classics of Western Spirituality (Mahwah, NJ: Paulist, 1983). Page numbers, when given, refer to this translation.

In this mystical experience, the subject, the object, the means of vision, are all light, and, one might say, all one in the light: in the vision of this divine uncreated light, everything is illumined and becomes light in the union with light.

For Palamas, as grace is granted to both the intellect and the body, the divine light should be seen equally by both. The transfiguration of Christ was the paradox of the vision of the uncreated light by created eyes: "Whilst it is not a sensible light, the apostles were counted worthy to perceive it with their eyes, but by power other than that of the sense" (*Triad* 1.3.28). Similarly:

> The disciples would not even have seen the symbol, had they not first received eyes they did not possess before. As John of Damascus puts it, "From being blind men, they began to see," and to contemplate this uncreated light. The light, then, became accessible to their eyes, but to eyes which saw in a way superior to that of natural sight, and which had acquired the spiritual power of the spiritual light. This mysterious light, inaccessible, immaterial, uncreated, deifying, eternal, this radiance of the divine nature, this glory of the divinity, this beauty of the heavenly kingdom, is at once accessible to sense perception and yet transcends it. (*Triad* 3.1.22, p. 80)

We are to see the divine light of God's self-revelation with our actual bodily eyes, but our eyes as they will have been transfigured by the Spirit; the immaterial light of God will be seen by material eyes, but through a power other than the natural power of vision.

And finally, as the divine light is the revelation of God himself (in his energies, rather than his essence — a conceptual distinction rather than separation), so also the light that shone on Tabor is the same as the light that will shine in the Kingdom to come. As Palamas writes:

> Is it not clear that the divine light is always one and the same, whether it be that which the apostles saw on Tabor, or that which purified souls now see, or that of the very reality of eternal blessedness to come? That is why the great Basil called the light which blazed on Tabor at the transfiguration of our Lord, a prelude to the glory of Christ in his second coming. (*Triad* 1.3.43)

It is the eschatological light of the Kingdom, which is already anticipated in this life. But in this present life, we only receive the vision of light as a pledge of the full vision to come:

This light at present shines in part, as a pledge, for those who through impassibility have passed beyond all that is condemned and through pure and immaterial prayer have passed beyond all that is pure. But on the last day, it will deify in a manifest fashion "the sons of the resurrection" who will rejoice in eternity and in glory in communion with him who has endowed our nature with a glory and splendour that is divine. (*Triad* 2.3.66, p. 67)

Palamas has a very keen sense of the inauguration of the eschatological kingdom; we are to participate in the eschatological life within this present life. The light of Tabor is the same light that illumines the hesychasts and others, who are therefore already living the eschatological life, anticipating here and now the resurrection with Christ, and this is something that is shared, already now, with the body.[2]

Two comments need to be made regarding this discourse of divine light. First, it should not be taken "literally." Palamas certainly insists on the reality of the divine light, seen and experienced by the saints of the church. But he also provides an important qualification regarding the term itself. When he reflects on the language that he is using, Palamas intimates that while the divine light itself is not to be understood as an image or a symbol of something else (but is the very encounter with God in and through his energies), the language that we use to express that experience should be taken symbolically. He begins this way:

Beyond the stripping away of beings, or rather after the cessation [of our perceiving or thinking of them] accomplished not only in words, but in reality, there remains an unknowing which is beyond knowledge; though indeed a darkness, it is yet beyond radiance, and, as the great Dionysius says, it is in this dazzling darkness that the divine things are given to the saints.

---

2. Cf. Palamas, *Hagioretic Tome* 6.10: "For if in the age to come the body is to share with the soul in ineffable blessings, then it is evident that in this world as well it will also share according to its capacity in the grace mystically and ineffably bestowed by God upon the purified intellect, and it will experience the divine in conformity with its nature. For once the soul's passible aspect is transformed and sanctified — but not reduced to a deathlike condition — through it the dispositions and activities of the body are also sanctified, since body and soul share a conjoint existence." *The Philokalia*, trans. G. E. H. Palmer, P. Sherrard, and K. Ware, vol. 4 (London: Faber & Faber, 1993).

That is, apophaticism leads to a union with God beyond knowing and un-knowing, in a darkness that is beyond light — a dazzling darkness. How-ever, to communicate this, we must have recourse to the words and expressions we have previously left behind. So Palamas continues:

> Thus the perfect contemplation of God and divine things is not simply an abstraction; but beyond this abstraction, there is a participation in divine things, a gift and a possession rather than just a process of nega-tion. But these possessions and gifts are ineffable: if one speaks of them, one must have recourse to images and analogies, not because that is the way in which these things are seen, but because one cannot adumbrate what one has seen in any other way.[3]

The theology of divine things, reality beyond expression, is expressed by Palamas in terms of light, not because this is what is actually seen, but be-cause one must have recourse to images and analogies (παραδειγματικῶς καὶ κατὰ ἀναλογίαν) to speak about ineffable things.

Palamas therefore recognizes that the transcendence of God relativizes the language that we use of him. This is an insight that seems to dovetail very much with the observation of Wittgenstein (though stated rather provocatively): "If we construe the grammar of the expression of sensation on the model of 'object and name,' the object drops out of con-sideration as irrelevant."[4] Experience is private; the language that we use of it, to be understandable, must be common, and therefore regulated by principles other than correspondence between the term and the experi-ence itself (should such even be possible).

This brings us to the second point that must be noted. For all the talk of divine light in later Byzantium, we should not forget the content of this. What this is was made clear by a figure from a few centuries before Palamas, St. Symeon the New Theologian, who more than any other figure wrote ex-tensively about his own experiences and the visions of light that he was granted.[5] In one of these accounts, he describes how his earlier experiences

3. Trans. I.iii.18, p. 36: Ἄρρητα δέ ἐστι τὰ λήμματα καὶ τὰ δόματα ἐκεῖνα, διὸ κἂν λέγωσι περὶ αὐτῶν, ἀλλὰ παραδειγματικῶς καὶ κατὰ ἀναλογίαν, οὐχ ὡς ὁρωμένων ἐκείνοις τούτων, οὰβυτως, ἀλλ' ὡς μὴ πεφυκότων ἄλλως δειχθῆναι τῶν ἐκείνοις ὁρωμένων.

4. L. Wittgenstein, *Philosophical Investigations*, trans. G. E. M. Anscombe (Oxford: Ba-sil Blackwell, 1968), vol. 1, p. 293.

5. Though, as with all autobiographical recollections, the context for recollecting is im-portant. See J. McGuckin, "Symeon the New Theologian (d. 1022) and Byzantine Monasti-cism," in A. Bryer and M. Cunningham, *Mount Athos and Byzantine Monasticism*, Papers

of the divine light always seemed incomplete, and how he was encouraged by his spiritual father to enter into a dialogue with the light: in his next vision of the divine light, he approached the light and "asked the One whom he saw: 'My God, is it you?' He replied and said, 'Yes, I am God who became man for your sake, and behold, I have made you, and I will make you into a god.'"[6] What ultimately matters for Symeon is not the light as light, but who the light is: appearing as Light is Christ himself, the Incarnate God. Eastern Christian spirituality is not photocentric, but fundamentally Christocentric. It is, again, the scriptural language of light that provides the common vocabulary for speaking of our encounter with God in Christ.

2. The Hermeneutics of Tabor

That the divine light coming into the world is tied to the Incarnation, the coming of Christ, is clear, as is the apparent reason for focusing on the transfiguration on Tabor as the paradigmatic moment or event for this revelation. But what is meant by this is, paradoxically, not clear, or at least needs to be unpacked further. There are two aspects that I would like to explore: first, the exegetical dimension in which the light of God is seen; and second, the connection between the command of God — "Let there be light" — and the design of God, to make human beings (*anthropos*) in his image. These two aspects will challenge the way in which we understand the direction of the "incarnational" movement and the direction in which the light shines.

When we speak of "Incarnation" we usually mean the assuming of human nature by a divine person, through his birth from a virgin, to become present among us and as one of us. However, it is striking that this is not

from the Twenty-Eighth Spring Symposium of Byzantine Studies, Birmingham, March 1994, ed. R. N. Swainson (Variorum, 1996), pp. 17-35; "St Symeon the New Theologian (969-1022): Byzantine Spiritual Renewal in Search of a Precedent," in *The Church Retrospective*, ed. R. N. Swainson, Studies in Church History, 33 (Ecclesiastical History Society, 1997), pp. 75-90; "The Luminous Vision in Eleventh-Century Byzantium: Interpreting the Biblical and Theological Paradigms of St Symeon the New Theologian," in *Work and Worship at the Theotokos Evergetis 1050-1200*, ed. M. Mullet and A. Kirby, Belfast Byzantine Texts and Translations, 27 (Belfast, 1997), pp. 90-123.

6. *Ethical Treatise* 5.287-316; Greek text in *Sources chrétiennes* 122, 129; trans. A. Golitzin, *On the Mystical Life* vols. 1-2 (SVS, 1995, 1996). See also *Catechesis* 36. 208ff.; Greek text in *Sources chrétiennes* 96, 104, 113; trans. C. J. de Catanzaro, Classics of Western Spirituality (New York/London, 1980).

known until after his passion, when he is no longer known according to the flesh but according to the Spirit (cf. 2 Cor. 5:16). This is most clear in the Synoptics (I'll return to John later): here, the disciples, despite having been with Christ for a number of years, seeing him transfigured on Tabor, working miracles, hearing his teaching (and whatever they heard from his mother about the circumstances of his birth) — despite all this, they abandon Christ at his Passion. Peter even denies him. Nor do they understand when they discover the empty tomb (an empty tomb is ambiguous after all). Nor even when they encounter the risen Christ on the road to Emmaus do they know him; in fact, they start to tell this stranger all that had happened and how some of their crowd had found the tomb empty (Luke 24). The disciples are usually depicted in the Synoptics as being rather slow to understand; but this time, their lack of understanding really defies belief, earning a sharp reproof for them and making an important point for us. Only when the "stranger" opens the Scriptures to show how the Christ had to suffer these things to enter into his glory do their hearts start to warm, and then after they persuade him to stay the night their eyes are finally opened in the breaking of bread. But at this point, he disappears from sight! Once they finally recognize him, finally know him to be the Son of God, the crucified and exalted Lord, he passes from their gaze. Christ was, is, and remains the "coming one," whose coming, whose presence, whose *parousia,* coincides with his passage, his *transitus,* his exodus, leaving us a trace: "through him you sought us when we were not seeking you, but you sought us that we might begin to seek you" as Augustine put it in his *Confessions.* Seeking him in this way, Christians from the beginning strive forward to meet the coming one, and in so doing, become conformed to his image, so that their bodies are transformed to the stature of his glorious body (cf. Phil. 3:20-21, etc.).

The starting point, then, for seeing Christ, the true Light, is the passion. The God who said "Let there be light" reveals his glory in the face of Christ through the light of the gospel (2 Cor. 4:4-6). Christ is not known (nor the light of God seen) through the usual methods of human knowledge — scientific analysis, historical inquiry, or philosophical reflection: these are inadequate when the desired object of knowledge is God, for God is not subject to human perception, whether physical or mental, but shows himself as and when he wills, just as the risen Christ comes and goes at his own pleasure, and, as we have seen, disappears from sight once he is recognized. It is, rather, as the one spoken of by the Scriptures and in the breaking of bread that the disciples come to recognize Jesus as the Christ, the

John Behr

Son of God, the Lord of glory.[7] And it is in terms drawn from the Scriptures (the Law, the Psalms, and the Prophets) that the evangelists then portray, give flesh to, the Christ they proclaim in the (canonical) Gospels.

Although the imagery of light does not play a significant role in the description of the Passion, the first writer to give considered space to the Transfiguration, the topos *par excellence* of the Byzantine theology of light, interprets this event in exactly the exegetical mode that we have just seen: the opening of the Scriptures to speak of Christ. According to Origen, when the disciples, seeing the Son of God on the mountain speaking with Moses, understood that it was he who said "A man shall not see my face and live" (Exod. 33:20), they were unable to endure the radiance of the Word, and so fell on their faces, humbling themselves under the hand of God. However, he continues,

> . . . after the touch of the Word, lifting up their eyes they saw Jesus only and no other. Moses, the Law, and Elijah, the prophetic element, became one only with the Gospel of Jesus; and they did not remain three as they formerly were, but the three became one.[8]

The vision of the transfigured Jesus, the Taboric light, is to see the Law and the Prophets no longer as something else, but one with the gospel of Jesus. It should also be recalled that the subject of discussion with Moses and Elijah upon the mountain was nothing other than Christ's "exodus," his *transitus* or departure, which he was to accomplish at Jerusalem (Luke 9:31).

The exegetical dimension of the Transfiguration, the divine light shining from the one of whom the Scriptures speak, is explored further in the fifteenth chapter of Origen's *Philokalia,* the anthology of his works prepared by Basil the Great and Gregory the Theologian.[9] To those who are

7. These are the two things, the context and the nourishment of the Christian tradition, that Paul specifically states that he has received and hands down or "traditions." Cf. 1 Cor. 11:23, 15:3.

8. Origen, *Commentary on Matthew* 12.43. *Origenes Matthäuserklärung,* I, *Die griechisch erhaltenen Tomoi,* ed. E. Benz and E. Klostermann, GCS 40, Origenes Werke, 10, two parts (Leipzig: Hinrichs Verlag, 1935, 1937); partial trans. in ANF 10 (1887; repr. Grand Rapids: Eerdmans, 1986), pp. 413-512.

9. *The Philocalia of Origen,* ed. J. A. Robinson (Cambridge: Cambridge University Press, 1893); ed., French trans., introduction, and notes M. Harl, *Origène: Philocalie, 1-20; Sur les Écritures, Sources chrétiennes* 302 (Paris: Cerf, 1983); trans. G. Lewis (Edinburgh: T. & T. Clark, 1911). Cf. J. Behr, *The Way to Nicaea,* The Formation of Christian Theology, vol. 1 (Crestwood, NY: St. Vladimir's Seminary Press, 2001), pp. 169-83.

not ready to ascend the mountain with Christ, but are attracted by the beauty of human words, such as the teachings of philosophers, rather than the Word of God, Origen says, Christ only shows "the foolishness of the preaching," so that because of this apparent foolishness they say "we saw him and he had not form nor beauty" (*Phil.* 15.18; 1 Cor. 1:21; Isa. 53:2). But to those who by following him have received the strength to ascend the mountain, he appears in a "more divine form," and those capable of such vision are indeed a "Peter, allowing the Church to be built in them by the Word" (*Phil.* 15.18). Origen then continues:

> Down below the Word has other garments; they are not white, they are not as the light. If you ascend the high mountain, you will see his light as well as his garments. The garments of the Word are the phrases of Scripture; these words are the clothing of the divine thoughts. As then down below he appears different, but having ascended he is transfigured, his face having become as the sun, so it is with his clothing, so it is with the garments, when you are below, they do not shine, they are not white, but if you ascend, you will see the beauty and the light of the garments, and will marvel at the transfigured face of Jesus. (*Phil.* 15.19)

To see the Lord transfigured in glory, the divine light of Tabor, is to no longer look upon Christ as merely human or in a merely human manner (as he was known before the Passion), but to read the Scriptures (the Old Testament), his garments, and see there the transfigured face of Jesus, no longer merely reading the words but understanding or perceiving their divine content. It is only through the flesh, the garments of the Word, that the divinity of the Word is made manifest, but only when they are understood and interpreted in a God-befitting manner and not in a merely human manner. Thus Origen continues:

> For we are told of what was said there and considered to be the Word of God, the Word made flesh, and who, as regards being God with God, emptied himself. Wherefore we see the Word of God humanly on earth, for he became man; for always in the Scriptures the Word became flesh, so that he might dwell among us. But if we recline on the bosom of the Word made flesh and are able to follow him when he ascends the lofty mountain, we shall say, "We saw his glory." (*Phil.* 15.19)

Those able to contemplate the Word in this manner, ascending Tabor or lying on his breast, "see his transfiguration in every Scripture," both those

John Behr

in which Jesus appears to the multitude in the literal sense of the text (where he has "become flesh"), and when he is transfigured on the mountain, and this, Origen concludes, "is the work of the highest and most sublime sense, containing the oracles of the wisdom hidden in a mystery, which 'God foreordained before the worlds unto the glory of his righteous ones'" (*Phil.* 15.19; cf. 1 Cor. 2:7). Jesus thus appears in a variety of forms, Origen notes, although this only refers "to the different periods of his life, to anything he did before the Passion and whatever happened after his Resurrection from the dead" (*Phil.* 15.20): that is, the unchanging identity of the Word of God is revealed through the cross, and everything else is understood as patterned upon this.

One further point of Origen's hermeneutical approach should be noted, i.e., that he insists that this illumination of the Scriptures by the light of the risen Christ, an exegetical dynamic illustrated by the event of the Transfiguration, is retrospective. Only in hindsight can Christians turn back to the Law and the Prophets to see them speaking of Christ, and so be illumined by the light of the gospel revealing the glory of the God who said "let there be light" shining in the face of Christ:

> Before the sojourn of Christ, the Law and the Prophets did not contain the proclamation that belongs to the definition of the Gospel, since he who explained the mysteries in them had not yet come. But since the Savior has come and has caused the Gospel to be embodied, he has by the Gospel made all things as Gospel.[10]

Not only does the light of God shine through the gospel in this manner, but in doing so, it causes all to be gospel, just as the Byzantine writers described how, in the light, all appears as light.

3. "It Is Finished"

Until the middle of the fourth century the church did not celebrate the crucifixion as a separate event from the resurrection as if they were two distinct actions or events, as if Christ died because he was human, but be-

10. Origen, *Commentary on John* 1.33, French trans., C. Blanc, ed., *Sources chrétiennes* 120 (Paris: Cerf, 1966); trans. R. E. Heine, *Origen: Commentary on the Gospel according to Saint John,* Fathers of the Church 80 (Washington, DC: Catholic University of America Press, 1989).

cause he is God he is able to get himself out of the grave — that would rend apart the inner unity of the Passion/Pascha, and separate the humanity and divinity of Christ in an unacceptable manner. It is rather by his death as a human being that Christ destroyed death; it is his humiliation that is his exaltation, the Pauline paradox that is made most clear in the Gospel of John. Even now, when the Christian tradition has, as it were, refracted the pure white light of the Lord's Passion into a spectrum of colors at the various events commemorated in Holy Week, it is still the victory on the cross that is celebrated at Pascha, Christ's trampling down death by death.[11]

This means that it is by his most human action, an action that expresses all the weakness and impotence of our created nature, that Christ shows himself to be God. Retrospectively (for at the time, the disciples abandoned Christ), once the Scriptures were opened and the bread broken, the cross of Christ, his death, is the revelation of God upon this earth. Christ shows us what it is to be divine by the manner in which he undergoes the only thing that we, as human beings, all have in common — death. He comes to us in his departure, and in doing so enables us to use the fact of our death (a given of the life into which we are born without choice) as the means of making Christ present now in this world, through a freely chosen sacramental death in baptism and a life of witness *(martyria)* thereafter.[12]

"It is finished" (John 19:30). Perhaps now we can hear the full scope of these words of Christ from the cross in the Gospel of John (and only there — in this "spiritual gospel" written by "the theologian"). The work of God is complete; and the one we now know as God rests from his works, in the tomb on the blessed Sabbath. Not only is he known as God, but as "the im-

---

11. The same point can be made from iconography. The images depicting the crucifixion throughout the early Christian period consistently depict the crucified Christ with a rigid body and eyes wide open, not because they were unable to depict a dead corpse (as usually assumed by art historians), but to make the theological point that the crucified one is the triumphant Lord: the cross itself is taken simultaneously as a reference to the crucifixion and to the risen Christ. Images of the "Anastasis" — the resurrection, appear only from about the seventh century (and then, it is not a depiction of Christ getting out of the tomb, but of the descent of Christ to raise up humanity, often mistakenly called the descent into Hades); a couple of centuries later Christ begins to be depicted dead on the cross, though the inscription, in Byzantine iconography, then reads "The Lord of Glory."

12. On the connections that lead from the tomb to the womb, from the Passion of Christ (on the 14 Nissan = March 25) to his birth (on December 25), and our (re)birth in the Virgin Mother, the church, see J. Behr, *The Mystery of Christ: Life in Death* (Crestwood, NY: St. Vladimir's Seminary Press, 2006), ch. 4.

age of the invisible God" he is, finally, the true human being on earth: "Behold the man" *(anthropos),* as Pilate unwittingly affirmed (John 19:5).

This connection between the completion of God's creative act, forming the human being, through a death in witness to Christ, to be born into the light and finally become human, is strikingly clear in the writings of St. Ignatius of Antioch. On his way to be martyred in Rome, he urges the Christians there not to interfere with his impending trial, not to try to get him freed from his martyrdom, but rather to keep silence: "For if you are silent concerning me, I am a word of God; but if you love my flesh, I shall be only a cry" *(Rom.* 2.1). Undergoing death in witness to Christ, the "perfect man" *(Smyrn.* 4.2) or the "new man" *(Eph.* 20), is a birth into a new life, to emerge as Christ himself, a full human being:

> It is better for me to die in Christ Jesus than to be king over the ends of the earth. I seek him who died for our sake. I desire him who rose for us. The pains of birth are upon me. Suffer me, my brethren; hinder me not from living, do not wish me to die. Do not give to the world one who desires to belong to God, nor deceive him with material things. Suffer me to receive the pure light; when I shall have arrived there, I shall become a human being *(anthropos).* Suffer me to follow the example of the passion of my God. *(Rom.* 6)

Entering through his passion into the light, the light of God's completed creation, Ignatius will also become a word of God and human being, of a stature that can only be attained by following the example of Christ (cf. Eph. 4:13). "The glory of God is a living human being, and the life of a human being is to see God," as St. Irenaeus of Lyons put it,[13] speaking of the martyr, who by his confession of Christ no longer lives by this world, but by the light that God has shone into the darkness, illuminating every human being (John 1:9). In this light, if we have the eyes to see, all will indeed appear as light.

---

13. St. Irenaeus of Lyons, *Against the Heresies* 4.20.7.

Light in the Thought of St. Augustine

Robert Dodaro, O.S.A.

Augustine has long been regarded in the Roman Catholic tradition as the "Doctor of Grace" and the "Doctor of Charity," because his teachings are recognized as foundational for later Western Christian doctrine concerning these themes. More recently, however, the French scholar Pierre-Thomas Camelot has called Augustine the "Doctor of Light."[1] Camelot explains that Augustine proposed an original interpretation of the concept of light *(lux, lumen)* in relation to God, creation, and the human being, one that was also highly influential in the Western Christian tradition. In this chapter I will summarize three aspects of Augustine's doctrine: (1) God as Father, Son, and Holy Spirit in relation to light; (2) the relationship of light to spiritual and material reality; and (3) the relationship of light to human intelligence. Before presenting this summary, however, I should offer some clarification of Augustine's use of the two Latin words that convey the English term "light": *lux* and *lumen.* Moreover, it will be useful to speak briefly about the sources of Augustine's reflection on light in relation to God, creation, and human intelligence.

Out of the over 5 million words that comprise the concordance of Augustine's works, the term *lux* and its inflected forms is used around 2720 times, and *lumen* around 1560 times.[2] As one familiar with Augustine's opus would expect, the terms are found with the greatest frequency in the following works: *Confessiones* (the classic account of his conversion to God), *De trinitate* (his major teaching on the Trinity), *De Genesi ad*

---

1. Pierre-Thomas Camelot, "Lumière. II: Etude patristique (jusqu'au 5e siècle)," in *Dictionnaire de spiritualité, ascetique et mystique,* vol. 9 (Paris: Beauchesne, 1976), cols. 1149-58.

2. See the CD-ROM, Corpus Augustinianum Gissense 2.

litteram (his commentary on Genesis), *De ciuitate dei* (his major teaching on the meaning of human history), *Enarrationes in Psalmos* (his commentary on the Psalms), and *In Iohannem euangelium tractatus* (his commentary on the Gospel of John), but also in two lesser-known essays of his, *De uidendo Deo* (an essay on seeing God) and *De praesentia Dei* (an essay on the presence of God). In general, the Latin term *lux* designates the more fundamental concept of "light," whereas *lumen* expresses "light" in the sense of a lamp or lantern or some other means of transmitting light, or of daylight.[3] Augustine, however, adapts his own usage to that of the Old Latin translation of the Bible, where the distinction between the terms is less clear, resulting in his use of *lux* and *lumen* interchangeably.[4]

Principal sources for Augustine's teachings regarding the theme of light are both philosophical and biblical.[5] Plato and Plotinus figure prominently among theorists of a worldview founded on the concept of light (φῶς). Plato's representation of the sun as the Good (*Republic* 6-7 passim) and, therefore, as the source and end of human knowledge (*Republic* 6,5057b-511a), and Plotinus's development of this epistemic theory (*Enneads* 5,3 [49], 7ff.), along with his identification of the first hypostasis, the One, with the light (*Enneads* 5,6 [24], 4), are examples of Greek philosophical treatments of light that strongly influence Augustine.[6] Moreover, Augustine seems to be aware of, and to subscribe to, one of the theories of vision from Greek philosophy. Briefly, according to Augustine, the eyes emit a flux of rays, and the sense of sight issues from the eye as from a lantern. The theory can be traced to Aristotle (*Sense and the Sensible* 437a-b),[7]

---

3. See W. Ehlers, "lumen," in *Thesaurus Linguae Latinae*, vol. 7/2, 1956-79, cols. 1810-23; "lux," in *Thesaurus Linguae Latinae*, vol. 7/2, 1956-79, cols. 1904-17.

4. So argues Marie-Anne Vannier, "*Lumen, lux*," in *Augustinus-Lexikon*, vol. 3, ed. Cornelius Mayer (Basel: Schwabe, forthcoming). I thank the *Redaktion* of the *Augustinus-Lexikon* at the *Zentrum für Augustinus Forschung*, Würzburg, Germany, for permitting me access to this unpublished article.

5. Patristic sources were also influential and will be mentioned *infra*. Also, I shall present arguments below that the Manicheans also influenced Augustine's concept of God as light.

6. See Vannier, "*Lumen, lux*." In the case of Plato, much of this influence upon Augustine is indirect and came to him through philosophical encyclopedias, not from his direct contact with the texts. See also Ronald H. Nash, "Some Philosophic Sources of Augustine's Illumination Theory," *Augustinian Studies* 2 (1971): 47-66.

7. See Augustine, *Gn. litt.* 1,16,31; 7,14,20; *s.* 362, 20: "Quid est ictus oculi? Non quo palpebris claudimus oculum vel aperimus: sed ictum dicit oculi emissionem radiorum ad aliquid cernendum." All abbreviations of Augustine's works are taken from *Augustinus-Lexikon*, vol. 1, ed. C. P. Mayer (Basel: Schwabe, 1986-), cols. xxvi-xl.

but it was first propounded by Empedocles (31B84 DK) and subsequently was refined by Plato (*Timaeus* 45b-d) and Aristotle (*Sense and the Sensible* 437-38), among others. On the other hand, Augustine rejects the theory of contraction and emission, which he understood as being described by the Greek Church Father Basil of Caesarea.[8]

The Bible, too, offered Augustine a series of significant theological reflections on light in relation to the divine nature and to creation. For example, at Genesis 1:3, "God said let there be light," while Micah 7:8 refers to the Lord as light. Most important among biblical texts for Augustine's teaching, however, were those verses of the Psalms treating the theme of light, in particular, Psalm 27:1: "God is my light"; Psalm 33:6: "come to him and be enlightened"; Psalm 35:10: "in your light we shall see light"; Psalm 66:2: "may he cause the light of his countenance to shine upon us"; and Psalm 138:11: "night shall be my light."[9] Among New Testament sources, the Gospel of John was the most important for Augustine's teaching, in particular, 1:4 "In him [i.e., the divine Word] there was life, and that life was the light of men," and 1:9 "There is one who enlightens every soul born into the world; he was the true light." Finally, Augustine also frequently cited 1 John 1:5: "God is light."

1. God as Light

When Augustine states in his commentary on Genesis that God is "unchanging and incorporeal light"[10] he is challenging a Manichean conception of god as light to which he had subscribed for nine years while he was a young man. According to this view, the divine essence consists in a material light, albeit one that is infinitely supple. This Manichean god of light was said to be engaged at all times in an active struggle against the influence of an equal and opposite god of darkness, one that was responsible for evil in the world.[11] Manicheans explained that the god of light

8. See Augustine, *Gn. litt.* 1,16,31. I am indebted to Dr. Ernesto Paparazzo of the Istituto di struttura della materia of the Italian Consiglio Nazionale delle Ricerche for his collaboration in the writing of this paragraph.

9. See Camelot, "Lumière," c. 1156.

10. See Augustine, *Gn. litt.* 1,1,3: ". . . incommutabile atque incorporale lumen, quod Deus est."

11. See R. J. Connelly, "Light and Reality in Saint Augustine," *Modern Schoolman* 56 (1979): 239; Byard Bennett, "*Iuxta unum latus erat terra tenebrarum:* The Division of Pri-

was able to extend itself to all inferior beings by means of participation.[12] The material component of this participation was responsible for a form of pantheism: god as light was materially present to some extent in all reality. Augustine acknowledges in his *Confessiones* that, while he was a Manichean, he believed in a form of this pantheism, a position he rejected only once he was able to conceive of God in terms of a spiritual (i.e., non-material) substance.[13]

Although Manichean cosmology clearly reflects the conflict between the twin gods of light and of darkness, as Augustine reports, he is nevertheless rightly accused of hardening the dualistic features of this conflict in his writings against Manichean religious belief.[14] Recent research demonstrates that Manicheans prayed exclusively to the god of light, so that Manichean theology, in the end, is monotheistic.[15] Thus, when Augustine insists in his anti-Manichean writings that God's light is unchangeable and utterly distinct from all visible, material forms of light, he also intends to distance his idea of God as light from the Manichean concept.[16] Nevertheless, the divergence between the two views does not negate the fact that Augustine's formulation of his position owes something for its inspiration to his long-term exposure to Manichean theology.[17]

If, for Augustine, God is light, then the Father, the Son, who is Christ, and the Holy Spirit are each the same light.[18] But whereas Augustine holds

---

mordial Space in Anti-Manichaean Writers' Descriptions of the Manichaean Cosmogony," in *The Light and the Darkness: Studies in Manichaeism and Its World*, ed. P. Mirecki and J. BeDuhn (Leiden: Brill, 2001), pp. 68-78. See also Erich Feldmann, *Der Einfluß des Hortensius und des Manichäismus auf das Denken des jungen Augustinus von 373*, vol. 1, unpublished dissertation, Universität Münster (Westfalen), 1975, pp. 616-31.

12. See Connelly, "Light and Reality in Saint Augustine," pp. 237-51, at p. 239.

13. For Augustine's views, see *conf.* 4,29; 4,31; 5,19-20; and especially 5,25 and 6,4.

14. See Basil Studer, *The Grace of Christ and the Grace of God in Augustine of Hippo: Christocentrism or Theocentrism?* trans. M. J. O'Connell (Collegeville, MN: Liturgical Press, 1997), p. 97.

15. See Studer, *The Grace of Christ*, p. 97, who cites in support of this conclusion, Erich Feldmann, *Die "Epistula Fundamenti" der nordafrikanischen Manichäer. Versuch einer Rekonstruktion* (Altenberge: Akademische Bibliothek, 1987), p. 39, and Julien Ries, "Dieux cosmiques et dieu biblique dans la religion de Mani," *Augustiniana* 41 (1991): 757-72, at pp. 770-71.

16. See Augustine, *conf.* 7,16: ". . . lucem incommutabilem, non hanc uulgarem et conspicuam omni carni nec quasi ex eodem genere grandior erat . . . non hoc illa erat, sed aliud, aliud ualde ab istis omnibus." See also Augustine, *mor.* 2,11; 2,22; *s. Dolbeau* 25,8.

17. So Studer, *The Grace of Christ*, p. 97.

18. See Augustine, *trin.* 7,4 and 6.

that God's light is inaccessible to human sense perception,[19] he also insists, citing John 1:4, that Christ enlightens the human mind with his divine light.[20] Augustine refers to Christ as the "sun of justice" *(sol iustitiae),* an allusion to the biblical text Malachi 4:2 and a Christian substitute for the Roman god "the unconquered sun" *(sol inuictus).*[21] In this context, he refers to Christ's role in revealing the form of divine justice, the complete content of which remains hidden from human beings prior to the final judgment and their complete redemption from the effects of original sin.[22] In conjunction with Christ's role in revealing the divine light, Augustine treats the expression, "light from light," *(lumen de lumine)* from the creedal statement of the Nicene Council (325 CE).[23] In the first of his works in which he quotes this expression, *De fide et symbolo,* he juxtaposes it with John 1:9 and interprets it as establishing that Christ shared the same divine substance, and therefore the same unchangeable and immaterial light of the Father, and that this fact distinguishes Christ as the divine light from human beings who are enlightened by Christ into a condition of wisdom *(sapientia).*[24]

2. The Relationship of Light to Spiritual and Material Reality

To understand how Christ enlightens the human mind and thus enables it to be wise, some explanation is required of the relationship of divine light to spiritual and material reality in Augustine's thought. To understand this relationship, one has to understand what Augustine thinks happened

---

19. See Augustine, *uid. deo* 44-46, citing 1 Timothy 6:16. The Platonic philosophical background to the affirmations in this text is apparent.

20. See Augustine, *Io. eu. tr.* 1,18, *trin.* 4,3, along with Camelot, "Lumière," c. 1156.

21. On the general background for this treatment of Christ, see Martin Wallraff, *Christus Verus Sol. Sonnenverehrung und Christentum in der Spätantike* (Münster: Aschendorff, 2001).

22. See, for example, Augustine, *ep.* 55,8. On the background to this approach to justice in Augustine, see, in general, Robert Dodaro, *Christ and the Just Society in the Thought of Augustine* (Cambridge: Cambridge University Press, 2004).

23. See Augustine, *f. et symb.* 6; *trin.* 6,2-3; 7,2; 7,4; 15,9; 15,23; *c. s. Arrian.* 9; *Io. eu. tr.* 29,5; 31,4; 34,4; 39,1; 40,3; 71,1, along with Marie-François Berrouard, *"Deus de Deo, Lumen de Lumine,"* in *Œuvres de saint Augustin,* vol. 72: *Homélies sur l'Évangile de saint Jean XXII–XXXIII,* traduction, introduction, et notes par M.-F. Berrouard (Paris: Desclée de Brouwer, 1977), p. 842.

24. See Augustine, *f. et symb.* 6; *trin.* 4,27.

when God said, "Let there be light" (Gen. 1:3). First, however, it is important to remember that prior to reporting these words, Genesis records that
God "created heaven and earth," and "earth was still an empty waste, darkness hung over the deep, but already the breath of God stirred over the waters" (Gen. 1:1-2). Augustine interprets these biblical passages as signifying
that God created original matter from nothing,[25] and that it was of two
kinds: material being (corresponding to the Genesis phrase "an empty
waste") and spiritual being (corresponding to the Genesis phrase "darkness hung over the deep").[26] However, both of these kinds of matter were
unformed, meaning that they did not yet correspond to any identifiable
being, and that they were inherently changeable and prone to degeneration
into nonbeing.[27] By giving this unformed matter a determinate form, God
endowed it with identity and stability.[28] This divine endowment of form
upon an original formless matter is what Augustine believes happened
when God said, "Let there be light."[29]

Augustine reasons, in part, on the basis of John 1:3 ("it was through
him that all things came into being"), that when God said, "Let there be
light," it was Christ as the divine Word through whom God pronounced
these words and thereby brought into existence all spiritual and material
beings (including created, visible light).[30] But because Christ, the divine
Word, is also divine light, the process of creation, which consists in en-
dowing formless matter with form, involves an illumination of every spiritual and material being. Augustine explains that this divine illumination is
responsible for an orientation or conversion of all beings towards God.

25. See Augustine, *uera rel.* 36.

26. See Augustine, *Gn. litt.* 1,1,2-3.

27. See Augustine, *conf.* 12,6; 12,8. Connelly, "Light and Reality in Saint Augustine,"
p. 241. Unformed "matter" is therefore not matter in the sense of material being, but a pre-
condition to material and spiritual being. See the explanation of Connelly, "Light and Reality
in Saint Augustine," p. 240.

28. See Augustine, *conf.* 12,28. However, these two processes — the creation of unformed matter and the bestowal upon it of form — should not be construed as taking place
at two distinct moments in time for Augustine. See Augustine, *conf.* 13,48; 12,40, along with
Connelly, "Light and Reality in Saint Augustine," pp. 241-42.

29. An essential work for understanding Augustine on this point is Marie-Anne
Vannier, *"Creatio," "conversio," "formatio" chez S. Augustin,* 2nd ed. (Fribourg: Presses
Universitaires, 1997).

30. See Augustine, *Gn. litt.* 1,2,6-4,9.

3. The Relationship of Divine Light to Human Intelligence

In rational human beings, the form that conveys this conversion is called wisdom *(sapientia),* because it reflects the divine light which is divine wisdom.[31] At the foundation of Augustine's conception of the illumination of human beings one finds the Platonic principle of participation, by which beings share in the character of their eternal archetypes (forms or ideas).[32] For Augustine, the rational human mind participates in the divine mind through the "forms" *(formae)* or ideas that are impressed in the human mind through divine illumination.[33] In fact, according to Augustine, that the human mind is rational at all is due to divine illumination and the forms that inhere in the mind as a result of it.[34] It is this divine illumination that separates human beings from other animals.[35] Augustine holds that all human intellectual activity, including sensing, imagining, reasoning, knowing, remembering, and believing, all thinking, speaking, and acting, depends upon this illumination.[36]

How does Augustine think the divine illumination of the human mind happens? Key to answering this and related questions is Augustine's reflection on Genesis 1:26, "And God said, 'Let us make man wearing our own image *(imago)* and likeness *(similitudo)*.'" On the basis of this biblical verse, he posits that the forms in the mind of God are different from, while similar to, those in the human mind: they exist in a logically and ontologically prior way in the divine mind and derivatively in the reasoning capacity of the human mind.[37] As Augustine explains this relationship, the created, mutable light of human knowledge is a reflection of the uncreated, divine light.[38] But the relationship between the two sets of forms is more than can be accounted for by a simple likeness. To quote Augustine, "Our illumination is the partaking of the Word, namely of that life which is the

31. On this point, see especially Augustine, *Gn. litt.* 1,9,17; *uera rel.* 66; and *trin.* 7,4-6, along with Connelly, "Light and Reality in Saint Augustine," pp. 243-44.

32. See Plato, *Phaedo* 74a-75d. Cf. Augustine, *trin.* 4,4: "inluminatio quippe nostra participatio uerbi est, illius scilicet uitae quae lux est hominum."

33. Augustine's classical exposition of this principle is found at *diu. qu.* 46.

34. See, for example, Augustine, *ciu.* 11,10; *trin.* 4,3.

35. Augustine, *trin.* 4,3

36. See especially Augustine, *ep.* 120,10.

37. This explanation is offered by Ronald H. Nash, *The Light of the Mind: St. Augustine's Theory of Knowledge* (Lexington: University Press of Kentucky, 1969).

38. See Augustine, *c. Faust.* 20,7.

light of men."[39] Hence, Christ's involvement in human illumination occurs not only in human creation through the divine Word, but in every human intellectual activity that tends towards Truth, whether the individual human being is a Christian or not. In at least one passage of his writings, Augustine dismisses those who deny that certain Platonist philosophers who were not baptized Christians were nevertheless able to perceive "the light of the unchangeable Truth."[40]

However, in the case of Christians, Augustine holds that divine illumination of the human mind is not only cognitive, but moral or spiritual as well, in that it involves a progressive dynamic through which the mind gradually comes to resemble God.[41] In this way, divine illumination describes for Augustine what takes place when the Christian grows in the practice of genuine virtue, especially in relation to righteousness *(iustitia)* or holiness *(sanctitas).* Divine illumination in this context is interchangeable with the Augustinian concept of grace by which the human intellect and will are healed of the impeditory effects of original sin and are thus enabled to seek the highest Good, which, for Augustine, is God.

In this context, too, it is possible to speak in Augustinian terms of the role of the Holy Spirit in divine illumination. We have seen that in describing the function of illumination in cognition, Augustine speaks about Christ as enlightening the human mind so that it arrives at a true judgment. However, when Augustine speaks about divine illumination in conjunction with the Christian's moral or spiritual growth, he treats the activities of both Christ and the Holy Spirit. Thus, for example, when he refers to the Holy Spirit's role as expressed at Romans 5:5 in spreading love *(caritas)* in our hearts, he equates this love with light *(lux).*[42] Specifically, he suggests that the Holy Spirit forms in the minds of believers a delight *(delectatio)* in God as the supreme Good, accompanied by a love *(dilectio)* for God as that Good. Augustine holds that both of these affections, delight and love, draw believers into an ardent desire to participate in the true light, which is God. As a consequence, they seek to live a just and a holy life.[43]

39. Augustine, *trin.* 4,4, alluding to John 1:4.

40. See Augustine, *trin.* 4,20. Augustine grounds his reasoning here on the Scriptures: Habakkuk 2:4; Romans 1:17; Galatians 3:11; Hebrews 10:38; 2 Corinthians 5:7.

41. See Augustine, *trin.* 12,4; *Gn. litt.* 1,5,10, and Connelly, "Light and Reality in Saint Augustine," pp. 246-47.

42. See Augustine, *ep.* 140,54: ". . . profecto caritas lux ipsa est, quae diffunditur in cordibus nostris per spiritum sanctum qui datus est nobis."

43. See Augustine, *spir. et litt.* 5. He also quotes Romans 5:5 in this section in reference

In book 8 of *De trinitate,* Augustine offers an expanded explanation of the process through which the human mind is attracted to God by means of the reflection in it of God's light. In this account he implicitly makes clear that because God is both love (1 John 4:8) and light (1 John 1:5), these terms are interchangeable in reference to God: God's love is his light. For Augustine, this means that when human beings experience love in its correct form *(uera caritas),* as they do when they love their fellow human beings with a love that has the others' best interests at heart (understood as their union with God), they experience in their minds a true reflection of God's light. Augustine states that by loving others in this way, human beings love both others and God at the same time and with the same love with which God loves. Augustine concludes that when human beings love in this manner, they simultaneously dwell in God's light.

This way of proceeding is not an indulgence in poetic thinking on Augustine's part. In drawing out this analysis through several chapters of *De trinitate,* book 8, he presses his readers to focus on the feeling they experience when they love others in the right way. He leads his readers to this point first by posing the question, Why is it that Christians love the apostle Paul?[44] He answers the question by observing that what Christians love about Paul is his just soul *(anima iusta).* Continuing his analysis, he invites his readers to reflect upon the questions "What is justice?" and "How do we recognize it?" He answers that human beings recognize justice when they see it displayed in just persons such as Paul, because all human beings can recognize the "form" of justice when it is mediated to their minds, as it is for Christians in the case of Paul, among others. The mediation of the form of justice to the human mind is a function of divine illumination, as I have explained above. Later, Augustine states that when Christians reflect upon Paul's justice, as they do when they read in Scripture about his just deeds, they burn inwardly *(exardescire)* with love for him.[45] Augustine identifies this sensation with love for the form of justice and, consequently, for God.[46] He says that this sensation is what it is like to dwell in God's

to the Holy Spirit. See also Johannes Jacobus Verhees, *God in Beweging. Een onderzoek naar de pneumatologie van Augustinus* (Wageningen: H. Veenman & Zonen, 1968), pp. 216-17.

44. See Augustine, *trin.* 8,9.

45. See Augustine, *trin.* 8,13.

46. See my discussion of these texts at Dodaro, *Christ and the Just Society,* pp. 157-59. See also Rowan Williams, "*Sapientia* and the Trinity: Reflections on the *De trinitate,*" in *Collectanea Augustiniana. Mélanges T. van Bavel,* ed. B. Bruning et al. (Leuven: Augustinian Historical Institute, 1990), pp. 316-32.

light.[47] Hence, when human beings recognize the feeling that they experience when they love their fellow human beings correctly, they recognize God's love acting in them; specifically, they recognize the reflection of God's light in their own minds. Augustine further identifies this experience of divine light (= divine love) with wisdom.

Arriving at this point in their analysis of Augustine's illumination doctrine, some scholars have then turned their attention to the relationship in his thought between wisdom *(sapientia)* and knowledge *(scientia)*.[48] Ronald Nash concludes that for Augustine the divine ideas in the human mind are a priori and virtual preconditions of *scientia*. They are a priori preconditions insofar as they cannot be derived from experience; they are virtual preconditions in the sense that they are present to the mind even when they are not objects of thought. For Augustine, knowledge is possible only when these divine ideas are applied to sense knowledge.[49] In a later work, Nash reiterates Augustine's view that, taken by itself, the human mind is incapable of recognizing the truth, an act that requires "the constant, immanent and active presence of God."[50]

We have seen that Augustine's treatment of light distinguishes between uncreated light, which he identifies with God, and created light, which he understands in two distinct senses, physical light and the light of the human mind. This latter light is the means by which man carries out all of his intellectual functions, including his moral and spiritual development. Though Augustine calls it created light, he nevertheless holds that it is a reflection of the divine, uncreated light, and that it involves a participation by the human mind in that divine light. Given these assumptions, is Augustine's use of the term "light" in these latter cases metaphorical or analogical? It is clear from his texts that his use of light in speaking of "divine light" or of the "light of the human mind" is not limited to the metaphorical. Augustine is not just saying that God's activity in the human mind works "something like" light works in the physical world. Instead, he posits the reality of divine light and of its reflection in the human mind, and he distinguishes these realities from that of physical light. For Augustine, to say that something is real is to say that it has substance *(substantia)*, but

47. See Augustine, *trin.* 8,12-13. See also Robert Dodaro, "*Deus caritas est* nell'esegesi agostiniana sulla Prima Johannis," *Lateranum* 73 (2007): 333-55.

48. See, for example, Connelly, "Light and Reality in Saint Augustine," pp. 246-47.

49. See Nash, *Light of the Mind*, ch. 8, citing Augustine, *inm. an.* 4.

50. See Ronald H. Nash, *The Word of God and the Mind of Man* (Philadelphia: Presbyterian and Reformed Press, 1992), ch. 8, citing *Gn. litt.* 21,31,59.

this is not to say that it is physical in the sense of our conventional concepts of matter and energy. To a limited extent, Augustine inherited from the neo-Platonists a certain understanding of spiritual substance. He could therefore posit a nonmaterial, nonphysical *substantia* or reality. Understood in this way, both his conceptions of uncreated light and of the divine illumination of the human mind can be understood along the lines of analogies with physical light. He would assume that these analogies are grounded in the revealed biblical teaching that employs terms associated with "light" in order to speak of God and of divine activity in the world. However, Augustine also assumes that scriptural language is figurative and that what this language signifies (the *res* behind the scriptural signs, *signa*) is intentionally shrouded by God to the human intellect. Hence, Scripture provides human beings only with a coded language about divine reality. Nevertheless, Augustine also assumes that scriptural language is based on analogies and that these analogies are true, if partial, representations of the relationship (and not merely of the distinction) between uncreated reality and created reality. Hence, for Augustine, we may not fully understand what Scripture means when it asserts that "God is light"; however, because we know light in a human, i.e., in a physical, empirical way, we possess a true idea (a true analogy) of what God is when we think of God as light, as well as a true idea/analogy of the relationship between divine light and human intellection.

4. By Way of Conclusion

Are there correlations between Augustine's theory of divine illumination and the contemporary physics of light? The first point of connection has to be stated in terms of the "humble approach" exhibited both by Augustine and by certain contemporary physicists who examine light. In another chapter of this volume, Markus Aspelmeyer and Anton Zeilinger suggest that some quantum phenomena are inconsistent with physicists' intuitive understanding of how the world should work, and that these phenomena may require "a change in our epistemology and our ontology." In terms of his theology, whether Augustine is treating the question of God as uncreated light, or the doctrine of divine illumination of the mind, he is careful not to propose more than he believes the limits of knowability allow him to state. Central to Augustine's epistemology is the concept of divine mystery *(sacramentum/mysterium)* that limits the human ability to know anything concerning God in more than a partial way.[51] For example, Augustine admits that he cannot reconcile God's infinite justice with his infinite mercy.[52]

A second connection between Augustine's approach and that of some contemporary physicists can be found in Aspelmeyer and Zeilinger's description of the "observer" in a quantum experiment who can no longer be thought of as existing independently from the phenomena he is observing. The experimenter's choice of measurement instruments radically affects the outcome by determining which properties of a quantum system become reality. Hence, for these physicists the clear distinction between observer and observed reality breaks down to a certain extent; the observer in a sense determines the reality he perceives. In Augustine's thinking there is a similar kind of involvement on the part of the theologian in the doctrine he seeks to define. In a remarkable passage from the closing chapter of *De trinitate*, Augustine candidly acknowledges that the defects in human intellection as a consequence of original sin limit the truth claims of what he (or any theologian) can assert about the Trinity. He concludes that God's grace alone will gradually enable him to readjust his conception of the "rule of faith" that determines for Catholic believers what their faith requires them to believe concerning God. By implication, Augustine is arguing that the ability to perceive the objective standard of Christian dogmatics (the *regula fidei*) is conditioned by the subjective moral condition of the "observer."[53]

---

51. See Robert Dodaro, "Mysterium," in *Augustinus-Lexikon*, vol. 3, ed. C. Mayer (Basel: Schwabe, forthcoming). See also the excellent treatment of this matter by E. Cutrone, "Sacrament," in *Augustine through the Ages: An Encyclopedia*, ed. A. Fitzgerald et al. (Grand Rapids: Eerdmans, 1999), pp. 741-47.

52. See Augustine, *perseu.* 18: "hoc non dico: si quaeris quare; quia fateor me non inuenire quid dicam. si et hoc quaeris quare; quia in hac re sicut iusta est ira eius, sicut magna est misericordia eius, ita inscrutabilia iudicia eius."

53. See Augustine, *trin.* 15,51: "Ad hanc *regulam fidei* dirigens intentionem meam quantum potui, quantum me posse fecisti, quaesiui te et desideraui intellectu uidere quod credidi et multum disputaui et laboraui. domine deus meus, una spes mea, exaudi me ne fatigatus nolim te quaerere, sed quaeram faciem tuam semper ardenter. tu da quaerendi uires, qui inueniri te fecisti et magis magis que inueniendi te spem dedisti. coram te est firmitas et *infirmitas* mea; illam serua, istam sana. coram te est scientia et *ignorantia* mea; ubi mihi aperuisti suscipe intrantem; ubi clausisti aperi pulsanti. meminerim tui; intellegam te; diligam te. auge in me ista donec me reformes ad integrum." *Infirmitas* and *ignorantia* are, for Augustine, the classic, enduring defects of the soul as a consequence of original sin. For an explanation with indication of additional scholarly literature, see Dodaro, *Christ and the Just Society*, pp. 27-30.

Clearly, the most difficult area in Augustine's speculations concerning light is found at the boundary between uncreated and created light insofar as it involves the human mind in divine illumination. With a clear debt to neo-Platonic thought, Augustine employs terms such as illumination *(illuminatio)*, divine indwelling *(inhabitare)*, and participation *(participatio)* to describe the human mind's access to the eternal forms. Augustine thus conceives of human knowing, willing, and loving as transcendent operations that involve the mind in a created light that is influenced by an uncreated light. Clearly, for Augustine, human intellection depends upon uncreated light in a manner analogous to the human being's physical dependence upon sunlight.[54] We saw Augustine develop this theory in his analysis of the feeling of love that one person feels for another. He maintains that when this love is aimed at the other's true good, it is God's love acting in the human heart. Augustine also holds that this divine love is interchangeable with divine (uncreated) light. Hence, human love and divine love interact in the human mind, just as the reflected light of the human mind interacts with the divine light. Augustine cannot explain how these two orders of reality interrelate, but he believes that they do. His theoretical approach to human intellection, based as it is in two distinct orders of light, thus pushes against modern conceptions of realism in an analogous manner to the way that quantum optic physics, as discussed by Aspelmeyer and Zeilinger, pushes against it.

54. This latter point is stressed by Andrew Steane in the chapter he contributed to this volume.

Uncreated Light: From Irenaeus and Torrance to Aquinas and Barth

George Hunsinger

1

Knowing that "God is light" and that "in him there is no darkness at all" (1 John 1:5), and knowing further that the light in which God dwells is an "unapproachable light" (1 Tim. 6:16), Irenaeus of Lyons once wrote this remarkable passage about God:

> He is simple, non-composite, not made up of different members, altogether like and equal to himself, because he is wholly intellect, wholly spirit, wholly mind, wholly thought, wholly reason, wholly hearing, wholly seeing, wholly light, and the whole source of all that is good. That is how persons of religion and piety speak of God. But he is above all these properties too and therefore indescribable. He is rightly called the all-comprehending intellect, but he is not like the intellect of human beings. He is most aptly called "light," but he is nothing like the light we know. (*Against Heresies,* II.13.3-4)[1]

Several points in this passage stand out. First, the idea of divine simplicity seems to be something that Irenaeus can simply take for granted. In

---

1. As found in *The Scandal of the Incarnation,* ed. Hans Urs von Balthasar (San Francisco: Ignatius, 1990), p. 19. Cf. R. M. Grant, *Irenaeus of Lyons* (New York: Routledge, 1997), p. 109.

I would like to thank Gerald O'Collins, Kathryn Tanner, John Bowlin, Keith Johnson, Paul Molnar, Matthew Levering, and Wentzel van Huyssteen for helpful comments as I was drafting this chapter.

other words, as early as the second century, divine simplicity was already an idea that was presupposed by Christian writers without argument, as is evident not only in Irenaeus but also in Clement of Alexandria, Origen, and perhaps Tertullian. From a very early stage it seems to have been accepted by Christian writers that being simple or noncomposite was fundamental to the definition of God's being. Simplicity, we might say, was a "nonmoral" divine attribute distinguishing God from all that he had made.[2] It was an ontological marker separating the created from the uncreated.[3] By definition, God, unlike his creatures, was "simple, noncomposite, not made up of different members."

Second, Irenaeus was also prepared to draw the appropriate metaphysical corollary. If divine essence was essentially simple, then it was necessarily identical with each of its predicates. If these predicates fell into a long list — mentioned were intellect, spirit, thought, reason, hearing, seeing, light, and goodness — then the divine essence would be identical with each of these predicates by virtue of divine simplicity. The predicates could not be understood merely as parts adding up to a larger whole. Given divine simplicity, it would be improper to think about them in quantitative terms. If God was mind, then he was "wholly mind"; if light, then "wholly light"; if goodness, then "wholly goodness."

Third, Irenaeus did not ask whether these predicates would also be identical with each other by virtue of being identical with the divine being. Were they simply expressions of human perception as constrained by the

2. On the other hand, simplicity would not merely be a nonmoral attribute. Without parts, whatever is simple must be immutable, and, by at least some measures, immutability indexes goodness. I owe this point to my colleague John Bowlin.

3. It seems unlikely that second-century Christian writers could have adopted this assumption so readily if it had not already been established in Judaism. There are in fact texts where Philo says or implies that God is simple. While neo-Platonism, in some form, would also be an obvious source, Plotinus at least is ruled out because his dates are too late (c. 204-270 CE). Christopher Stead suggests a possible source in Xenophanes (c. 570-485 BCE). See Stead, *Divine Substance* (Oxford: Oxford University Press, 1977), p. 188. See also the discussion in Rowan Williams, *Arius, Heresy, and Tradition* (Grand Rapids: Eerdmans, 2002), pp. 119-22. Williams points to Philo and to the neo-Pythagoreans as influenced by Plato's *Parmenides* (370 BCE), in which the idea of the One that is indivisible and has no parts appears. It might also be noted that Parmenides himself (c. 520-450 BCE), who may have studied under Xenophanes, defined the One as indivisible and beyond parts, and that Aristotle (384-322 BCE) regarded the "Prime Mover" as a being that was eternal, indivisible, without parts, and without magnitude (*Physics*, VIII; *Metaphysics*, K). In short, since the idea of divine simplicity was in some sense already present in Philo, it probably enjoyed a general and established accessibility for Irenaeus from both Greek and Jewish sources of tradition.

imperfections of finitude, or were they true and actual also for God? Was their metaphysical status real or merely nominal? Augustine and Thomas Aquinas would later accept some version of the nominalist option while Karl Barth would defend the realist view. Irenaeus did clearly assert, however, that the divine operations were identical with each other (*AH* II.13.8).[4]

Fourth, the idea of divine simplicity was regarded as a matter of religion and piety. How Irenaeus understood this connection — i.e., between the simple divine object and piety — is not entirely clear. Did he think that divine simplicity — as a way of differentiating the creature from the Creator — distinguished Christian piety from pagan idolatry? Or did he think that believing in divine simplicity was merely distinctive of Christian piety, while not necessarily unique to it? Did he mean that confusing or combining the being of God with that of the world would be impious? Furthermore, did he regard the radical metaphysical otherness of God as implied in divine simplicity to be a datum given by natural or by divine revelation (i.e., by "general" or "special" revelation)? At a minimum, Irenaeus seemed to claim that a proper religious disposition was not possible apart from some sense of God's metaphysical otherness. "That is how persons of religion and piety speak of God."

Fifth, Irenaeus implied that language about God was irreducibly paradoxical. God was comparable, and yet also incomparable, to any predicates rightly ascribed to him. Predicates of the divine being were accessible to human apprehension but only in the form of pure inaccessibility. They could not properly be ascribed to God without ineffability. They were proper to God, and yet God transcended them absolutely. For example, God was rightly called "all-comprehending intellect" or "light," and yet he was "above all these properties too and therefore indescribable."[5]

Sixth, it followed that language about God was also analogical in some realist sense. Because certain predicates were "rightly" ascribed to God, theological language was not merely equivocal. On the other hand, because God transcended every predicate, neither was it merely univocal. The only alternative would be that theological language was somehow analogical, and that the analogies were at once appropriate while yet also being inadequate. Although inherently inadequate, theological language

4. See Stead, *Divine Substance,* p. 189. Stead comments: "This is, in all essentials, the doctrine of Augustine and Aquinas."

5. "For God's intellect and light are not at all like our intellect and light (2.13.4), which means that negation and eminence are necessary to each other." Eric Osborne, *Irenaeus of Lyons* (Cambridge: Cambridge University Press, 2001), pp. 37-38.

about God somehow transcended its limitations. "He is most aptly called 'light,' but he is nothing like the light we know."

Seventh, although the divine predicates were utterly "indescribable," that did not prevent them from being the absolute "source" of their creaturely correlates. The uncreated, though wholly other, was also wholly the source of all created being. The divine goodness, for example, was seen as "the whole source of all that is good." By extension, it seems that uncreated Light, though unlike any light that we know, would be the whole source of all created light.

Finally, what is said to make theological language possible is not human capacity but divine love. As we read a little further on: "In fact, in every respect, the Father of us all is unlike the littleness of men. Although, because of his love, we can use these words to speak of him, we know because of his greatness, that he is above them" (*AH* II.13.4). Turning this statement around, we might say that despite the indescribable immensity of the divine and the infinitesimal smallness of the human, the wholly other God can nonetheless truly be known, spoken about, and loved. Knowledge of, speech about, and love for this God would be possible, just because he stoops down in love to make himself available, at the creature's own level, to a creature who was otherwise incapable of God. "The true light, which enlightens everyone, was coming into the world" (John 1:19). "Again Jesus spoke to them, saying, 'I am the light of the world. Whoever follows me will never walk in darkness but will have the light of life'" (John 8:12).

If the idea of uncreated Light is unpacked according to these points from Irenaeus, the following results are obtained.

- The one indivisible being of God is wholly a being of light.
- God's transcendence as uncreated Light is something for religion to acknowledge and piety to adore.
- The light in which God dwells is unapproachable and indescribable.
- To affirm God as uncreated Light is no mere creaturely projection.
- God is comprehended truly and properly when comprehended as incomprehensible Light.
- God alone is light in the true and proper sense.
- All creaturely light, despite its metaphysical otherness, finds its supreme source in God.
- Created light is entirely contingent upon uncreated Light.
- Created light is what it is only as a remote, imperfect copy and by inconceivable extension.

- Uncreated light can be known for what it is only because God is love and because in love God wills to be known.
- Proper statements about uncreated Light must take a form that is not only paradoxical but also analogical: "God is light, and yet God is unlike any light that we know."

This statement, we may note, can be turned into a useful formula: *God is "x," and yet God is unlike any "x" that we know.* The value of "x" might then be any number of different ascriptions: for example, "Father," "merciful," "righteous." The advantage of the formula is that it requires us to define the predicate in light of God as attested in Holy Scripture, and not the other way around. It blocks any attempt to start from our experience and then project it onto God, as though our language about God were somehow merely univocal. Thus, for example, we might say: *God is Father, and yet God is unlike any Father that we know.* The same would hold true for statements like *God is merciful, God is righteous,* etc.

This way of understanding the grammar of the word "God" can be found in Aquinas: "When we apply 'wise' to God, it leaves the thing signified as incomprehended, as exceeding the signification of the name. . . . The same rule applies to the other terms" (*Summa Theologiae* 1.13.5 [hereafter *ST*]). God is wise, in other words, but God's wisdom is unlike any wisdom that we know. Aquinas concluded that because God is not an object in the universe, and therefore not the instance of a genus or a class, all our words about God "must be used equivocally" (*ST* 1.13.5).[6] We cannot specify their *modus significandi.*

The proper corollary was drawn by Hilary: *Non sermoni res, sed rei sermo subjectus est.* ("The thing is not subject to the word, but the word to the thing.") (*De Trin.* IV.14):[7]

> [H]uman feebleness cannot by any strength of its own attain to the knowledge of heavenly things; the faculties which deal with bodily matters can form no notion of the unseen world. Neither our created bodily substance, nor the reason given by God for the purposes of ordinary life, is capable of ascertaining and pronouncing upon the nature and work of

---

6. Quoted by Victor Preller, *Divine Science and the Science of God* (Princeton: Princeton University Press, 1967), p. 167, n. 10. Cf. Aquinas, *Summa Theologiae,* vol. 3, Blackfriars Edition, ed. Herbert McCabe (New York: McGraw-Hill, 1964), p. 63.

7. Hilary of Poitiers, "On the Trinity," in *Nicene and Post-Nicene Fathers,* vol. 9, ed. Philip Schaff (Grand Rapids: Eerdmans, 1983), p. 75.

God. Our wits cannot rise to the level of heavenly knowledge, our powers of perception lack the strength to apprehend that limitless might. We
must believe God's word concerning Himself, and humbly accept such
insight as He vouchsafes to give. We must make our choice between re-
jecting His witness, as the heathen do, or else believing in Him as He is,
and this in the only possible way, by thinking of Him in the aspect in
which He presents Himself to us. . . . The meaning of words shall be as-
certained by considering the circumstances under which they were spoken; words must be explained by circumstances not circumstances
forced into conformity with words. (*De Trin.* IV.14)[8]

For He whom we can know only through His own utterances is a fitting
witness concerning Himself. (*De Trin.* I.18)[9]

2

A famous formula from the Fourth Lateran Council ran as follows:

For between Creator and creature there can be noted no similarity so
great that a greater dissimilarity cannot be seen between them (*Consti-
tutions,* ii).[10]

Whatever this formula might mean, it is not necessarily in agreement
with the view taken by Irenaeus. Although both would posit an analogy
between the Creator and the creature, the Lateran formula, if taken
strictly, seemed to construe their metaphysical difference as a matter of
degree ("greater dissimilarity"), whereas Irenaeus, if taken strictly, appeared to adopt a more radical view. For him their difference would seem
to be absolute, as set forth through a pattern of negation and eminence,
not just a matter of degree. Uncreated Light, being wholly other than created light, was placed in a class by itself: God was "unlike any light that we
know."

The idea of divine simplicity seemed to generate a quandary. Defining
God as wholly other than any creatures seemed to rule out the possibility

8. Hilary of Poitiers, "On the Trinity," p. 75.
9. Hilary of Poitiers, "On the Trinity," p. 45.
10. Norman P. Tanner, *Decrees of the Ecumenical Councils,* vol. 1 (Washington, DC:
Georgetown University Press, 1990), p. 232.

of analogical discourse in theology. The idea of analogy, even as construed by the Fourth Lateran Council, seemed to posit that God and the creature were somehow metaphysically comparable. The dissimilarity between them, no matter how great, was finally a matter of degree. Divine simplicity, on the other hand, seemed to require a difference that was not merely relative but absolute. If so, it seemed to rule out the possibility of analogical discourse about God. Language about God, on these terms, could only be equivocal and apophatic. Analogical views of theological language that affirm divine simplicity, or God's radical difference from the world, need to deal with this dilemma.

The difficulty with the idea of a "greater dissimilarity" is well articulated by Denys Turner:

> [T]here can be no good sense . . . in any . . . calculation of the greater and lesser degrees of "distance" which lie between Creator and creatures as contrasted with that between one creature and another; for it is not on some common scale of difference that these differences differ . . . as if to say: it is this kind or that, only infinitely so. . . . [A] term of comparison . . . presupposes a common scale. . . . For if God is not any kind of being, then his difference from creatures is not a difference of any kind, hence is not a difference of any size, hence is not incomparably greater, but, on the contrary, is, simply, incommensurable. "Greater" and "lesser" cannot come into it, logically speaking.[11]

The same point was recognized long ago by Hyppolytus:

> For comparisons can be instituted only between objects of like nature, and not between objects of unlike nature. But between God the Maker of all things and that which is made, between the infinite and the finite, between infinitude and finitude, there can be no kind of comparison, since these differ from each other not in mere comparison (or relatively), but absolutely in essence.
>
> And yet at the same time there has been effected a certain inexpressible and irrefragable union of the two into one substance [ὑπόστασιν] which entirely passes the understanding of anything that is made. For the divine is just the same after the incarnation that it was before the incarnation; in its essence infinite, illimitable, impassible, in-

---

11. Denys Turner, *Faith, Reason and the Existence of God* (Cambridge: Cambridge University Press, 2004), p. 213.

comparable, unchangeable, inconvertible, self-potent [αὐτοσθενές], and, in short, subsisting in essence alone the infinitely worthy good.[12]

The purpose of this section is to suggest that an ambiguity can be discerned in the writings of Thomas F. Torrance. In his remarks about theology and science, it is not always clear how he expects to escape the horns of this dilemma. Sometimes his views seem in line with the Lateran formula, while at other times they lean toward Irenaeus. Torrance's ambiguities are subtle and elusive. No more than a sketch can be provided here. While his sympathies are finally Irenaean, he leaves some of the quandaries that they generate unaddressed.

Like Irenaeus, Torrance drew a distinction between uncreated Light and created light. He also accepted the idea of divine simplicity. Unlike Irenaeus, however, he did not associate uncreated Light with divine simplicity in any direct or explicit way. That may be one reason why he sometimes seemed to depart from the idea of God's radical difference from the world, even though elsewhere he strongly affirmed it.

Some tendencies of Torrance's theology are evident in the following remarks:

> God is Light, uncreated Light, and it is in the light of that invisible, uncreated Light that the created lights of the world are visible. Thus, we understand the rationalities of nature, or what I have called its contingent intelligibility, in light of the uncreated Rationality of God. You understand created light in the light of uncreated Light. It is because God's Light is constant that we believe in the ultimate stability and reliability of the universe which he has correlated to his Light. So we have a remarkable analogy between the unique metaphysical status of physical light in the contingent universe and the unique status of the Light that God is, from a theological point of view.[13]

In this remark there are two terms and a relationship. The terms are God and the world, and the relationship between them is not necessarily one of radical or absolute difference.

God is described as Light, indeed as uncreated Light. This Light is said to be invisible. God as uncreated Light is then linked with two further

---

12. Hyppolytus, "Against Beron and Helix," in *The Ante-Nicene Fathers*, vol. 5, ed. Philip Schaff (Grand Rapids: Eerdmans, 1986), pp. 231-32.

13. Thomas F. Torrance, *The Ground and Grammar of Theology* (Charlottesville: University Press of Virginia, 1980), pp. 129-30.

ideas. First, uncreated Light is glossed by the idea of uncreated Rationality. Moreover, God's Light is said to be constant.

Looking back to the passage from Irenaeus, some similarities and differences are evident. Like Torrance, Irenaeus also wrote of God not only as Light, but also as intellect, mind, and rationality. Although the latter terms were perhaps more nearly correlated with the divine Light than equated with it, they were all explicitly determined by the idea of the divine simplicity. Therefore, Irenaeus could strongly affirm that the divine rationality and divine Light were incomparable, being unlike any that we know.

Torrance did not wish to deny that God's being was incomparable. Indeed, elsewhere he explicitly affirmed it.

> God alone is unceasing and self-sufficient in his power to live, eternally existing in himself in a way that is beyond all comparison and infinitely surpasses our power to comprehend. He is by nature underived, without beginning and without end.[14]

It is perhaps noteworthy, however, that while God's being is here said to be underived, unceasing, and self-sufficient, infinitely surpassing our power to comprehend, no mention is made of its being simple in the sense affirmed by Irenaeus as metaphysically noncomposite.

When we attend to Torrance's initial remarks, we also need to pick out what was stated about the world. The world as such is said to be the site of created lights, which are described as visible rather than invisible. Nature is then said to have its own rationalities, which are summed up under the heading of "contingent intelligibility." The universe is finally said to possess properties of ultimate stability and reliability. Created light is thus conceived as visible, intelligible, stable, contingent, and reliable in a way that points to these features as eminently instantiated by God. Since the passage from Irenaeus was concerned only with describing God, it offered no comments about features constitutive of the world.

How, then, does Torrance think God and the world, uncreated Light and created light, are related? This is of course a very large question, to which only the most cursory of answers can be suggested here. Broadly speaking, however, two lines of inquiry stand out. First, how might created light be understood in light of uncreated Light? (This question is suggested in the main remark given above.) Second, and more important here, what

---

14. Thomas F. Torrance, *Transformation and Convergence in the Frame of Knowledge* (Grand Rapids: Eerdmans, 1984), p. 335.

about the reverse movement? Does created light have anything to tell us about uncreated Light? It is with this second line of questioning that Torrance sometimes ran into difficulties.

Without going into detail, the kind of answer that Torrance gives to the first line of inquiry can be noted. Christian theology in general and natural scientists who happen to be Christians in particular, Torrance liked to suggest, are in an advantageous position to understand the natural world. Christian theology, for example, helped demystify the world in a way that made it susceptible to scientific investigation. Moreover, the sensibilities of a Christian and a scientist like Clerk Maxwell equipped him, much as they did John Philoponus centuries before him, to think profitably about the natural world in relational terms.[15] This is an argument from theological sensibility to successful lines of scientific inquiry. On the premise that the created light of the world somehow corresponds to the uncreated Light of God, Christian theological sensibilities have arguably borne scientific fruit.

Nevertheless, Torrance acknowledged that because God differs radically from the world, created light cannot, in and of itself, serve as a basis for understanding uncreated Light. There is, Torrance wrote in this vein, "an absolute distinction between created and uncreated being."[16] It follows that "no argument from created intelligibility, as such, can actually terminate on the Reality of God, but in accordance with its contingent nature can only break off."[17] If God is wholly other than the world, then while the world can be understood in light of God (although the condition for this possibility needs to be spelled out more fully than it is in Torrance), God cannot be understood in light of the world, but only if at all in light of himself through his own self-disclosure.[18] Uncreated Light must be understood out of itself or not at all.[19]

---

15. For John Philoponus, see, for example, Torrance, *Ground and Grammar,* pp. 60-61. For Clerk Maxwell, see, for example, Thomas F. Torrance, *The Christian Frame of Mind* (Colorado Springs: Helmers & Howard, 1989), pp. 147-55 and *passim.*

16. Thomas F. Torrance, *The Trinitarian Faith* (Edinburgh: T. & T. Clark, 1988), p. 100.

17. Torrance, *Ground and Grammar,* p. 100.

18. In his *The Christian Doctrine of God* (p. 77), Torrance quoted several passages from Irenaeus to this effect: "Since it is impossible, without God, to come to knowledge of God, he reaches men through his Word to know God" (*Against Heresies,* IV.8.1). "No one can see God except God" (referring to God as revealed in the incarnate Son) (*AH,* IV.8.1). "The Lord has taught us that no one can know God unless God himself is the Teacher, that is to say, without God, God is not to be known" (*AH,* IV. 11.3). Cf. Thomas F. Torrance, "Kerygmatic Proclamation of the Gospel: *The Demonstration of Apostolic Preaching* of Irenaios of Lyons," *Greek Orthodox Theological Review* 37 (1992): 105-21.

19. "While it is in his Light that we see light," wrote Torrance, "the very splendour of

Torrance's account, however, is not without its ambiguities. A brief look at his ideas about "contingency" and "ontological stratification" can suggest what these ambiguities are.

The term "contingent" is itself ambiguous. It could simply mean that something is not necessary, and thus either need not have existed at all or might have been other than it is. It could also mean, however, that one thing is dependent on something else as a necessary or sufficient condition of its existence. In Torrance's discourse, "contingent" officially means "nonnecessary," but operationally, we might say, it often seems to imply that the natural world as investigated by science logically requires the uncreated reality of God as its necessary and sufficient condition. "Contingent" rationality, freedom, and stability, though in one sense nonnecessary, are in another sense seen as pointing to their necessary metaphysical ground in the uncreated (eminent) rationality, freedom, and stability of God.

While it would be one thing to affirm God as the ground of the world on the basis of God's self-revelation (a top-down approach, so to speak), it would be quite another to do so on the basis of the natural world as considered in and from itself (a bottom-up approach). Torrance's idea of "ontological stratification" sometimes seems to move in the latter direction.[20] The idea of ontological stratification, as derived essentially from Michael Polanyi, is that reality (and therefore truth) falls into "levels" that are open upwards but not reducible downwards, so that what exists at a lower level can be explained only by recourse to a higher level. "All meaning," according to Polanyi, "lies in the higher levels of reality that are not reducible to the laws by which the ultimate particulars of the universe are controlled."[21] Torrance commented: "The same principle, of course, applies to the universe as a whole, which is thus to be regarded as an essentially open system, for precisely as an intelligible whole it requires a sufficient reason be-

---

God's Light finally hides him from us. In the mystery of his self revelation God reserves the innermost secret of his eternal Being as God, into which, as Irenaeus insisted, we cannot intrude" (*Christian Doctrine of God*, p. 81).

20. The idea of stratification runs throughout Torrance's writings. A good brief account may be found in his *Reality and Evangelical Theology* (Philadelphia: Westminster, 1982), pp. 35-39. A longer account appears in his *Reality and Scientific Theology* (Edinburgh: Scottish Academic Press, 1985), pp. 131-59.

21. Michael Polanyi, *Scientific Thought and Social Reality: Essays,* ed. Fred Schwartz (Madison, WI: International Universities Press, 1974), pp. 136-37; quoted by Torrance, *Divine and Contingent Order* (Oxford: Oxford University Press, 1981), p. 20.

yond itself."[22] The need for ultimate intelligibility, Torrance stated at another point, "does more than raise a question, for it seems to *cry silently* for a transcendent agency in its explanation and understanding."[23] Or again, Torrance could write, "That the immanent rationality of the universe is unable to give any final account of itself is the obverse of the fact that the rational connection between the creation and God is grounded in God alone."[24] As Paul D. Molnar has pointed out, statements like these represent a subtle form of ambiguity in Torrance.[25] Contrary to his official view, they seem, in a certain respect, to understand uncreated Light or Rationality in light of the contingent light or rationality of the world.

In his book *Theism and Ultimate Explanation: The Necessary Shape of Contingency,* Timothy O'Connor gives an unambiguous argument that a necessary being must be the ground of contingent beings.[26] O'Connor does not base his conclusion on logical necessity but on "probable reasoning" of a more informal kind. At the same time — and this is crucial — he relaxes the classical emphasis not only on divine simplicity but also on the radical difference between God and the world. (For example, he argues that God's *nature* must in some strong sense be mutable.) Although in his less guarded statements Torrance gestures towards such moves while stopping just short of them, they suggest why he cannot have it both ways. Bottom-up inferences from the world to God — in particular, from created contingencies to a necessary divine being as their ground — cannot easily maintain God's perfection, God's self-sufficiency, and God's essential difference from the world, or else they can do so only in a significantly qualified and weakened sense.[27]

---

22. Torrance, *Divine and Contingent Order,* p. 20. It may be worth noting that Aristotle took the existence of the whole universe and its motion as a given that required no further explanation (*Physics,* VIII).

23. Torrance, *Reality and Scientific Theology,* p. 58; italics original.

24. Thomas F. Torrance, *Space, Time and Incarnation* (Oxford: Oxford University Press, 1969), p. 60. The fuller context in which this last statement appears does not entirely mitigate the point being made here.

25. Paul D. Molnar, *Incarnation and Resurrection* (Grand Rapids: Eerdmans, 2007), pp. 84-85. See also, more fully, Molnar, "Natural Theology Revisited: A Comparison of T. F. Torrance and Karl Barth," *Zeitschrift für dialektische Theologie* 20 (2005): 53-83.

26. Malden, MA: Blackwell, 2008.

27. O'Connor, like most philosophical theologians, would be averse to the kind of dialectical solutions proposed in this essay.

3

Our brief survey of created and uncreated light in Irenaeus led to the conclusion that he applied two countervailing principles to his understanding of theological language: negation and eminence. Negation without eminence would lead to a view of theological language that was merely apophatic. No positive statements about God could be made. Eminence without negation, on the other hand, while allowing for positive statements, would do so only (it would seem) at the expense of denying God's fundamental difference from the world. A God who was merely eminent might differ from the world only by degree of "greater dissimilarity" (no matter how greatly). The idea of divine simplicity in combination with certain divine predicates seemed to require a form of analogical discourse in theology in which negation and eminence were both necessarily affirmed and accorded equal weight.[28]

Like Irenaeus, Torrance affirmed God as uncreated Light. More than Irenaeus, however, he wished to coordinate the uncreated Light of God with the created light, or contingent intelligibility, of the world. Unlike Irenaeus, moreover, Torrance did not explicitly integrate his idea of uncreated Light with that of divine simplicity (though in separated places he affirmed both). If divine simplicity logically requires the idea that God's difference from the world is absolute, then God's rationality, freedom, and stability would need to be, as Irenaeus saw, unlike any that we know. In his desire to establish a positive connection between created and uncreated light, however, Torrance sometimes introduced a certain ambiguity into his discourse. He seemed to accord greater weight to the principle of eminence than to the principle of negation in his use of analogical theological discourse. Eminence at the expense of negation runs the risk of obscuring God's difference from the world.

---

28. For a very fine account of "divine simplicity" in historical and systematic perspective, see Brian Davies, "Classical Theism and the Doctrine of Divine Simplicity," in *Language, Meaning and God* (London: Geoffrey Chapman, 1987), pp. 51-74. For a philosophical discussion arguing that the idea of divine simplicity is neither incoherent in itself nor incompatible with the ideas of contingent divine volition and knowledge, see Jeffrey E. Brower, "Simplicity and Aseity," in *The Oxford Handbook of Philosophical Theology*, ed. Thomas P. Flint and Michael Rea (Oxford: Oxford University Press, 2009). Brower makes it clear that the idea of divine simplicity cannot properly be isolated from other unique features of God's being, such as perfection, incomprehensibility, aseity, and so on. See also Brian L. Leftow, "Simplicity and Eternity," unpublished dissertation, Yale University, 1984.

Neither Irenaeus nor Torrance, it might be suggested, offered a fully satisfactory account of how the countervailing principles of negation and eminence might be held together in the analogical discourse of theology. Irenaeus did suggest, however, that although we know, because of his greatness, that God is above the words we use of him, it is only by God's love that they can be used at all (*Against Heresies* II.13.4).

4

A note may be in order about how analogical discourse has been dealt with in Christian theology. It is of course a notoriously difficult question. Given that, by definition, God is absolute, infinite, and holy, while the human creature is finite, relative, and (as it happens) fallen, it would seem that God and the creature must be incommensurable — separated not only by an ontological divide but also by an abyss of impiety and wickedness — so that no common standard or frame of reference would exist by which they might be meaningfully compared. The incomprehensible God would seem to be enshrouded in holy darkness, while the alienated creature would be reduced to guilty silence — or empty words. The faith of the church presupposes, however, that it is both necessary and possible not only to speak *about* God truly, but also to speak *to* him properly, in theology, worship, and prayer. How then can such speaking be regarded as possible?

Simplifying greatly, two broad lines of solution have been proposed. Necessary conditions for speaking about God are found either in certain aspects of the created order or else exclusively in the sovereignty of God. The first solution is associated with Thomas Aquinas, the second with Karl Barth.

According to Gregory Rocca, who will be followed here, Aquinas's view of analogy involved a delicate balance between "positive" and "negative" theology.[29] Positive theology, as explained by Rocca, means that God made creatures in his own likeness whereas negative theology implies that the creature, being brought forth out of nothing, must nonetheless be radically unlike God. God was thought to be incomprehensible in a twofold sense, for God transcended a whole range of created qualities as well as all

29. Gregory P. Rocca, *Speaking the Incomprehensible God: Thomas Aquinas on the Interplay of Positive and Negative Theology* (Washington, DC: Catholic University of America Press, 2004); page references cited in the text.

created modalities.[30] True statements about God were possible but only with the proviso that their *modus significandi* could not be known.

Rocca advances three points of particular interest. First, for Aquinas analogy was "more a matter of judgment than of concept in the traditional sense" (p. 355). In other words, analogy was more about modes of reflection (meaning) than about modes of being (truth), though of course the two cannot be separated. Second, analogical discourse in theology presupposed truths about God to which Aquinas had already assented on the basis of faith, and those truths took primacy over truths of reason (p. 354). Finally, an important condition for the possibility of analogical discourse was "the creature's ontological imitation of the divine nature and properties" (p. 132).

Despite the creature's radical unlikeness to God, the creature nevertheless corresponded to God by nature so as to make analogical discourse possible. A real metaphysical similarity was in force between the human creature and God (p. 127). The statement from the Fourth Lateran Council regarding creaturely likeness in the midst of greater unlikeness, to which Aquinas subscribed, meant that "a real though deficient likeness to God" was inherent in the creature by God's design (p. 275). An inherent likeness in the midst of unlikeness helped make analogical discourse possible.

By contrast, Barth solved the problem of analogical discourse by appealing not so much to nature as to grace.[31] Although human language was inherently incapable of referring to God, it was nevertheless made capable of doing so. Human language, as sanctified by grace, was at once affirmed, annulled, and elevated — affirmed in its creatureliness and annulled in its incapacity, in order to be elevated beyond itself. This gracious process of affirming, nullifying, and elevating, of capacitating the incapacitated, was associated with being raised from the dead (II/1, p. 231). It was therefore miraculous and beyond comprehension. Barth's controlling metaphor was not creation but resurrection.

---

30. "Quality" pertains to the sort of thing an entity is; here, mainly to its essence, capacities, and limitations. Negative theology holds that some qualities are not possessed by God in any way, not even preeminently, as in the statement, "God is immaterial." "Modality," on the other hand, can be either "objective" or "subjective." Objectively, although God is preeminently good, the perfection of this modality in God is not the same as its perfection in a creature. Subjectively, furthermore, although human concepts must be used in speaking of God, they cannot be used of God in the same sense as of a creature. When used truly, they are not only used preeminently but also at the same time ineffably. See Rocca, *Incomprehensible God*, pp. 58-62.

31. See Karl Barth, *Church Dogmatics*, vol. 2, part 1 (Edinburgh: T. & T. Clark, 1957), pp. 224-43. Hereafter cited in the text as II/1.

Grace made possible, and continued to make possible, what was otherwise impossible. Analogical discourse was grounded not in some metaphysical similarity between God and the creature, but solely in the sovereign freedom of divine grace. Human language, without ceasing to be essentially inadequate, was extended to be made fully appropriate. To be made appropriate despite being inadequate meant becoming absolutely dependent on grace. It was a miraculous dependence that occurred perfectly and perpetually: not statically but dynamically, not merely once and for all, but continually, again and again.

Yet in elevating human language beyond its natural capacities, God "does not perform a violent miracle" (II/1, p. 229). The Creator enjoys an original and proper claim on human language, even though it has no such claim upon him. Neither human sin nor creaturely finitude could undo this primordial divine claim. Human language belongs to the good creation in and through which God knows himself as God. When the Lord God graciously elevates human words, concepts, and images to participate in the truth of his own self-knowledge, language is not alienated from its original purpose, "but, on the contrary, restored to it" (II/1, p. 229).

For Barth, because God and the creature are incommensurable, any ontological continuity between them — not only regarding predicates like goodness, reason, and wisdom, but also regarding "nonagential" predicates like being, beauty, and light — must be seen as miraculously given, again and again, from above. Ontological continuity with the reality of God does not belong to the creature qua creature. It does not belong to the creature as a given endowment or a fixed condition — not originally, and not even subsequently. The continuity does not exist except as it is continually given, and it is not given except miraculously through God's gracious operation. As continually though miraculously given, the continuity is not merely "occasional" (a common misunderstanding of Barth). It is rather a function of the perpetual operation of God's grace as grounded and centered in Christ from before the foundation of the world. As such the continuity is always at once real and yet also incomprehensible. Therefore the ontological difference between God and the creature is not seen as "infinitely greater" but as absolute. Any similarities between the creature and God — real though incomprehensible, incomprehensible though real — are not grounded in the creatureliness of the creature, but strictly and entirely (not just partially) in divine grace as a perpetual and miraculous operation from above.

If this general account is reasonably correct, then the central difference between Aquinas and Barth on analogy might seem to be the difference between a bottom-up and a top-down approach. However, just as Aquinas relies on important top-down elements, so also does Barth appeal to elements that are intriguingly bottom-up.

A top-down element in Aquinas appears when he presupposes prior assent to the truths of faith. Because these truths form a premise from which he works, there is a sense in which he already knows in advance that the defects of nature can be, must be, and are perfected and exceeded by grace. Otherwise, true human judgments could not possibly correspond to the transcendent reality of God. Grace from above remains the paramount factor, because natural similarities, being metaphysically deficient, are not enough.

Furthermore, since God remains incomprehensible, faith can know that although its assertions about God are true, it must do so without knowing how. Therefore, for Aquinas analogical discourse depends indispensably on grace in two ways: not only to elevate nature (here, in the form of human language) beyond its deficiencies, but also to bring analogical assertions into ineffable correspondence with God. The bottom-up function of nature depends on the top-down operation of grace.

Likewise, Barth finds that he cannot be top-down without also being bottom-up. The created order in general, and human language in particular, belong originally and properly to God. The Lord God graciously places himself at the disposal of human language by elevating it to himself. Presumably, since God is wholly other than the created order, this gracious elevation of the creature would have happened even in an unfallen world, but after the Fall it must happen in another, more drastic way.[32]

Nevertheless, the divine affirmation, annulment, and elevation of human language to a higher plane (Barth's *Aufhebung*) does not alienate language from itself. It only restores it to a destiny originally intended for it. Language has no capacity — we might say, no passive potency — for being elevated in this way, not before the Fall, and certainly not after it. Its elevation is always necessarily miraculous (whether as *metathesis* or *anastasis*) but not without divine foresight and provision. Analogical discourse for

32. Metaphorically speaking, the difference, perhaps, though Barth does not spell anything out, might be between *metathesis* and *anastasis*: *metathesis* in an unfallen world (direct "translation" or "transposition," as with Enoch in Heb. 11:5), and *anastasis* after the Fall ("resurrection" from the dead, as with Jesus). *Metathesis* and *anastasis* would both be miraculous forms of elevation, but the latter might be considered the more drastic. (Although occurring after the Fall, the story of Enoch [Gen. 5:24; Heb. 11:5] might be regarded as a kind of *analepsis*, or flashback, gesturing towards what might have been.)

Barth depends on the final goal originally planned for nature (here again, in the form of human language) by means of grace. Human language was created to be sanctified, elevated, and perhaps, in a certain sense, deified. The top-down operation of grace presupposes an indispensable bottom-up fulfillment as predestined for nature.

The differences between Aquinas and Barth, while not unimportant, should therefore not be overstressed. Both theologians would see the elevation of human language as very much a miracle of grace, and both would see it as mysterious in its *modus significandi*. For Aquinas, the miracle of grace was somehow more relative or less drastic than for Barth, for whom it was always revolutionary and absolute. For Aquinas it occurred as grace worked with a metaphysical likeness already implanted, albeit deficiently, in nature by creation; whereas for Barth it occurred as grace operated on an original incapacity in nature that could be overcome only, so to speak, by redemption from death. For Aquinas the elevation of language was perhaps finally something like a transition from illness to health, whereas for Barth it was more like being raised from death to life. Nevertheless, both theologians saw the elevation of human language as something that greatly perfected and exceeded its limited capacities in a way that would scarcely be possible without a new work of grace.

Indeed, Gregory Rocca finds exactly the same threefold pattern in Aquinas as we have noted in Barth. For Aquinas, too, according to Rocca, "a positive predicate is first affirmed of God, then denied, and finally affirmed once again in a supereminent fashion."[33] If so, then even if Barth's moment of negation were somehow the more radical, the convergence between the two theologians regarding analogical discourse would be considerable. "No positive perfection can be predicated of God," Rocca states of Aquinas, "unless it has been filtered through the corrective lenses of the threefold way."[34] Precisely this threefold way, for both Aquinas and Barth, could thus be interpreted as making explicit the grammar otherwise implicit in Irenaeus's seminal statement that "God is light and yet God is unlike any light that we know." According to this grammar, light as a positive divine predicate would first be affirmed of God, then denied, and finally reaffirmed in a supereminent and ineffable fashion. This threefold pattern would set forth the grammar governing negation and eminence.

33. Rocca, *Incomprehensible God*, p. 73.
34. Rocca, *Incomprehensible God*, p. 73.

5

Finally, two views of revelation may also be sketched, particularly with reference to the concept of light. (We are here shifting from modes of judgment to modes of revelation.) According to one view, created light would enjoy a remote metaphysical likeness with uncreated Light. It would thus possess a certain capacity for revealing uncreated Light, even if that revelation were deficient in itself. As a real though inferior source of divine revelation, created light would function independently of uncreated Light and alongside it. It would be a relatively autonomous source, even if its revelation would need to be supplemented, perfected, and exceeded in order to be made suitable for religious and theological purposes.

According to the other view, by contrast, created light would not be relatively autonomous. As a source of revelation, it would always be dependent rather than independent. It would thus be subordinate rather than alongside and separate. Created light would possess no particular revelatory power in itself (i.e., no "passive potency" for revealing uncreated Light). Only on the prior condition that uncreated Light had already acted of its own accord to reveal itself could created light be seen as reflecting it. Any metaphysical likeness of created light with uncreated Light would not be sufficient in itself for the latter to be revealed by the former. The secondary revelation of uncreated Light by created light, when actualized by the former, would be seen as "fitting" without being metaphysically inherent in created light as such.

A parallel (though an imperfect one) might be drawn with eucharistic conversion as interpreted by Aquinas. Aquinas states that the bread and the wine possess no "passive potency" for being converted into Christ's body and blood, since the eucharistic conversion happens "solely through the active power of the Creator" [*non . . . per potentiam passivam creaturae sed per solam potentiam activam Creatoris*] (*ST* 3a. 75, 8).[35] Eucharistic conversion would thus be "fitting" without being inherent in the elements. Because the two correlates are both means of nourishment, it is "fitting" for the bread to be converted into Christ's life-giving flesh. But this broad similarity in function does not mean that a "passive potency" exists in the bread for becoming Christ's life-giving flesh. Fittingness need not imply the existence of a passive potency.

35. Thomas Aquinas, *Summa Theologiae*, 3a. 73-78, vol. 58, *The Eucharistic Presence*, ed. William Barden (Cambridge: Cambridge University Press, 2008), pp. 90-91.

Likewise, it would not be incoherent to hold that created light can become a fitting vehicle for revelation without possessing a capacity for it. Created light would lack all "passive potency" for revelation apart from the "active potency" of uncreated Light. But given the actual operation of uncreated Light in its capacity for self-revelation, created light, despite its incapacity, could (under certain circumstances) become a secondary, fitting, and dependent source of revelation as well. Because both are sources of illumination, this use of created light by uncreated Light would be fitting.

The top-down active potency of uncreated Light would be infinite in this event, even if the bottom-up passive potency of created light, as a revelatory source, were zero. As Réginald Garrigou-Lagrange explains, "Now, since active potency, active power, must be greater in proportion to its passive correlative, it follows that when passive potency is reduced to zero, the active potency must be infinite."[36]

In short, according to the second view of revelation, zero passive potency would be an aspect of nature, in certain respects, while infinite active potency would be an aspect of grace. But the zero passive potency of created light would not prevent it from becoming a secondary, dependent, and fitting vehicle of revelation. For it would be made so by the infinite active potency of uncreated Light.

6

In pondering the *analogia entis* question, it is fascinating to discover that a strand of Aquinas scholarship exists in which it is denied that Aquinas actually subscribed to the kind of *analogia entis* that has commonly been attributed to him and that appears in neo-Thomism.

Laurence Paul Hemming, for example, states that "there is no formal *analogia entis* in Aquinas. . . . [His] analogical way of speaking . . . provides no basis for ontological inference from us to God."[37]

Hemming's remarkable conclusions were anticipated nearly forty years earlier in *Divine Science and the Science of God* by Victor Preller.[38]

36. Réginald Garrigou-Lagrange, *Reality: A Synthesis of Thomistic Thought* (St. Louis: Herder, 1950), p. 159.

37. Laurence Paul Hemming, *Postmodernity's Transcending: Defining God* (Notre Dame: University of Notre Dame Press, 2005), pp. 133-34.

38. Victor Preller, *Divine Science and the Science of God* (Princeton: Princeton University Press, 1967).

Preller argues that in Aquinas the famous five ways already presuppose the knowledge of faith, and that the resulting "natural theology" is so highly formal (a kind of speculative algebraic notation) that it is completely empty of specific content. If so, then again there can be no inference from natural to revealed theology, nor can natural theology provide a substantive basis on which any revealed knowledge of God could rest. Nor could natural revelation be "correlated" with special revelation, as if the former were independent of the latter and alongside it.

Hemming and Preller both urge that Aquinas possessed a radical sense of God's "metaphysical" otherness. In his book *Speaking the Incomprehensible God,* Gregory Rocca also argues, as we have seen, that what Aquinas sets forth as the knowledge of reason already rests, in important respects, on the knowledge of faith.

These readings of Aquinas would seem to be intriguingly compatible with Barth. Preller, in particular, would seem to merit a detailed and careful assessment. A good beginning along these lines is the volume titled *Grammar and Grace,* edited by Jeffrey Stout and Robert MacSwain.[39] In this posthumous *Festschrift* for Preller, the measured essays by David Burrell and Fergus Kerr in particular point to some ways in which the truths of reason for Aquinas were grounded, implicitly and explicitly, though often only implicitly, in the truths of faith. Although this line of Aquinas interpretation is bound to remain controversial, here again we potentially have a remarkable convergence of Aquinas with Barth. It may well be that Barth was not so much mistaken about the *analogia entis* as that neo-Thomism was mistaken about Aquinas.

David Burrell is among those who gesture positively toward Karl Barth in a way that brings Aquinas into unexpected convergence with him.[40] Most important, he affirms that in Aquinas we find the "Barthian" themes of an "infinite qualitative difference" between the Creator and the creature (p. 256), the absence of any "common feature" uniting the two (p. 258), and the presence of a "hidden element" by which truths of faith function as the tacit ground for truths of reason about God (pp. 256-57). The category of "being," states Burrell, cannot be stretched to include the Creator as well as the creature (p. 262), and faith is "deeply intertwined" in

---

39. *Grammar and Grace: Reformulations of Aquinas and Wittgenstein,* ed. Jeffrey Stout and Robert MacSwain (London: SCM Press, 2004).

40. See David B. Burrell, "From Analogy of 'Being' to the Analogy of Being," in *Recovering Nature,* ed. T. Hibbs and J. O'Callaghan (Notre Dame: University of Notre Dame Press, 1999), pp. 253-65 (hereafter page references in the text).

carrying out philosophical inquiry (p. 261). "All discussion of 'analogy of being' or of 'analogous concepts' is utterly foreign to Aquinas" (p. 259). Moves like these, Burrell rightly observes, "would have warmed Karl Barth's heart" (p. 254). Without perhaps satisfying him completely, they would certainly have brought him into sufficient hailing distance with Aquinas so as to give them a common set of opponents.

Ralph McInerny, who spent his life writing about analogy, argued that for Thomas the term should be restricted to semantics and barred from ontology.[41] That is, Thomas thought the term "analogy" described a mode of discourse, not a mode of being. McInerny is followed in this interpretation by theologians like Hemming and Burrell. They don't think the term "analogy" is germane to describing ontological relations. That is one reason why they can deny that an *analogia entis* is found in Aquinas.

A Barthian position on some of these matters might be suggested in the following terms. For Barth, just as we cannot understand the *modus significandi* in true statements about God, so also we cannot comprehend the *modus participationis* — if we want to use the idea of participation, as Thomists do — when it comes to the creaturely forms of the good, the beautiful, the true, and so on. "Participation" is thought by Thomists to be a necessary category if creaturely exemplifications of such transcendental predicates is going to be made "intelligible."

For Barth, however, it would always be a matter of *incomprehensible* intelligibility, that is, of intelligibility in the midst of radical (not "infinitely greater") unintelligibility, since God is not an object in the universe and so is "wholly other" in himself and in all his perfections (as Burrell, White, Preller, and others, so far as it goes, would agree).

Because of the neo-Platonic origins of the Thomistic idea of "participation," it inevitably carries "substantialist" connotations with it, and these are unfortunate. They may not be entirely intended or even required, however. As Burrell rightly argues, being in Aquinas is a matter of "pure act" and so is something dynamic and living.

A Barthian position could dispense with the whole idea of "ontological participation" without needing to worry overmuch about its use by Thomists. The Barthian view, however, would finally be more actualist that substantialist, more coherentist than correlationist, and more miraculous than participationist. Miracle and mystery always went hand in hand

41. Ralph McInerny, *Aquinas and Analogy* (Washington, DC: Catholic University of America Press, 1996), pp. 162-63.

for Barth, for whom it would make little sense to search for "nonmiracu-lous" or "metaphysical" forms of "intelligibility" in theology.

That is why, in affirming real predications of God, Barth was appar-ently closer, in the end, to Irenaeus and Hilary than to Thomas. According to Victor White and Brian Davies, our knowledge of God, for Aquinas, was finally agnostic. "According to Aquinas," wrote White, "'we do not know what God is.' [*ST* 1.1.7] . . . It is a sobering thought that, when we talk about God, we do not know *what* we are talking about. . . . It is sufficient . . . to point out that we do not know what the subject, *Deus*, is; but it is also true that we do not know what *est*, as predicated of God, is either."[42] "[Aqui-nas's] position on our knowledge of God," concurred Davies, "is decidedly agnostic."[43] The move from creation to the Creator, through God's "effects" as perceived by reason, offered a firmer basis for negation than for emi-nence. For the bottom-up approach, although God was somehow light, he was unlike any that we know.

For Barth, on the other hand, our knowledge of God was not decid-edly agnostic. He did not believe that creaturely forms of God's transcen-dental perfections — like goodness, truth, beauty, or being — could be successfully grounded "metaphysically" by means of unaided reason. He was, of course, interested in comprehending the incomprehensibility of God. But the divine incomprehensibility could not be made comprehensi-ble through the metaphysics of unaided reason. It could only be made comprehensible — without sacrificing either God's self-revelation or God's radical incomprehensibility — through the concept of miraculous grace. Comprehensibility in incomprehensibility could only be grounded in "the free activity of God" (I/1, p. 9) as revealed by grace to faith. Only through revelation, and not through unaided reason, could we, in speaking of God, be prevented from "committing ourselves to an enigma in regard to which we cannot conclusively know" (II/1, p. 325).

> It is dangerous and ultimately fatal to faith in God if God is not the Lord
> of glory, if it is not guaranteed to us that in spite of the analogical nature
> of the language in which it all has to be expressed, God is actually and
> unreservedly as we encounter Him in His revelation: the Almighty, the
> Holy, the Just, the Merciful, the Omnipresent, the Eternal, not less but

42. See Victor White, "Prelude to the Five Ways," in *Aquinas's Summa Theologiae: Criti-cal Essays*, ed. Brian Davies (Lanham, MD: Rowman & Littlefield, 2005), p. 37.

43. Brian Davies, "Aquinas on What God Is Not," in *Aquinas's Summa Theologiae*, p. 142.

infinitely more so than it is in our power to grasp, and not for us only, but in actuality therefore in Himself. (II/1, p. 325)

The stress fell neither on metaphysical agnosticism nor on a common scale of similarity but on "incomprehensible similarity" (II/1, p. 227). Eminence, in our knowledge of God, was not less valid than negation but more so. For the top-down approach, God was indeed light, actually and unreservedly light, despite being unlike any that we know.

In short, on this reading the differences between Aquinas and Barth can be regarded as more nearly a matter of emphasis than of substance. Both, in effect, made the necessary affirmations, not only that "God is light," but also that "God is unlike any light that we know." Nevertheless, differences in method led inevitably to different inflections. Where negation was essential for the one, eminence was decisive for the other. Theology after Aquinas and Barth might do well not to remove this tension but to operate dialectically between the two.

7

Three reflections may be in order by way of conclusion.

First, "uncreated Light" as a metaphor in Christian theology is best correlated with concepts whose form is paradoxical. God's uncreated Light is not only brilliant and glorious, it is also blinding and profoundly unapproachable. This holy and searing, this uncreated Light is described by faith as being revealed in its hiddenness and hidden in its being revealed. That may be one reason why the tradition speaks so paradoxically about God's blinding radiance and luminous darkness. The relationship of created to uncreated Light is one of mystery and inconceivable similarity. God is not partially but totally hidden under the creaturely forms that reveal him, and yet under those forms God is also truly and graciously revealed. Despite the radical limitations of these forms, faith may trust that God is not other than he has revealed himself to be in them. The Lord God is free to disclose himself under creaturely forms without ceasing to be God, even as they are used by him for this purpose without ceasing to be creaturely. Faith has confidence in the midst of the inexpressible, because it is convinced that these paradoxes suggest something of how God has revealed himself in Jesus Christ.

Second, created light as described by quantum mechanics offers an unexpected but striking metaphor for uncreated Light. According to quantum mechanics, a photon is an elementary particle that does not consist of parts. As the basic unit of light and all other forms of electromagnetic radiation, it is irreducible to any other elements. Photons are therefore simple and noncomposite. In the history of Christian theology (from Irenaeus, say, to Torrance), the idea of uncreated Light is commonly associated with the divine essence, which has itself been seen as simple, irreducible, and noncomposite. Photons and the divine essence therefore share, intriguingly, the attribute of irreducible simplicity. Of course this parallel should not be pressed too far. Unlike God, for example, photons may be refracted by a lens or exhibit wave interference with themselves. Unlike photons, moreover, the Trinitarian essence of God, though absolutely simple, is inseparable from the three divine "persons" which belong to it, and from their eternal *perichoresis* (or dynamic coinherence). The divine essence, therefore, though noncomposite, is internally and ineffably complex. The triune God, although irreducibly simple, is also at the same time intrinsically three — another (and fundamental) example of how uncreated Light, as confessed by faith, must finally be described in terms of an inconceivable *coniunctio oppositorum.*

Finally, as John Polkinghorne has suggested, a parallel between created light and uncreated Light might also be drawn between photon entanglement and the Trinity. Photon entanglement refers to what happens when one photon is split into two in such a way that instant communication takes place between them. Could this be, Polkinghorne wonders, something like the perichoretic exchange of love within the Trinity? In photon entanglement, furthermore, the one photon can no longer be described without full mention of its counterpart. This interrelationship might seem reminiscent of the Trinity insofar as the Father is not the Father except in relation to the Son, nor is the Son the Son except in relation to the Father, so that (leaving the Holy Spirit aside) the two are defined by their relations of origin, and neither can be described without mention of the other. Polkinghorne reflects, however: "I think that to claim analogy here might be too strong an assertion to make, but there is certainly a satisfying degree of consonance discernible between the relationality of the physical world and the Trinitarian character of its Creator." This statement seems admirable for its reticence. Perhaps the most to be expected from the dialogue between physics and theology would not be strong analogies but satisfying degrees of consonance.

Appendix: On the Reason and Revelation Chart

Some recent interpreters of Aquinas seem to think that his "proofs" for God's existence presuppose certain truths of faith, but that on that basis one can extract "truths of reason," which (once extracted) stand on their own. These independent rational truths about God, though they are merely formal, can be used as an apologetic bridge by which to move from the formal to the substantial. The initial (substantial) truths of faith, once the bridge is crossed over to them, can then be supplemented by further (substantial) truths of faith. (This would be the "Transitional version" of Type 2.)

This "supplementalist" idea is, in effect, a sophisticated and highly refined version of the older, cruder "foundationalist" conception. According to the older foundationalism, the truths of reason did not first require truths of faith in order to be known, and they were themselves substantial, not merely formal. The (substantial) truths of reason provided a "foundation" upon which the (substantial) truths of faith could then build. (This would be the "Foundational version" of Type 2.)

In his 1934 essay "No," Barth associated Emil Brunner with foundationalism (the old Type 2), though he also rejected "correlationalism" (Type 3). He presupposed, but did not greatly develop (until much later), "coherentism" (Type 4). Dowey and Gerrish seem to interpret Calvin as being Type 3, whereas Barth seems to think that the spirit, if not always the letter, of Calvin is most in accord with Type 4.

I don't think the newer argument from reason (e.g., Preller) works, if it contends that one "must" move from rational reflection to the formal (i.e., empty and "algebraic") conception of "deity," so that the existence of the world, taken as a whole, can be made "intelligible." I would grant, however, that the word "must" could be changed to "might," i.e., the world *might* be made intelligible in this way. I would regard the more tentative version to be a stronger argument. The existence of the world, taken as a whole, *might* be made "intelligible" by appealing to an ultimate ground for it in "God" as a transcendent Creator. This Creator, however, would (as the Thomists concede) remain "incomprehensible" in itself. ("We know *that* 'God' is, but not *what* 'God' is." *Deus non est in genere.*) The existence of the world would thus be made "intelligible" by an appeal to incomprehensible transcendence.

- Type 2 presupposes some sort of significant continuity between the independent truths of reason and the revealed truths of faith.

- Type 3 retains the idea that both types of truth are mutually independent, while no longer insisting on a bridge of continuity by which one could cross from the one to the other.
- Type 4 takes all natural or secondary sources of revelation as entirely dependent, for their proper use, on the truths of faith, so that no valid theological truths are logically independent of and alongside those of faith. Natural revelation, for example, would not be denied but could only be properly apprehended and acknowledged on the basis of faith.
- Type 4 posits a discontinuity between the truths of faith and all ideas about God derived from natural reason — whether substantive or formal, and whether originally derived or not from faith. These independent rational ideas, however, can sometimes be critically appropriated on the basis of faith so that they are then reconfigured, and are no longer independent of faith's knowledge but dependent on it. There is thus no way from reason to faith, but there is a way from faith to reason. The original discontinuity is overcome on the basis of special revelation.

The conclusion to my chapter posits that Type 4 is not necessarily incompatible with a version of Type 3. If Type 3 involved two *independent* circles (one greater and the other lesser), rather than an ellipse with two foci, then they might be seen as standing in a relation of correlation. The larger circle would include everything in Type 4. The lesser circle would represent, in effect, a chastened version of what Type 2 thinks can be gained on the basis of natural reason. It would be a chastened version because it would involve only a set of questions about the *possibility* of the existence of a Deity, not a set of necessary conclusions. Insofar as Thomas can be interpreted in the direction of this chastened version (with or beyond White, Preller, and perhaps others), his position would not stand in conflict with Barth's robust version of Type 4. The views of Thomas (on the theological truths of reason) and Barth, seen as two mutually independent circles, could be (critically) correlated in Type 3 fashion without positing a continuity or eventual synthesis between them.

Reason and Revelation

	TYPE 1	TYPE 2	TYPE 3	TYPE 4	TYPE 5
	Reductionist	Supplementalist	Correlationist	Coherentist	Fideist
	Revelation within the Limits of Reason Alone	Revelation as Perfecting Reason	Reason and Revelation in Creative Tension	Reason within the Limits of Revelation Alone	Revelation Alone
	Reason as self-sufficient	Reason as independent of and preparatory for Revelation	Reason as independent of and alongside Revelation	Reason as internal to and dependent on Revelation	Revelation as noncognitive and extrarational
	Faith as merely symbolic	Reason → Revelation	Reason → Revelation	Reason → Revelation	Revelation as a matter of inner experience and a form of life
	Pattern of Reduction	Pattern of Completion and Synthesis	Pattern of Coordination	Pattern of Inclusion and Subordination	Pattern of Incommensurability
		Foundational version: Trapezoid plus Triangle	Image: Ellipse with Two Foci	Image: Circle with Center and Periphery	
		Traditional version: Narrow Bridge from the Formal to the Substantial	Two Circles, Independent and Separate		
		F → S			

Contributors

Gerald O'Collins, S.J., a prolific author in Christology, was, for more than three decades, professor of systematic and fundamental theology at the Pontifical Gregorian University (Rome). He taught at the Weston School of Theology (Boston Theological Institute) in Cambridge, Massachusetts, and the Jesuit Theological College in Melbourne for five years before joining the Gregorian faculty in 1973. He has initiated and co-chaired international ecumenical symposia on the resurrection (1996), the Trinity (1998), the Incarnation (2000), the redemption (2003), and the legacy of Pope John Paul II (2008) and co-edited their proceedings. In 2006, he was made a Companion of the Order of Australia. Among his fifty-six books are *Christology: A Biblical, Historical, and Systematic Study of Jesus Christ* (1995; 2nd updated ed. 2009), *Following the Way* (2000), *Living Vatican II: The 21st Council for the 21st Century* (2006), *The Lord's Prayer* (2006), *Christ Our Redeemer: A Christian Approach to Salvation* (2007), *Jesus: A Portrait* (2008), *Salvation for All: God's Other Peoples* (2008), *Catholicism: A Very Short Introduction* (2008), and, most recently, *Jesus Our Priest: A Christian Approach to the Priesthood of Christ* (2010).

Mary Ann Meyers is a writer and the senior fellow at the John Templeton Foundation. For more than a decade she served as Secretary of the University of Pennsylvania, where she taught American civilization courses in the history of religion in America. She was subsequently president of the Annenberg Foundation. Earlier in her career, she was an assistant to the University of Pennsylvania's president and taught at Haverford College. She is author of *Art, Education and African-American Culture: Albert Barnes and the Science of Philanthropy* (2004 and 2006) and *A New World Jerusalem: The Swedenborgian Experience of Community Construction* (1983), as well as a co-author of *Religion in American Life* (1987), *Coping with Serious Illness* (1977), and *Death in America* (1975).

OTHER CONTRIBUTORS

Markus Aspelmeyer is a senior researcher at the Institute for Quantum Optics and Quantum Information (IQOQI) of the Austrian Academy of Sciences. His investigations have focused on quantum optics and quantum entanglement. His current investigations probe quantum effects in massive mechanical systems, thought to be describable in terms of classical physics, and open up a new arena for studying the diffuse "border" between classical and quantum worlds. The winner in 2007 of the Fresnel Prize of the European Physical Society and the Ignaz L. Lieben Prize of the Austrian Academy of Sciences, he was awarded the Fritz Kohlrausch Prize of the Austrian Physical Society and the START Prize of the Austrian Ministry for Science and Research in 2008. In addition to papers published in leading science journals, Dr. Aspelmeyer is the co-editor (with Keith Schwab) of *Mechanical Systems at the Quantum Limit* (2008).

John Behr is professor of patristics and dean at St. Vladimir's Orthodox Theological Seminary in Crestwood, New York. He writes about early church history, especially the development of theological reflection, asceticism, and Christian anthropology. In addition to publishing articles in scholarly journals, he is the editor (with Andrew Louth and Dimitri Conomos) of *Abba: The Tradition of Orthodoxy in the West* (2003) and the author of five other books, including *St. Irenaeus of Lyons: On the Apostolic Preaching* (1997), *Asceticism and Anthropology in Irenaeus and Clement* (2000), a two-volume study of the formation of Christian theology, *The Way to Nicaea* (2001) and *The Nicene Faith* (2004), and, most recently, *The Mystery of Christ: Life in Death* (2006). He is currently working on a monograph titled *The Case Against Diodore and Theodore: Texts and Their Contexts,* an edition, translation, and commentary on the extant fragments of the writings of Diodore of Tarsus and Theodore of Mopsuestia. Dr. Behr is an Orthodox priest.

Marco Bersanelli is a professor of astronomy and astrophysics and director of the Ph.D. School in Physics, Astrophysics, and Applied Physics at the University of Milan, where he does research in observational cosmology. Previously, he was a visiting scholar at the Lawrence Berkeley Laboratory, University of California, and worked at the Istituto di Fisica Cosmica, Consiglio Nazionale delle Ricerche, Milan, as senior scientist. He has participated in a number of experiments in cosmology, including two expeditions to the Amundsen-Scott South Pole Station in Antarctica, and is one of the leading scientists of the Planck space mission, the European Space Agency project studying the early universe. In addition to numerous scientific papers, he has published scientific and interdisciplinary essays and books, including *From Galileo to Gell-Mann* (2009).

Robert W. Boyd is Canada Excellence Research Chair in Quantum Nonlinear Optics at the University of Ottawa and is also M. Parker Givens Professor of Optics and Professor of Physics at the University of Rochester. His research focuses on nonlinear optical interactions and nonlinear optical properties of materials, as well as the application of nonlinear optics, including quantum and nonlinear optical imaging. A fellow of the Optical Society of America and of the American Physical Society, he was recently awarded the Willis E. Lamb Award for Laser Science and Quantum Optics and the Humboldt Research Award for his breakthroughs in manipulating the properties of light. His research was selected by *Discover* as one of the top one hundred research stories in 2006 — and one of only six from physics chosen by this science and technology magazine. In addition to papers published in scientific journals, Dr. Boyd is the editor (with M. G. Raymer and L. M. Narducci) of *Optical Instabilities* (1986), (with Govind P. Agrawal) of *Contemporary Nonlinear Optics* (1992), and, most recently, (with Svetlana G. Lukishova and Y. R. Shen) of *Self-Focusing: Past and Present* (2009). He is also the author of *Radiometry and the Detection of Optical Radiation* (1986) and *Nonlinear Optics* (1992, and a new third edition, 2008).

David Brown, the Wardlaw Professor of Theology, Aesthetics and Culture at St. Mary's College, University of St. Andrews, has focused his research and writing on the relations between theology and the wider culture, initially in relation to philosophy and, in recent years, as expressed through the arts, both historically and at the present time. He also has published on more general doctrinal issues and contributed to ongoing discussions in ethics and philosophical theology. An Anglican priest, he formerly served as a university lecturer in ethics and philosophical theology at Oxford University and as Van Mildert Professor of Divinity at Durham University. He is a member of the British Academy. The editor of eight books, he is the author of twelve others, including *Choices: Ethics and the Christian* (1983), *The Divine Trinity* (1985), *Continental Philosophy and Modern Theology* (1987), *Invitation to Theology* (1989), *The Word to Set You Free: Living Faith and Biblical Criticism* (1995), *Through the Eyes of Saints: A Pilgrimage through History* (2005), and a major five-volume series linking biblical revelation and other experiences of God to the arts and to culture more broadly: *Tradition and Imagination* (1999), *Discipleship and Imagination* (2000), *God and Enhancement of Place* (2004), *God and Grace of Body* (2007), and *God and Mystery in Words* (2008).

Robert Dodaro, O.S.A., is president of the Augustinian Patristic Institute in Rome. He specializes in the writings of the Latin Fathers, especially those of Augustine of Hippo, the philosopher, theologian, and preeminent Doctor of the Church. He formerly served on the faculty of theology of the Pontifical Lateran University. In addition to publishing numerous papers in scholarly journals, he is the co-editor of two books, (with George Lawless) *Augustine and his Critics: Essays in Honor of Gerald Bonner* (2000) and (with E. Margaret Atkins) *Augustine: Political Writings* (2001), and the author of *Christ and the Just Society in the Thought of Augustine* (2004).

Michael Heller is a professor of philosophy at the Pontifical Academy of Theology in Cracow (Poland) and an adjunct member of the staff of the Vatican Observatory. A Roman Catholic priest and winner of the Templeton Prize in 2008, he is the founder and director of the Copernicus Centre for Interdisciplinary Studies in Cracow. He is the author of more than twenty books, including *Is Physics an Art?* (1998), *Creative Tension* (2003), and *Some Mathematical Physics for Philosophers* (2006).

George Hunsinger is the Hazel Thompson McCord Professor of Systematic Theology at Princeton Theological Seminary and a leading interpreter of the thought of Karl Barth. He currently serves as president of the Karl Barth Society of North America and was awarded the 2010 Karl Barth Award by the Union of Evangelical Churches in the Evangelical Church in Germany. Dr. Hunsinger formerly taught at New Brunswick Theological Seminary and Bangor Theological Seminary, and for four years, he served as director of the Center for Theological Inquiry at Princeton. A Presbyterian minister, he was the principal author of the new Presbyterian catechism adopted in 1998. He is the founder of the National Religious Campaign Against Torture (NRCAT), and, in recognition of his work with that organization, he received the Bishop James K. Matthew Award of the Washington-based Churches' Center for Theology and Public Policy. He is the co-editor of two books and the editor of three others, most recently, *Torture Is a Moral Issue: Christians, Jews, Muslims, and People of Conscience Speak Out*, which was published by Wm. B. Eerdmans in 2008. Dr. Hunsinger is also the author of *How to Read Karl Barth: The Shape of His Theology* (1991 and, in German translation, 2009), *Disruptive Grace: Studies in the Theology of Karl Barth* (2000), *The Eucharist and Ecumenism: Let Us Keep the Feast* (2008), and *Theological Commentary on Philippians* (2009).

John Polkinghorne, K.B.E., F.R.S., the former president of Queens' College, Cambridge, and the winner of the 2002 Templeton Prize, has been a leading figure in the dialogue of science and religion for more than two decades. He resigned his professorship of mathematical physics at Cambridge University to take up a new vocation in mid-life and was ordained a priest in the Church of England in 1982. A Fellow of the Royal Society, he was knighted by Queen Elizabeth II in 1997. In addition to an extensive body of writing on theoretical elementary particle physics, including *Quantum Theory: A Very Short Introduction* (2002), he is the editor or co-editor of four books, the co-author (with Michael Welker) of *Faith in the Living God: A Dialogue* (2001), and the author of nineteen other books on the interrelationship of science and theology, including *Belief in God in an Age of Science* (1998), a volume composed of his Terry Lectures at Yale University, *Science and Theology* (1998), *Faith, Science and Understanding* (2000), *Traffic in Truth-Exchanges between Theology and Science* (2001), *The God of Hope and the End of the World* (2002), *Living with Hope* (2003), *Science and the Trinity: The Christian Encounter with Reality* (2004), *Exploring Reality: The Intertwining of Science and Religion* (2005), *Quantum Physics and Theology: An Unexpected Kinship* (2007), *From Physicist to Priest* (2007), *Theology in the Context of Science* (2008), and *Questions of Truth: Fifty-one Responses to Questions about God, Science, and Belief* (2008).

Andrew M. Steane is university lecturer in physics at Oxford University, where he is a fellow of Exeter College. He has made central contributions to understanding how the laws of nature place constraints upon, and allow opportunities for, the storage, conveyance, and processing of information. His research involves fundamental questions about the nature of quantum mechanics. A fellow of the Institute of Physics, he received its Maxwell Medal and Prize in 2000 for his discovery of quantum error correction. His work included not only proofs of the main ideas of one of the foundational concepts of quantum information physics and quantum computing but also explicit constructions of codes and the networks to generate them and to use them to stabilize fragile quantum systems without disturbing their stored quantum information. He is the author of many papers published in scientific journals.

Kathryn E. Tanner, a professor of systematic theology at Yale Divinity School, relates past thought from the history of Western theological traditions to areas of contemporary concern using critical, social, and feminist theory. She was formerly the Dorothy Grant Maclear Professor of Theology at the University of Chicago Divinity School, where she taught for fifteen years, after earlier serving as a member of Yale's religious studies faculty. Co-editor (with Delwin Brown and Sheila Davaney) of *Converging on Culture: Theologians in Dialogue with Cultural Analysis and Criticism* (2001) and (with John Webster and Iain Torrance) of *The Oxford Handbook of Systematic Theology* (2007), she is editor of *Spirit in the Cities* (2004) and the author of six other books: *God and Creation in Christian Theology: Tyranny of Empowerment* (1988), *The Politics of God: Christian Theologies and Social Justice* (1992), *Theories of Culture: A New Agenda for Theology* (1997), *Jesus, Humanity, and the Trinity* (2001), *The Economy of Grace* (2005), and *Christ the Key* (2010).

Kallistos Ware, Metropolitan of Diokleia (Timothy Ware) was the Spalding Lecturer in Eastern Orthodox Studies at Oxford University for thirty-five years until his retirement in 2005. He joined the Orthodox Church in 1958, was ordained a deacon and given the new name of "Kallistos" seven years later, and ordained to the priesthood in 1966. He took monastic vows at the Monastery of St. John the Theologian in Patmos, Greece, and remains a member of that community. The founder of the Greek Orthodox Parish of the Holy Trinity in Oxford, he was consecrated titular Bishop of Diokleia, the first Englishman to become a bishop within the Orthodox Church since the eleventh century — in 1982. In 2007, he was elevated to titular Metropolitan of Diokleia. Long active in the work of Christian unity, Metropolitan Kallistos was a member of the Anglican-Orthodox Joint Doctrinal Discussions for eleven years and also served as the Orthodox co-chair of the Preparatory Commission for the Orthodox-Methodist Theological Dialogue. In addition to publishing articles in scholarly journals, Bishop Kallistos is the co-translator of two Orthodox service books and of *The Philokalia,* a collection of texts written between the fourth and fifteenth centuries by Orthodox spiritual masters. He is the author of eight books, including *The Orthodox Church* (1963; rev. ed. 1993). Two of a projected six volumes of his collected works have been published as *The Inner Kingdom* (2000) and *In the Image of Trinity* (2006).

Anton Zeilinger, one of the world's leading researchers in the foundations of quantum mechanics, is professor of physics and director of the Experimental Physics Institute at the University of Vienna and scientific director of the Institute of Quantum Optics and Quantum Information of the Austrian Academy of Sciences. His pioneering investigations of multi-particle entanglement received international attention in 1997 when he and his colleagues at the University of Innsbruck, where he was then directing the Institute of Experimental Physics, confirmed the possibility of quantum teleportation by demonstrating, through the use of pairs of entangled photons, that the properties of one particle can be instantly transferred to another over an arbitrary distance. Dr. Zeilinger's quantum interference experiments with "buckyballs" (molecules whose shapes resemble the geodesic domes designed by R. Buckminster Fuller), so far the largest objects to have demonstrated quantum behavior, have proven that clusters of more than one hundred atoms obey quantum-mechanical rules, thus extending the quantum domain farther than ever before. More recently, he has become interested in tests of Leggett-type, nonlocal theories, as well as in fundamental phenomena in quantum entanglement of ultra-cold atoms among other scientific problems. The former president of the Austrian Physical Society, Dr. Zeilinger was named Austrian Scientist of the Year in 1996, and his other honors include the Senior Humboldt Fellow Prize, Germany's Order pour le Mérite, the 2000 Science Prize of the City of Vienna, the 2005 King Faisal Prize, and the Isaac Newton Medal of the British Institute of Physics. In 2010 he shared the Wolf Prize in physics for elementary conceptual and experimental contributions to quantum physics. He is a fellow of the American Physical Society, an honorary member of the Slovak Academy of Sciences, a foreign member of the Serbian Academy of Sciences, and an honorary professor of the University of Science and Technology of China. In addition to publishing in major scientific journals, he is the editor (with Dirk Bouwmeester and Artur Ekert) of *The Physics of Quantum Information* (2000) and (with Chiara Macchiavello and G. Massimo Palma) of *Quantum Computation and Quantum Information Theory* (2001). He is also the author of two books, *Einsteins Schleier* (2003) and *Einsteins Spuk* (2005).

Index

absolute time, 19-21
acoustic waves, 98-99
active potency, 227
affirmation, way of, 151
Alexander of Alexandria, 117
Ambrose, 117n.25
analogia entis, 18, 227-29
analogical discourse, 210, 214, 221-22, 223-25
analogy, 6-7, 18-19, 22, 137
anastasis, 224
Andrew of Crete, 132
angels, 106n.3
anisotrophies, 94-96, 98
apaugasma, 114
Apollinarius, 125
apophatic theology, 133, 143-44, 187, 220
Apophthegmata, 148-49
architecture, 11
Aristarchus, 81, 94
Aristotle, 2, 22, 81, 173, 196-97
Arius, 117
art, 11-12, 163-64, 168-73
artisan analogy, 11, 126-27
ascent, way of, 151
Aspelmeyer, Markus, 4, 5, 6, 9, 205-6, 207
astrology, 74
astronomy, 89
Athanasius, 2, 114n.19, 115, 117-18, 123, 124
Augustine, 5, 12, 74, 106n.3, 112, 120, 128-29, 158, 173-74, 182, 189, 195-207, 210

"backward light," 70-71
Balla, Giacomo, 174-76
Baptism, 157
Barlaam the Calabrian, 154
Barth, Karl, 12-13, 221-25, 228-31, 233-34
Barzel, Ammon, 176
Basil of Caesarea, 118, 119, 149, 190, 197
beauty, 111, 112
Behr, John, 6, 12, 154
Being as Communion, 25
Bell, John, 60
Bell theorem, 60
Bersanelli, Marco, 10
Big Bang, 2, 8, 17, 25-26, 28, 39
Birgitta of Sweden, 11, 172, 182
blackbody radiation, 21
block universe, 20
Bloy, Léon, 31
Boccioni, Umberto, 174
Boehme, Jakob, 153
Boethius, 20
Bonaventure, 11, 120, 128
Bondi, Hermann, 40
Book of Common Prayer, 158
Bohr, Niels, 64
bose statistics, 25, 27
"bottom-up" approach, 5
Boyd, Robert, 4, 6, 9, 105
Bragg, William, 81
Brancusi, Constantin, 181
Brower, Jeffrey E., 220n.28
Brown, David, 11, 18, 107, 120, 139

Brukner, C., 66
Brunner, Emil, 233
burning bush, 105, 139, 150
Burns, Robert, 17-18
Burrell, David, 228-29
Byzantine vision of light, 183-94

Calvin, John, 233
Camelot, Pierre-Thomas, 195
Cappadocians, 119, 149
Caravaggio, 172
Carrà, Carlo, 174
cataphatic theology, 143
causality, 9, 68, 71-79
cave analogy (Plato), 1, 138
celestial bodies, 80
chaos, 136, 161
Chartres cathedral, 169
Chora fresco, 103
Christian mysticism, 112
Christmas, 112
Christology, 149
church, 157
classical physics, 24
Clement of Alexandria, 134, 143, 144-45,
    150, 152, 209
clock synchronization, 73-74
cloud, 109, 139-40, 142, 161, 166-68
COBE satellite, 94, 96
coherentism, 233
Congar, Yves, 119
consubstantiality, 116
contemplation, 132
contingency, 12
contingent beings, 219
contraction and emission, 197
Copernicus, 94
correlationism, 233
correlations, between science and theol-
    ogy, 6
Cosmic Background Radiation, 8, 26
cosmic expansion, 10, 92-93
cosmic microwave background (CMB),
    91-98
cosmic properties, of light, 25-26
cosmology
    of Grosseteste, 83, 99
    modern, 8, 10, 99-100
Council of Chalcedon (451), 1, 23

Council of Constantinople (381), 1, 118
Council of Nicaea (325), 2, 115, 116, 199
covenant, 161
Cowper, William, 171
created light, 12, 133, 204, 207, 211, 215-17,
    220, 227, 231-32
creatio ex nihilo, 161
creation, 221-22
    as continual process, 54
    light analogy for, 126-28
Crombie, Alistair, 82
crucifixion, 135, 192
curvature of spacetime, 46, 99
Cyril of Jerusalem, 118

Dalì, Salvador, 12, 176-77
Damascus Road, 104, 165
Dante Alighieri, 10, 85-88, 93-94, 99,
    100, 120, 182
"dark energy," 26
darkness, 11, 33, 107, 136, 111, 187. *See also*
    thick darkness
    of crucifixion, 135
    as evil, 108, 136, 160
    as mystery, 140, 159
    in New Testament, 142
    of night sky, 91-92
    as part of created order, 135
    in Platonism, 138
    on Sinai, 11, 132, 135, 139-41, 150, 152,
        161, 164, 183
darkness symbolism, 142-43, 151-52, 153
"dark night of the soul," 136, 166
Davies, Brian, 220n.28, 230
death, 38, 107, 193, 194
decoherence, 52
deism, 9, 54
delight, 121, 202
Democritus, 99n.52
Descartes, René, 174
descent, way of, 151
Desert Fathers, 148, 158
de Sitter, W., 34-35, 36
Diadochus of Photice, 146-48, 154
Dionysius the Areopagite, 18, 119, 143,
    151-52, 156, 165-66, 168
dipole anisotropy, 94
Dirac, Paul, 22
distant causality, 73-74

divine indwelling, 207
divine simplicity, 208-15, 220
Divisionists, 174, 181
Dodaro, Robert, 5, 12, 112, 158
Dowey, Edward A., 233

Easter, 103-4, 112
Eastern Christian tradition, 12
Eckhart, Meister, 166
Eddington, A. S., 33, 34, 38, 73
Einstein, Albert, 2, 19, 21, 24, 33-34, 37-
    38, 61, 74-75, 77, 89
Eiseley, Loren, 3
electromagnetic fields, 46, 88
electromagnetic radiation, 2, 44, 45-47,
    232
electrons, 46-47
eminence, 220-21, 225, 231
Empedocles, 173, 197
Empyrean, of Dante, 86-87, 99
enlightenment, from truth, 108
entangled state. *See* quantum entangle-
    ment
environment, 44, 53-54
epiphanies, 178
Epiphany, 112
epistemology, 9, 64, 205
Eriugena, John Scotus, 119-20
eschatological light, 184-86
Eucharist, 157, 226
Evagrius, 143, 146-47, 153n.63, 154, 183
Everett, Hugh, 51
evolutionary biology, 53-54
Exodus, 139
expansion of the universe, 35-36, 38, 41-
    42, 79
experience
    of God, 5-7, 107, 121, 181
    mystical/spiritual, 7, 20, 23, 119, 133-37,
        143, 146, 159, 165-66, 185-88, 203-4
    of St. Paul, 104, 132-33
    of war, 29, 30-31

Feast of Booths, 110
Feast of the Transfiguration, 157
fermi statistics, 25
fine-tuning, 26
fire, 113-14, 115
firmament, 84

Flavin, Dan, 12, 178-81
forms, 83, 127, 141, 144, 146, 168-69, 174,
    201, 207, 230-31
foundationalism, 233
Fourth Lateran Council, 12, 213-14, 222
Fox, George, 137
Francis of Assisi, 158
Friedman, Alexander, 34-35, 37
Futurists, 12, 174, 181

Galileo, 80-81
Gamow, George, 39
Garrigou-Lagrange, Réginald, 227
Geerten, Tot Sint Jans, 172
generation, of the Son, 115, 124, 126-27
geometric cosmology, 38
Gerrish, B. A., 233
GHZ theorem, 60
Glashow-Weinberg-Salam model, 2
glory, 105-6, 109, 112, 142, 162, 184
go-between, light as, 47
God
    aid in illumination, 173-74
    associated with darkness, 11, 132, 136-
        37, 160, 161-62, 165, 181-82
    as cloud and shade, 11
    as creator, 54-55, 106-7
    incomprehensibility of, 136, 140-41,
        144, 150, 230, 233
    as light, 1-2, 81, 85, 86, 107-8, 183, 197-
        99
    love of, 203, 207
    presence of, 81, 85, 128-29, 140, 184
    relationship with world, 9
    sovereignty of, 221
    transcendence of, 152, 187, 211
Godart, Odon, 28, 39, 41
Gold, Thomas, 40
Gothic architecture, 168-73
grace, 202, 222-25, 227
grand unified theory (GUT), 2
gravitational fields, 94
"greater dissimilarity," 12, 213, 214, 220
Greek Fathers, 3, 11, 132
Greek philosophy, 11, 81, 138, 196-97
Greenberg, Clement, 178
Greenberger, D., 60
Gregory of Nazianzus, 2, 118, 125, 134,
    143, 145-46, 149, 164, 190

Gregory of Nyssa, 11, 118, 119, 120, 128, 129, 143, 149-51, 152, 154, 156, 164-65, 166
Gregory Palamas, 11, 12, 113, 132-34, 143, 153, 154-57, 184-87
Grosseteste, Robert, 2, 10, 82-85, 88, 89, 92, 95, 99, 100
ground of being, 55
group velocity, 68, 70, 76
Grünewald, Matthias, 103

haloes, 172-73
harmonizing tendency, 41-42
Harries, Richard, 54
heaven, 86-87, 104
Heisenberg's uncertainty principle, 26
hell, 137n.13
Heller, Michael, 8-9
Hemming, Laurence Paul, 227-29
hesychasts, 113, 154, 155, 184, 186
Hilary of Poitiers, 120, 123, 212-13, 230
Hildegard of Bingen, 120
holiness, 106, 202
Holy of Holies, 140, 162-64
Holy Spirit, as light, 10, 113-14, 10, 118-20, 122, 202
Homilies of Macarius, 143, 147-49, 154, 155
homoousios, 104n.1, 115, 116, 117, 119
Horne, M. A., 60
Hoyle, Fred, 40
Hubble, Edward, 90
"Hubble's constant," 36
Hubble Space Telescope (HST), 90-91
Humble Approach Initiative (Templeton Foundation), 3-4, 13
Hunsinger, George, 7, 12, 112
Huygens, Christiaan, 2
hypersphere, 88, 93
Hyppolytus, 214-15

Ignatius of Antioch, 194
illumination, 118, 122, 128-29, 145, 149, 152, 157
Augustine on, 200, 201-5, 207
image of God, 188
Incarnation, 188-89
incompatibility theorem, 61
incomprehensible intelligibility, 229

indistinguishability, of quantum entities, 24-25
"infinite qualitative difference," between Creator and creature, 228
inflation, 96
information, finiteness of, 66
information velocity, 76, 79
inner, personal experience, 156
"Inner Light," 137
intellectual light, 138
interactions, 44, 47, 53, 54
interval, 21
Irenaeus, 11, 12, 142-44, 148, 155, 194, 208-15, 216, 220-21, 230

Jammer, M., 74
Jerusalem, as zone of light, 107
Jesus Christ
    glory of, 109
    human and divine natures of, 22-23, 26
    as "Light from Light," 1, 10, 108-11, 112, 114-17
    as "sun of justice," 199
    as "tabernacling" among us, 164
John Chrysostom, 134
John of Damascus, 120, 122, 126, 185
John of the Cross, 136, 166
Jones, David, 106n.3
Joyce, James, 178
justice, 199, 203
Justin Martyr, 10, 115

Kepler, Johannes, 91
Kerr, Fergus, 228
King's College Chapel (Cambridge), 170
knowledge, 201, 204, 205-6
Koester, Craig, 114

Lambert, Dominique, 28, 30, 36
Langton, Stephen, 120
laser lights, 25
Leggett, A. J., 61
Lemaître, Georges, 8-9, 28-42
Leo XIII, Pope, 32
light. *See also* created light; uncreated light
    as intelligible in itself, 4-5
    and matter, 84-85, 92-93

as metaphor, 7-8, 10, 133
as source of corporeity, 83
and space, 83-84
as symbol, 44-45, 47, 160
transforming effect of, 153, 156
truth claims about, 5
light and darkness, 131-59, 162-66, 181-82
light-by-light scattering, 69
light fields, 69
"light from heaven," 104
light mysticism, 11, 140, 142-49
light on Mt. Tabor. *See* Transfiguration
local realism, 57-61, 64
logarithmic model of the universe, 35-36, 37
logic, 22, 78
Logos, 164
Lonergan, Bernard, 23
"looking up" and "looking down," 43
love, 202-4, 207
lumen, 195-96
luminosity, 45
"luminous darkness," 150, 151, 152
lux, 195-96

MacSwain, Robert, 228
Manicheans, 196n.5, 197-98
material being, 200
Matheson, George, 11, 167-68
matter, and light, 84-85, 92-93
Maximus the Confessor, 2, 134, 153n.63
Maxwell, James Clerk, 2, 19, 88, 217
McInerny, Ralph, 229
measurement problem, 61-64
metaphor, 6-7, 17, 137, 181
metathesis, 224
microwave background radiation, 41
Milton, John, 170-71
mind, 204, 205, 207
Minkowski space, 75
miracle, 110, 189, 223, 225, 229-30
modalism, 19
Molnar, Paul D., 219
monastic life, 6
Mondrian, Piet, 181
Moses, 132, 135, 139-41, 150, 152, 161, 183
Motovilov, Nicolas, 149
Mount Sinai. *See* Sinai
Mount Tabor. *See* Tabor

mystery, 140, 144, 159, 164, 205, 229-30
mystical experience, 7, 20, 23, 119, 133-37, 143, 146, 159, 165-66, 185-88, 203-4
mystical union, 136, 158, 159

Nash, Ronald, 204
natural law, 53
natural revelation, 234
natural theology, 228
necessary being, 219
negation, 151-52, 220-21, 225, 231. *See also* apophatic theology
neo-Platonism, 112, 205, 207, 209n.3, 229
neo-Pythagoreans, 209n.3
neo-Thomism, 42, 227
new life, 23, 194
Newman, Barnet, 178, 181
Newtonian physics, 19, 22, 65
Nicene-Constantinopolitan Creed, 149
Nicene Creed, 43-44, 104, 122, 149
Nicolas of Cusa, 151
nocturnal mystics. *See* darkness symbolism
nominalism, 210
nonbeing, 200
nonlinear optical effects, 68, 69-71
Novalis, 159
nurture, vs. genetics, 54

observer, framework of, 65-67, 206
O'Collins, Gerald, 6, 10
O'Connor, Timothy, 219
Olbers paradox, 91n.29
ontological participation, 229
ontological stratification, 218
ontology, 56, 205
optics, 82
Origen, 104n.1, 116, 118, 143, 145, 164, 190-92, 209
original sin, 202, 206
Otto, Rudolf, 140
"outer darkness," 137

pantheism, 198
Parmenides, 209n.3
participation, 7, 207, 229
particle theory of light, 2, 21-22, 89
passion of Christ, 189-93
passive potency, 224, 226-27

Pauli, Wolfgang, 65
Pelikan, Jaroslav, 114n.19, 115
Penzias, Arno, 41, 91
perfection, 156
perichoresis, 232
phase velocity, 69
Philo, 140, 143, 144-45, 150, 152, 209n.3
Philoponus, John, 2, 217
photon beamsplitter, 62-63, 65
photon entanglement, 232
photons, 22, 23, 24-25, 46, 89, 98, 177
  polarization of, 57-60
  simplicity of, 232
physical realism, 9, 44, 56-61, 67
physical theory, 64-65
Planck, Max, 21, 89, 177
Planck satellite, 95, 96-98
Plato, 1, 138, 143, 145, 173, 196-97, 209n.3
Platonism, 138, 140, 202
Plotinus, 1, 138, 143, 144, 153, 154, 196,
  209n.3
Poincaré, Henri, 30, 31
Polanyi, Michael, 218
Polkinghorne, John, 5, 6, 8, 105, 137, 232
Pope, Alexander, 171
positive theology, 221
positivism, 31
prayer, 6, 156-57
predicates, of divine being, 209-12, 225
predictions with certainty, 60
Preller, Victor, 227-29, 233, 234
Previati, Gaetano, 174
Primeval Atom hypothesis, 29, 38-39, 41
primordial light, 10, 41, 84, 97
"proper time," 21
Pugin, A. W. N., 169
purgation, 136
purification, 152
Pythagoras, 81

quantum electrodynamics, 46-47
quantum entanglement, 3, 8, 9, 20n.3, 24,
  27, 45, 49-51, 57-59
quantum fields, fields, 45-46
quantum state, 48
quantum theory, 8, 9, 17, 19, 21-23, 24,
  44, 46, 48-51, 231-32
  and measurements, 51-52, 61-64, 65,
  66

quarks, 23, 46-47

radiance, Son as, 117-18
radiation, 33, 40, 41
rainbow, 85
randomness, 66
realism, 57, 207. *See also* physical realism
reason and revelation, 233-35
redemption, 199, 225
relationality, 24-25, 47. *See also* interactions
relativistic cosmology, 34
relativity, 19-21, 46. *See also* theory of
  relativity
Rembrandt, 172-73
Resurrection, 148, 192, 222
revelation, 5, 226-27, 233-35
Richard of St. Victor, 121
Ricoeur, Paul, 18
rider on the clouds, 167
righteousness, 202
Rocca, Gregory, 221-22, 225, 228
Rufinus of Aquileia, 116
rule of faith, 206
Ruskin, John, 169-70

Sabbath, 193
Schrödinger, Erwin, 57-58, 64
science, and theology, 43
scientific method, 82
Second Law of Thermodynamics, 45
Seraphim of Sarov, 149, 158
Severen, Joris Van, 29, 30-31, 32
Severini, Gino, 174
shadow, 161, 166-68
Shekinah, 140, 142
sin, as darkness, 136
Sinai, 132, 135, 139-41, 150, 152, 161, 164,
  183
Sloan Digital Sky Survey (SDSS), 90
"slow light," 70
solar mystics. *See* light mysticism
Son, generation of, 115, 124, 126-27
space, 19-21, 83-84, 98
special relativity, theory of, 61
speed of light, 2, 9, 19-20, 68-79, 88-89
Speiser, Andreas, 88
spiritual being, 200
spiritual substance, 205

Index

state vector, 48
static state, 35, 38
Stead, Christopher, 209n.3, 210n.4
steady state cosmology, 40-41
Steane, Andrew, 6, 9, 105, 137
stigmata, 158
Stout, Jeffrey, 228
subatomic world, 24
substance, 204-5
  light as supreme, 82
  and the Trinity, 104n.1, 114-19, 123, 124, 199
Suger, Abbot, 168-69
Sullivan, W. T., 176
sun, 47, 80, 81, 84, 174, 196
  divine analogy, 2, 122-38, 146, 115-18
  no need for in the New Jerusalem, 111
superabundance, 151, 152
superluminality, 72-73, 75
superposition states, 22, 63-64
supplementalism, 233
symbol, 6-7, 18, 160
Symeon the New Theologian, 6, 10, 11, 119-20, 143, 153-55, 187-88
Symeon the Studite, 154n.65
symmetry/symmetries, 2, 37, 46, 99

Tabor, 132, 133-34, 142, 184-85
tachyons, 77
Tanner, Kathryn, 7, 10, 105, 112, 120-21
Temple, 11, 105, 162-64
Templeton Foundation, 3-4, 13
Templeton, John, 4
Tertullian, 115-16, 118, 209
theism, as coherent, 54
theophany, 139, 150
theory of relativity, 2, 19, 33
thermodynamics, 38
thick darkness, 132, 135, 136, 139-41, 144, 145, 150, 152, 183-84
Thomas Aquinas, 12-13, 18, 112n.13, 120, 126-28, 174, 178, 210, 212, 221-31, 233-34
Thomism, 42
Tillich, Paul, 170, 181
time, 19-21, 35, 39, 65, 73-79, 106
time dilation, 73-74
"top-down" method of theology, 5
Torrance, Thomas F., 12, 215-21

Transfiguration, 17, 109, 132, 133-34, 142, 143, 148, 155, 157-58, 184-85, 188, 190, 192
Trinity, 10, 25, 113-26, 149, 232
Two-degree-Field (2dF) Galaxy Redshift Survey, 90
Turner, Denys, 214
Turrell, James, 176

uncreated light, 12, 22, 133-35, 204, 205, 207, 211-17, 220, 227, 231
uniform motions, 47-48
union with God/mystical union, 136, 143, 152, 158, 159, 165, 184-85, 187
Updike, John, 12, 177

vacuum, 26, 46
  speed of light in, 9, 68-72, 75, 76, 79, 88
Vanacker, Daniël, 28-29
Vaughan, Henry, 151
velocity of light. See speed of light
visibility, 19

Ware, Kallistos, 5-6, 11, 107, 111, 113
water, 110, 164, 182
wave/particle duality, 21-23, 26, 105
wave theory of light, 2, 21-22, 88
Westcott, B. F., 163
White, Victor, 230, 234
Williams, Rowan, 209n.3
Wilson, Robert, 41, 91
wisdom, 82, 124, 129, 171, 199, 201, 204, 212, 223
Wittgenstein, Ludwig, 187
WMAP satellite, 94-95, 96
wonder, 7, 80, 120, 140, 145, 159, 182
world
  as acausal, 77-78
  openness of, 9, 67
World War I, 30-31
Wren, Brian, 121

Xenophanes, 209n.3

Zeilinger, Anton, 4, 5, 6, 9, 60, 66, 205-6, 207
"zero point motion," 26